"One of the most pathbreaking and origi- books on the history of political theory .t has been published in many years." So tes Dr. W. Y. Elliott, Professor Emeritus Harvard, in his Foreword to *Political ·th and Epic*, by Gilbert Cuthbertson.

Dr. Cuthbertson examines fifteen great roic myths to present a new philosophy of tory—the epic myth as a culture-shaper d its relation to the concepts of political ory. He studies in detail the classical epics m *Gilgamesh* through the *Ramayana* to ltaire's *Henriade*, maintaining that po- cal myth is a primary but neglected source political theory. Political myths perform same key legitimizing, legalizing, and bilizing functions in the primitive com- nity that political theory performs in the ore advance system. Based upon a far- nging comparison of anthropology, art, erature, and politics, the book views poli- s itself as a working relationship and eraction of myth-power-value.

Focusing upon the model of the epic hero the epitome of cultural values, Cuthbert- n constructs an essentially new model for development of political culture. In the ncept of epic political myth he finds a sis for the revival of traditional theory.

"Why are the forms of political myth more nstant, when bounded only by human agination, than the forms of human his-

(*Continued on the back flap*)

nued from the front flap)

d by human experience?" he swer lies in the intimate con- een art, society, and politics, renders a mythless culture a in terms. However, not only s share the quality of having ey also preserve essentially the yth, including tested heroism, f the hero to the underworld, lden fruit. Similar mythic forms ical political functions whether th Plato, Tibet, and the Incas; and the Zuñi Indians; or the nd the "cargo cults." The con- litical myth, which argues a ancy in human nature, serves on for cultural comparison and rstanding.

DR. GILBERT CUTHBERTSON is Associate Professor of Political Theory at Rice University and Resident Associate of Will Rice C e Univer- si mmerfield S Harvard, w n Fellow. H , *Political Power*, yth-power-value relationship, as well as a number of articles for scholarly journals.

Sept. 10—

Political Myth and Epic

Political Myth and Epic

• • • • • • • • • •

by
GILBERT MORRIS CUTHBERTSON

MICHIGAN STATE UNIVERSITY PRESS

1975

Library of Congress Card Catalogue Number: 74–75801
ISBN: 0–87013–185–0
MANUFACTURED IN THE UNITED STATES OF AMERICA

★

★

★

★

★

To PROFESSOR W. Y. ELLIOTT

"omnium facile acutissimo et sine
ulla dubitatione doctissimo"

Cicero, *Academia*

Acknowledgements

Dr. W. Y. Elliott directed the preparation of my thesis at Harvard. The inspiration is his; the errors, mine.

The Woodrow Wilson National Fellowship Foundation supported my work financially. Dr. Benjamin Colby gave helpful advice on current developments in anthropological theory. Dr. Judith Shklar, Dr. Francis Heller, Dr. J. Eldon Fields, Dr. Walter Sandelius, and Dr. Ethan Allen contributed the foundations of my interest in Political Theory

Thanks is also due to my colleagues at Rice and to the University Fellowship Program for underwriting my research work.

Table of Contents

FOREWORD

• • •

A new philosophy of history—the epic myth as a culture-shaper and its relation to the concepts of political theory and particularly theories on human nature—is embodied in the fifteen great epics chosen by Gilbert Cuthbertson in this important contribution. He really treats many other epics in his wide-ranging notes of comparison.

Given the enormous range of philosophies of history, it is truly astonishing *how few of any importance have been devoted essentially to the epic myth as a culture-shaper.* This is particularly true in view of the fact that all of the great religions of the world are in their true essences epic myths—i.e., they are the testing of a hero, usually divinely descended or connected, to represent the successful formulation by his own example by trials met, and by his ability to learn through the trials that have beset him as a matter of his divinely ordered fate: the resulting pattern of conduct and of moral example which becomes the overwhelming formulator and conditioner, one might add, of the civilizations which adopt these religious cultures, whose founders are something more than merely human and political heroes.

If there is one point in this book that I think needs further exploration it is the relation of the political epic to the religious epic, though Dr. Cuthbertson clarifies many aspects of the differences. There is a very great connection in instances like the Moslem epic on which pretty clearly Baber and Akbar, and, for that matter I suppose, a good many of the Mogul Moslem rulers in India were carrying out as faithfully as they could under the circumstances depicted by the divinely ordered example of Mohammed in the Koran. The role of the caliphate and the Sheriff of Mecca during the whole existence of the Mohammedan church-state union—for such in fact it very nearly was—is an example of this. One might make a considerable number of parallel instances without exhausting the possible lists, since the myths and religions in their early forms were very closely connected; and it is obvious that in many ways the Norse legends had this characteristic of being both political and religious myths, and a good deal of the Greek mythology had the same character.

Indeed a considerable part of the Greek tragedies, particularly of Sophocles and Aeschylus, were devoted to stripping off some of the cruder forms of the older religious teaching that the Greek tragedies of the fifth century B.C. were criticizing in plays like the *Oresteia* trilogy, the substitution in *The Eumenides* of the laws of Athens for the Furies (the Erinyes), in the concluding part of that trilogy. This greatest trilogy of Aeschylus portrays a protest, as does his *Prometheus Bound,* and the role of Heracles in finally setting Prometheus free from the unjust punishments of Zeus, harried as the king of gods was by his jealous wife, Hera.

Euripides in one of his few great tragedies, from the point of view of its spiritual content, makes the same kind of criticism by implication of Hera's interference through sending the nymph, Frenzy, to turn Heracles into a manic-state, or state of real madness: *Heracles in a Frenzy* is the usual translation of the title of this great tragedy, which makes the eponymous hero of the Greeks, Heracles, kill his whole family, practically speaking, before his mind is clarified and he realizes what he has been forced to do this horrid slaughter by the savage wrath of Hera and her messenger, the nymph Frenzy, whom she has sent to cast her spell upon him.

In this tragedy, of course, fortunately Heracles comes to his senses and is brought to Athens to pass his old years by being persuaded to return with Theseus, whom he has rescued at an earlier time from the underworld.

Theseus, in turn, invites Heracles to come and become one of the patron deities of Athens, as Athena is later acclaimed by the Athenians. In Euripides' play Heracles accepts this role as to avoid the stigma of suicide and the shame that this would have brought upon him by Hera, as Theseus brings out clearly.

The interesting thing is the differentiation of the political epic, fifteen examples of which are chosen by Professor Cuthbertson for what I think is one of the most pathbreaking and original books on the history of political theory that has been published in many years. It is an elaborate and well-documented effort to show that these political epics, which are essentially to govern the shaping of the tone of the whole society, rest basically but not entirely on its religious institutions for the kind of cultural and purposive tone that every great religion sets through the example of its founder and the teaching of the priests who inculcate this religion. More note might be taken of how mothers who teach religion to their children at their knees and priests in the churches combine these religious and political strains.

The political epic is of a somewhat different character than the great founding religious epics. It is the melding of this basically divine order by which human beings are indoctrinated through the example of the founder, and through the theology that is institutionalized in the ritual of the church and in its basic beliefs and in its hold on its membership. Beyond this the political myth uses an exemplar of the same order in some ways because the founding father takes on in many cases the attributes of at least a partially divine leader or one guided by the degrees of revelation. Who shall say that Moses is not both a political and a religious leader? Or that, for that matter, David is not also of this order and that most of the Old Testament is embodying the religious doctrines in the political figures who become political epic leaders, and whose examples are very much one of teaching the survival of the children of Israel under the harsh conditions surrounding them of dealing with very much greater powers?

It is extraordinarily interesting and basically revealing of the true source of legitimate rule that it is this guidance by God, so to speak, that makes their political system survive through long periods of what amounts to defeat (often slavery) and captivity and many other humiliations—even its dispersion. Today the linkage of culture to religion in guiding power is reappearing in new political epics quite as much as through old or new religious epics, as in the new leadership that the children of Israel are finding once more in the reoccupation of "their" holy land. The same struggle is going on with the Arabs all about them. That is all traditional; but it is interesting that it is complicated and made much more important in a world scale by the fact that the totalitarian system of the Soviet is now bent upon using the Arabs to destroy the West through the destruction of the oil resources of the East, to which Palestine's power role is in some degree a key.

What is equally instructive perhaps is that the political leadership of the Israelis is backed up by the most astonishing change in the warlike character and activities of the Jewish leaders in reoccupied Palestine; and in an entirely different attitude toward the things of this world than that which guided still most of the Jews of the Diaspora, who still have had to win their controlling power by becoming masters over the world's wealth and influence; or even of direct political power in the Western systems leading, of course, to reactions like those of the

Nazis in Germany and to a degree of antisemitism which is not at all lacking in many countries today.

The astonishing part about that, however, is that the political epic that is most vivid in men's minds is probably connected with the magic formula epic, not a usual form for an epic, of Marx and Engels, particularly of Marx, whose hold on Communism and through Communism on a very large part of the globe's human inhabitants is a substitute for religion in some respects; and it combines (as totalitarianism must) a sort of orthodoxy in the interpretation of its creed and the power of the leader who has difficulties in remaining free of the military pressures and of the pressures of his secret service and party personnel; as well as in the survival of the system given its Mosaic epic of conquering at all costs and of the fact that coexistence for the Arabs, to begin with, means coexistence on what amounts to Communist Marxian terms that ultimately mean the destruction of any system that is not thoroughly collectivist in its control and is not governed during the transition period of a dictatorship over the proletariat, at least. Israel professes today no ambition beyond the now occupied territories. So did Hitler. Never Lenin and his successors.

This work of Professor Cuthbertson's introduces a much richer background because it takes in a range of heroic myths that run the whole gamut from the Norse legends, the *Kalevala,* the *Araucana,* the *Divine Comedy,* and *Paradise Lost,* as well as Camoëns' the *Lusiads* and the *Henriade,* as well as offshoots like the *Cid* and less than, I should stress, the English and continental *(Parsifal)* Arthurian legends. These have a most powerful hold on the imaginations, not only of England's great period as in Spenser up to Tennyson; but through their diversification in plays like Wagner's *Parsifal* through at least their shadow in Germany and in Europe. The *Nibelungenlied* is not given perhaps as large a place in Professor Cuthbertson's collection as it deserves in some ways; but the whole theory of Hitler was very much pervaded by the *Gotterdämmerung* atmosphere of the Wagnerian reproduction of these basic myths: For that matter more could—by spending a lifetime—be made of the Middle Eastern myths, the Egyptian and similar myths, and to a greater degree of the Hindu myths of India. All these take on various political characters which Dr. Cuthbertson has carefully introduced in the short but very pithy study that he has made. This book is a new beginning and a trial framework for further testing.

Though it is obviously just a beginning, it is still a very important beginning. It is a beginning that is at once the most original and fruitful approach to showing what the types of conflict were out of which came the British Empire, with the introduction of a different order of myth which finally placed its hopes of royalty in a crown that became more a crown symbolic. I wrote about that in a book on the *New British Empire,* particularly in the appendix on the *Lion and the Unicorn,* showing how symbolic that leadership had become and how it lost in some ways the epic qualities that the older Shakespearean rivalries of the British dynasts showed in the struggle for the crown and the throne. Shakespeare's additions in his own great tragedies to the epic side of Greek tragedies is a road that leads to ever new insights into the deepest cultural aspects by the epic myth.

The astonishing thing about this book is that it has not been written earlier or that the effort has not been made more systematically. Ernst Cassirer, Lord Raglan, Sydney Hook, and many others wrote about the myth of the state. But few of them wrote, except in outline as did Hermann Schneider, about political epics; and the last thing in Cassirer's view was that "myth" was used in a bad sense and not in the sense of a shaping and indoctrinating deeply with abiding impact. The theory was that we had outgrown all myth making á la Auguste Comte, and that Rousseau was trying to reintroduce some of it by the back door and preparing the way for the French Revolution when he wrote about the *Moi Commŭn,* the common self, La Volonté Générale, plus the "infallibility" of the general will, as he called it: But Rousseau was equally interested in the justification of authority and the need for introducing it by "The Great Legislator." He stressed the need of something that the old Roman law principle required, as Cicero noted in working out something that would give a basis for *consensus juris* that could be embodied in principles that were *personified.* These got their embodiment in a finality of law which we in our system, for all our constitutionalism and its vaunted dependence on checks and balances and restraints on power and things of that sort, nevertheless put into the mouths of the Supreme Court as if they had been oracles.[1] We have had witness of that oracular role of the Supreme Court which has been perhaps a little painful in its extreme taking over of power, even the power of amending the Constitution freely, if not quite at will, as Warren's Court certainly did. The whole play of myths suggests that the study that I gave of the *Constitution as the American Social Myth*[2] in this little book, *The Constitution Reconsidered,* edited by Conyers Read as a sesquicentennial edition, tries to prove, and more recently brought somewhat up-to-date by a revised and supplemented edition.[3] *The Constitution as the American Social Myth* was bound to have some sort of a spokesman.

The law speakers were reverting to the priests, and the priesthood became the aristocracy of the robe, and this, in turn, gave an astonishing new flexibility in the change of the fundamental laws and in the change of the ethos, the basic justification of law by what was just law, *consensus juris,* as Cicero called it, a fundamental agreement on what was "right" law. The ambiguity of the word "law" in all European languages is not unintentional, it's both law and right—justice is an indication of that—one of the few English terms in which we use this ambiguity purposely. *Jus* means both law and right; *Droit* means that same thing; so does *Recht* in German.

It is interesting that this defense of the justice of law required a different kind of myth and it is extraordinarily interesting that the chivalric myth had to put some limits on power by the chivalry of the Round Table, for instance, because chivalry made the stronger protect the weaker in many ways. The loyalty of feudalism was a carefully arranged affair to fit political needs, and it did offer buffers against unlimited power. Not only did it put restraints on, the assumption of the crown, which got more and more to have a religious overtone in some measure, in its duties, etc. It also put oaths of office and things of that sort into a very prominent and morally restraining position in the whole working of the political system.

Perhaps this aspect of the political myth has not been adequately developed in this volume of Dr. Cuthbertson's. I hope he will devote future time to it along with other developments and comparison of the later things that he writes. It is certainly something that is occupying the time of another one of my recent younger students from American University—Donald Williamson, as it also concerns my son, Ward Elliott, a lawyer as well as a political theorist. Both are concerned with the "co-organic characters," as I have called it, i.e., the purposive character of law which approaches legitimacy of the law from that angle in trying to understand why we are having such a revolt against educational systems in which this combination of force and morality plays an essential part in political dynamics.

Legitimatizing the feudal basis of authority had been worked up to a more satisfactory conclusion than we have been able to do in our own arrangement of the deification of civil *disobedience*, to a point far beyond what Thoreau really would have carried it. The current erection of violence has made it the tool of something that started off with a profession of nonviolence. This is not accidental.

I want to conclude by pointing out that the *epic hero* has ceased to be a figure of prestige and of universal acclaim with the "teaching value" of setting the model for society to the degree that the epic tradition required in the early structuring of our political systems.

These systems were in varying degrees *always* haunted by the eternal rivalries of special interests, as against public interests raising all the different interpretations of public interest in terms of class interests that all the Greek classical political theory was devoted to. The separation of powers, the division of powers, the notion of federalism, the fundamental laws against ordinary laws, and the different ways in which laws should be formulated, that require different degrees of consensus, different degrees of majority and different degrees of active consent of the majority.

All these things are, of course, not entirely explained by the presence or absence of epic myth, but it is, I think, significant in the United States that we turn back for our exemplars for the founding fathers not only to people such as Washington or to Lincoln, as the savior of this country, if you like, of a different era, but that we find so few people whom we can hold up as exemplars of this character in our own times. But even in the earlier part of the twentieth century there were certainly figures with more robustness of leadership and more call to duty and to the formulation of this, and there were hangovers of some degree in the times of Roosevelt and Truman who had some of these characters. There were even nostalgic reminiscences of it in some of the attitudes that were taken by Eisenhower, not Milton but his more robust and military brother.

It is of extraordinary interest to the students of politics to contemplate what form of modern epic could take that could be a political culture-shaper in times which are being so punished as ours are and which are looking, because of their very hardships and severities of testing of the system, for a rarity that will be not worse than the disease but that will cure the disease and put us back in the path of creative public policy that represents a *consensus juris* backed by not only the *utilitatis communio* that Cicero talked about ("a community of utility"). This includes both a common defense with general welfare that is more than welfare politics that go to the basis of the original meaning of the word *res publica* and that brings back some tradition of constitutionalism to our sorely tested republic.

W. Y. Elliott

Notes to Foreword

1. See my essay several times referred to by Dr. Cuthbertson on "The Constitution as the American Social Myth" in *The Constitution Reconsidered,* reissued in 1968, and the chapter on "The Supreme Court as Censor or Umpire" in *The Need For Constitutional Reform,* 1936.

2. This is frequently referred to in notes by Dr. Cuthbertson.

3. New edition (added chapters by editor, Richard B. Morris, and by John Roche) reissued in 1968 (Harper Torchbooks).

PREFACE

• • •

"Mythomania is always a rather disturbing thing"—
MALRAUX

When people first asked about the subject of this work, I told them the truth. It is a study of myth as the mechanism of political dynamics and of the relationship of politics to epic literature. It is an attempt to establish a co-organic theory of myth and to treat political science as an architectonic discipline. My thesis was presumptuous enough to suggest that community of myth may serve as a basis for international understanding.

In spite of such ambitious pretensions, it was difficult to explain to laymen how dirty old-fashioned politics could get itself involved with epic myths. What, after all, was *The Divine Comedy* to Boss Plunkitt of Tammany Hall? Well, unless the Boss needed the Italian vote, not much. Yet the whole structure of political myth conditions our thinking about political power. Myth serves as the vehicle of political ideas.

Getting further into the problem, political scientists tend to act like those well-insured and much advertised Hindu scholars of an Eastern tale. In treating myths, one group grasps the trunk and gets a singularly truncated view. Another group grips the foot and engages in a pedantic discourse. Others trail off into "posterior analytics."

Like other disciplines, modern political science is suffering from a large number of difficulties, congenital and inherited. Take, for example, the problem of meaning. We have been taught always to look beneath the surface. Rip the mask off the politician. The author really doesn't mean what he says. Jonah, swallowed by a whale?!

Criticism has become so acute that it is devastating to learn that a poor man sometimes means what he says. The average political scientist or literary critic can conjure up as many meanings as a spiritualist situated above a Rappite congregation can summon up a multitude of spirits.

Political scientists also suffer from a corollary ailment, distinguished by Dr. J.S. Galbraith as *Froude's Disease,* the inherent inability to get the facts straight. The British historian Froude was criticized for his demographic description of Adelaide. The attack continued through a succession of historians, all borrowing from each other, with none examining the original sources. Froude's description was, of course, essentially correct.

Another problem related to scholarly elephantiasis is the modern obsession with power and behavior. Power alone is not sufficient to understand the operations of human society. Power is amorphous; myth gives it form. Behavior is also closely structured by myths. Intellectual Jivaroism, which is a marked tendency toward single factor determinism, and the Aristotelean classification complex create additional difficulties.

This classification should warn the reader about what he may be in for. There is also Pascal's syndrome. You may recall that Pascal said that most of man's troubles stemmed from the fact that he could not sit still in a room for ten minutes straight. Pascal's own excuse was that dreadful fiery chasm which opened next to him at the dinner table.

One quarter of our political scientists dread this abyss as if it were the inner circle of the Antenora—but they are only part of the problem. The other three quarters resemble the greatly mortal Empedocles and are prepared to jump into the first Etna which comes along. . . . And so we jump *in media res* into the problems of myth and epic: society, religion, anthropology, law, literature, and POLITICS.

I. INTRODUCTION

• • •

"Loomings"

Thomas Mann has written, "The question of the human conscience is presented to us essentially in its political form."[1] Ernst Cassirer amplifies this thought:

> Perhaps the most important and the most alarming feature in this development of modern political thought is the appearance of a new power; the power of mythical thought. The preponderance of mythical thought over rational thought in some of our modern political systems is obvious. . . . We should carefully study the origin, the structure, the methods, and the techniques of the political myths. We should see the adversary face to face in order to know how to combat him."[2]

The translation of myth into political terms recalls the Faustian problem of the relationship between *Wort, Kraft,* and *Tat.* The Homeric *mythos,* which was a spoken word, has absorbed connotations of political power and has served as a stimulus to social action.

The search for the political myth poses a number of basic questions. What are the meanings of myth and epic for political theory? What are the practical functions of myth in the community? As Jakob Grimm promises, "I shall indeed interpret all that I can, but I cannot interpret all that I should."[3]

In this book the subject is divided into four parts, each of which explores an aspect of the myth as political. In the first section, myth is defined in political and co-organic terms as an entity which creates moral consensus and prohibitions, thereby structuring the community. The political myth is placed in the context of interdisciplinary materials. The problems of modernity and universality of myths are discussed.

In the next part the development of myth systems, or epics, is considered. The political content of epic is related to the mythic content. Comparative politics is studied by means of comparative literature.

The third part contains a discussion of the political functions of the eponymous hero. The hero is an embodiment of the myth, the binding unit of the community.

In the final part of the book, the types of political myths are studied. The myth categories are: messianic, cultural catastrophic, legitimizing, legalizing and community-forming, power and value-creating, iconoclastic, nationalistic, and educational. Myths dealing with history and the idea of freedom are also analyzed. Such political myths are correlative to the prevailing political conditions.

In *The Birth of Tragedy*, Nietzsche had this to say on the cultural impact of myths:

> Without myth . . . every culture loses its healthy creative natural power; it is only a horizon encompassed with myths that rounds off to unity a social movement.[4]

Epic constitutes the system of myth which serves as the ordering basis for culture. Myth itself is the foundation of the community. Myth is an articulation of symbols; it contains an essential truth value and is co-organic, having the political function of creating moral consensus or taboos in the community.

All sorts of lexicons have defined myth. A graphic definition is the nineteenth century Japanese etching which depicts myth as a matronly type. Myth is a Magna Mater, a kind of Queen Victoria incarnate.

Myth may expand in meaning until it becomes almost synonymous with literature, or until a "myth of myth" is reached. Perhaps the real "myth of myth" is the theme of this book. Since myth compensates for lack of political power, it becomes peculiarly suspect as an intellectual fabrication, or spiritual pacifier —a scholarly self-assertion. According to Valéry, "Myth is the name for everything that exists or subsists, only to the extent that speech is its cause."[5] The *Encyclopédie* ironically remarks that a myth may be "whatever one's interests lead one to think it is."[6]

Myth may contract in meaning until it becomes a story about the gods in their dealings with man and nature.[7] Myths belong to an order of knowledge, neither psychological, nor logical, but genuinely *mytho-logical.* Kerényi illustrates this point with the Polynesian tale of Hainuwele, who is murdered because of her generosity.[8]

Märchen, folk tales, and fables are not easily separable from myths in their political form. Sir Walter Scott writes that "the mythology of one period would appear to pass into the romance of the next and into the nursery tales of subsequent ages."[9] Categories such as those of Wundt seem arbitrary and inflexible, especially when developed in an evolutionary sequence.[10]

Malinowski, however, offers these reasonable distinctions:

> The *folk-tale* . . . is a seasonal performance and an act of sociability. The *legend,* provoked by contact with unusual reality, opens up past historical vistas. The *myth* comes into play when rite, ceremony, or a social or moral rule demands justification, warrant of antiquity, reality or sanctity."[11]

Myth possesses several main characteristics: it is an articulation of symbols or a communication; it contains an essential truth value; and it is co-organic.

These qualities which characterize myths can be compared with Schorer's typical literary definition of myth in *William Blake: The Politics of Vision:*

> (i) A myth is "a large controlling image" founded in man's experience (not a concept detached and abstracted from all sensible referents) (ii) not false by definition it may be as "true" as it can be (iii) it is not anti-intellectual (iv) mythic images are the elements, however submerged, by which thought is sustained and propelled, and by means of which ideas, those systems of abstraction, for example, that we call ideologies—activate behavior (v) our own civilization seems to be struggling toward a myth that will be explicitly ethical, even political.[12]

Characteristics of Myths

Graves has referred to myths as "verbal iconographs," Fromm speaks of "the forgotten language," and Max Müller of the "disease of language."[13] Not only are myths transmitted orally, but they also contain a tension-resolving internal dialogue that deals with ultimate questions. As Cassirer writes in *Language and Myth:*

> For a person whose apprehension is under the spell of this mythico-religious attitude, it is as though the whole world were simply annihilated; the immediate context, whatever it be, that commands his religious interest so completely fills his consciousness that nothing can exist beside and apart from it . . . when, on the other hand, the entire self is given up to a single impression, is "possessed" by it, and, on the other hand, there is the utmost

> tension between the subject and its object, the outer world; when external reality is not merely viewed and contemplated but overcomes a man in sheer immediacy with emotions of fear or hope, terror or wish fulfillment: then the spark jumps somehow across, the tension finds release, as the subjective excitement becomes objectified, and confronts the mind as a god or a demon.[14]

Part of the energy contained in myth is captured in the poetic "spontaneous overflow of powerful emotions."[15] Within the context of power, communication, and language, the spoken word assumes added significance for primitive society.

The spoken word may be attributed with a creative power as in the sacred words of the ceremonial of the Columbian Uitoto tribe.[16] The test of Marduk's power in the Babylonian creation epic, *Enuma elish,* also parallels the oral tradition of *mythos.*[17]

A secret or archaic language may be part of the mysticism which maintains the authority of the priesthood.[18] The word as name may be considered inseparable from the object. Knowing the "name" may give power to the hero. In an Egyptian tale he obtains power by the *drinking of a sentence.*[19] In fact, he imbibes a whole book of magic soaked in beer.

The traumatic separation of name from object may be tantamount to destruction. The nagging question "What is your name?" forces Lohengrin to depart in the swan-boat. When the sacred name is forgotten or used by improper persons, the result is the chaos of Lucian's sorcerer's apprentice.

Examples of the relationship between myth and language may be drawn from the revivalistic "speaking in the tongues," cabalistic formulas, "heavenly letters," and oracles.[20] Myth embodies the element of oral communication—a fusion of words and symbols poetically into a meaningful whole.

While the spoken word is mythically creative, the written word is potentially destructive as in the many tales of messengers sent bearing "strange symbols which have power to kill," Homer's Bellerophon. An important world myth theme is "the perverted message" in which the communication between man and god, the myth itself, collapses. Susan Feldmann comments on an African version:

> The Perverted Message, in particular, strikes the tragic note of some of Kafka's parables. God wants man to live and so dispatches to mankind the message of life, but due to the distance between man and god, the necessity for intermediaries, the contingencies attending the transmission of the message, man is cheated out of immortality. Once the wrong message is delivered, it stands; god himself is powerless to revoke it. In several versions of the story, however, it says that god endorsed the false message because *men believed it.*[21]

Essential "Truth" of Myths

The Faustian problem of the "Word" is closely associated with the question as to *was am Anfang steht.* The alchemic search for the *quinta essentia* is repeated in the efforts of mythologists to isolate the nuclear truth of the myth. The earliest tradition in the purgation of the false and fantastic from myth is the classical criticism. Pindar, Ephorus, Theopompus, and Euhemerus all sought the real elements, historical, moral, or physical in myths.[22]

Thucydides extracted mythology from history and established a pattern for later historical scholarship. Myth was rejected as a source for the study of culture. Modern intellectual historiography has barely begun to emancipate itself from Thucydides' scientific approach. Two millenia of scholars have been engaged like Lucian's Menippus, who scientifically investigates myths in Hades.

The search for a myth-explaining philosopher's stone has resulted in as many unusual theories as the search for the touchstone. These theories will be reviewed in later sections.

A modern parallel to the Greek criticism is the Biblical *Entmythisierung* with its "higher criticism." Such attempts to reduce myths to fact symptomize a critical scientific spirit; they also betray a nihilistic poverty of belief. The weird pantomime has ushered in such mummeries as the "worship of reason" and the "death of God."[23]

Any such effort to denature myth suggests this pertinent question: Is it possible for a society to distinguish between its own myths and nonmyths? The truth of myth can be examined only from a given social or political matrix, but the analysis does not proceed on coldly objective grounds.

There is an important piece of evidence presented by the typical Sudanese story-telling session:

> "I'm going to tell a story," the narrator begins.
> "Right!" the audience rejoins.
> "It's a lie."
> "Right!"
> "But not everything in it is false."
> "Right!"
> "We do not really mean . . . that what we are going to say is true." is the traditional beginning of every Ashanti tale.[24]

The scholarly hunt for the demythologized myth has a counterpart in the popular treatment of myths as fictitious narratives.[25] An extreme case defines myth as "that which has no real existence. . . . It is said that in politics, justice, and good faith are myths."[26]

Political myth, however, is true in the Aristotelean sense that poetry is often truer than history. As Butcher comments:

> Poetry expresses most adequately the universal element in human nature and in life . . .. It liberates us from the tyranny of

physical surroundings . . . . Poetry in striving to give universal form to its own creations reveals a higher truth than history, and on that account is nearer to philosophy.[27]

Carlyle argues in the same vein:

> Some speculators have a short way of accounting for the pagan religions, mere quackery, priestcraft and dupery say they. . . . They all have had a truth in them.[28]

The truth of myths may be evaluated at several levels: historicism, cognition, poetic metaphor, modernity and universality.

Historicism. At the most rudimentary level, myths may contain historical data, geographical descriptions, genealogies, migration patterns. (The problematic relationship between myth and history is reserved to the final chapter.) Arnold Toynbee considers mythology to be a valuable source for historical writing. He describes myth as "a primitive form of apprehension and expression in which . . . the line between fact and fiction is left undrawn."[29]

Cognition. Aside from the debatable historical truth of myths, myths do possess a cognitive truth value. Myths are meant to be believed and usually purport to be true. On the cultural level, the myth may create a psychic reality which insulates the culture from external "truths." This seems hardly the place to sermonize on the power of negative thinking or the psychosomatic consequences of voodoo. However, the case of the Maoris, who literally died of fright because of a broken taboo, is not isolated.[30]

Poetry, Metaphor, and Science. Besides belief, another element of mythic power is the poetic context, "the more than usual analogy," which permits the hearer to grasp a fundamental truth. In the spiritual realization of metaphor, myth serves as a way to the truth, which has been analogized to the Hindu concept of *marga.*[31]

MacIver describes the myth-picture as a composite of particular symbols by means of which the artist creates a "heightened perceptiveness."[32] Well-known symbols forge a common bond between the artist and the viewer—the citizen and the nation. In the political function of myth, these symbols are integrated into the *credenda* and *miranda* of political power.

In some aspects this process is like the fusion of scientific symbols. Myth may even appear to resemble scientific hypothesis. Indeed, W. B. Yeats has called science "the critique of myths."[33] Myths appear on the fringes of science—where scientific methods are frustrated in the effort to predict—where poetic intuition is necessary to progress. An example is the new sevenfold way to the periodic table.

Science and myth operate according to a similar metaphoric process but in opposite directions. Science strains for a detached objectivity; myth demands emotional participation, often ritual. Poetic myth moves far toward anthropomorphism, apostrophy, allegorical truth, Ruskin's "pathetic fallacy." The phrase, "have I not reason to lament what man has made of man" is ceaselessly repeated with varying syntax but with humanity constant.

Science moves toward the "apathetic fallacy," or mechanization of humanity. In literature, the product is a *1984,* or, as Ehrenburg has described, the "socialist realism" of the average Soviet novel:

> The author tells you from the very outset about the occupations of the hero and the heroine. Both work in a steel plant. The heroine is bold and full of pioneering spirit. The hero is honest, but tends to cling to routine. The heroine devises a new method of production which results in a six-per-cent economy. . . . We have such novels. . . . We have plays in which the actors must play

> the roles of puppets, discoursing about coal, steel, or cotton fabrics . . .[34]

Such a Mephistophelean spirit is the great antimyth, "the spirit of denial."

Modernity of Myths

The reliance on science to destroy the poetic concept of myth raises this question: Is myth disappearing in modern times? Nietzsche echoes Herder's concern regarding the mythlessness of modern man. Recent students of myth, including Allen Tate, have postulated a similar mythless quality.[35] Of course, to the Comtian positivists, myth and modern are antithetical terms. Myth supposedly disappears with the approach of their *état mystique.*

Modern man is not mythless, but perhaps he does seek the sensation of mythlessness as he seeks weightlessness. He splenetically attempts to destroy old myths and create new ones. Modern myths may be manipulated in political propaganda or assume the favored forms of Sisyphus and Prometheus. Modern literary interpreters find myths in Kafka, Mann, Yeats, Zola, Giradoux, Cocteau, and Gide, to mention a few.[36]

Wallace Stevens has written: "We live in an intricacy of new and local mythologies, political, economic, poetic."[37] Jung discusses "living mythologems." He exemplifies with psychic case studies in which dreams parallel such antique myth as Europa and the Bull.[38] Mircea Eliade asks a question vital to the political analysis of myths: "What has become of myths in the modern world? Or more precisely, what has taken the essential place occupied by myth in traditional societies?"

> For if certain "participations" in myths and collective symbols still survive in the modern world, they are far from filling the central part played by the myth in traditional societies; in comparison with these, our modern world seems destitute of myths. It has even been held that the diseases and crises of modern society are rightly attributable to the absence of a mythology appropriate to them. When Jung entitled one of his books, *Modern Man in Search of a Soul,* he implied that the modern world . . . is in quest of a new myth which alone could enable it to draw upon fresh spiritual resources and renew its creative powers.[39]

Others suggest that the modern novel "is the response to the internal anguish that can find no constraint in the form of myth."[40] Myth, however, is omnipresent in modern folklore and literature. Marxism, capitalism, nationalism, and constitutionalism all conceal the missing modern political myths.

Universality of Myths

Closely related to the problems of myth's modernity is the myth in its spatial distribution, universality. Having myths is a shared characteristic of all societies. Indeed myth is the prerequisite of society. In addition, there is a universal repetition of certain myth-themes.[41]

Some parallels can be explained by D'Alviella's "migration of symbols" and the diffusionist theory. Several related theories maintain the uniqueness of myth-creation: Bastian's *Elementargedanke,* or elementary ideas; Preuss' *Urdummheit,* primeval stupidity, and Jung's *urtümliches Bild,* or archetype. The diffusionist school asserts that the world of myths is a unified field. Then they disagree as to whether Babylonia or Egypt is the "cradle of myth." The "plagiarists" hold that myths are borrowed from the Bible.[42]

Other theorists have approached the universality of myth through multilinear evolution, repeated psychological necessity, or similar physical environment. These students of myth feel that the disjunctive distribution of themes is more than an entailed inheritance from the primeval. The distribution of the pan-Asiatic bear cult is therefore explained by the distribution of bears.[43] The key question in contemporary anthropology is not so much the source of the parallels as the cause for the repeated adoption of certain themes.

The difficulty in tracing the diffusion of myth-themes is underscored in such situations as the recovery of a legend resembling that of Rhampsinitis, reported in Herodotus, in modern Egypt. The source was a copy of Maspero's *Les contes populaires de l'Égypte ancienne,* which had been lent to a teacher in Upper Egypt.[44]

Co-Organic Nature of Myths

Diffusion, survival, and syncretism are organic qualities of myths. Myths also serve to create moral consensus for the community. This moral purposiveness combined with the organic structure qualifies myths within the theory of Dr. W.Y. Elliott in *The Pragmatic Revolt in Politics.* Myths are co-organic.[45]

As co-organic material, myths inherently possess a political function. Myth is an intellectual product of the organic group. The conditions of society dictate the prevalent form of social myth. Within the political framework of myth, key considerations are: legitimacy, maintenance of social order, social catharsis, moderation of individual assertions and the imposition of conformity and orthodoxy, legal sanctions, propaganda and cultural defense mechanisms, racial and ethnic myths. Political myths and customs have a consensual function; they also establish social prohibitions.

The ordering basis for society is a group of myths which may be referred to as a "charter myth" or "political formula."[46] Epics are also myth systems and serve a similar purpose. Epics bring to focus cultural ideas and political values. In epic, myth is fused with social history through poetry.

In primitive societies, myths serve the function of a constitution. Much of the mythic quality is preserved in the constitutions of advanced states. If the backward country merely transfers the demythologized document and the formal power structure, a terrible travesty occurs. Gawking sans-culottes, one remove from cannibalism, wear the top hats and fanfares of power and not much else.

Jenks exposes such an imitation during the Middle Ages:

> The Frank Empire was . . . a sham Empire. It aimed at reproducing the elaborate and highly organized machinery of the Roman State. Just as a party of savages will disport themselves in the garments of a shipwrecked crew, so the Merowingian and Karolingian kings and officials decked themselves with the titles . . . They broke down under the strain; and their breakdown is the first great tragedy in modern history, the parent of many tragedies to follow. Those who doubt the possibility of such an explanation, may be referred to the "Parliaments" and "Cabinets" of Samoa, and to the "Polynesian Empire."[47]

The power structure is a faithful reproduction of the Western model, but the corresponding myth structure is absent. In the duplicate, ritual is divorced from myth. The observer stands back in a state of shock. Even worse, the indigenous myth structure has been weakened by the onslaught of Westernizing natives and missionaries. The result is the absence of a unifying center, except the negative opposition against foreign beliefs.

Homogeneity of myths, as Sebba indicates, reinforces the constitutional structure of advanced states in times of severe stress:

From this viewpoint, the most rationalistic modern states appeared to be *mythically* superior to some antirationalistic totalitarian states that had to impose a myth of the state from above precisely because no political myth held the body politic together.[48]

Myth legitimizes and minimizes the exertion of political power. The study of myth's operation has long been reserved to the anthropologist; epic, to the classicist. My own approach to the myth is centripetal to the study of politics, driving toward POLITICAL MYTH from the peripheral disciplines. As Lévi-Strauss has rather sarcastically admonished:

> Precisely because professional anthropologists' interest has withdrawn from primitive religion, all kinds of amateurs who claim to belong to other disciplines have seized this opportunity to move . . . into what we had left as a wasteland.[49]

Myth and epic have been neglected by economic determinists, who have pigeonholed them in the superstructure, by behaviorists, and by social scientists.

Myths can determine the structure of society in a way which no economic forces can. In fact, myth often sustains the economic order. Marxism is a specialized complex of myths. Other random examples are available in which myth sustains the economic order. There is the communality of the Navaho sandpaintings and the destructive potlatches of the Kwakiutl. The Norse heroes also destroyed treasures to make certain that they would undertake new conquests. Malinowski describes the property structures of the Trobriand islanders:

> Should there arise land quarrels, encroachment in magical matters, fishing rights, or other privileges, the testimony of myth would be referred (to). . . . In most places economic monopolies are thus traced to the autochthonous emergence.[50]

Behaviorists have likewise neglected myths—the elements of behavior rooted in the epic structure; yet myths as value-creators control human behavior. Sociologists have made some effort to study myth, but only in isolated articles.[51] W.H.R. Rivers defines myth as "a narrative which gives an account of the coming into being of man himself, or any feature of his environment, natural or social." He relates a Melanesian myth about the taklai bird, which sounds like a nice animal fable, but actually accounts for the clan organization on the Island of Santa Cruz.[52] Such a myth is meaningless outside of its social context. John Dollard substitutes "magic" for "social myth": "Magic accepts the status quo; it takes the place of political activity, agitation, organization, solidarity, or any real moves to change status."[53]

Students of politics have neglected myths, although myth has been treated as a construct in political theory since the time of Plato. Political mythology, however, is rarely analyzed in specific terms. Bacon, writing "On the Wisdom of the Ancients," offers several examples of "political mythology" and "public idols." Typhon becomes a political revolutionary. The story of the Cyclops deals with base court officers; the River Styx, with compacts and confederacies.[54]

Locke, like Hesiod and Plato, recognizes the role of reason, passion, and superstition in governing mankind.[55]

Bodin was influenced by astrological myths. Hobbes recognized the paramount importance of manipulating "fear." Rousseau equated a people's "gods" with its laws. "Prejudices," of course, played an important role in Burke's political philosophy.

In modern political theory, Karl Deutsch and Quincy Wright study the attachment to symbols as part of nationalism. Hannah Arendt mentions "legends." Ernst Cassirer deals with étatist theory and "the struggle against myths in political theory."

Francis Delaisi has contributed "An Outline of Political Mythology" in his *Political Myths and Economic Realities.* He insists upon several fundamental points: the essential function of myth is to create willing obedience; myth creates legality; and myth is intensely conservative. According to the last theory, when myth is connected with the state, it becomes a supreme guarantee of both security and salvation. Therefore, to attack myth is to attack the foundations of the state. The standard examples are the suppression of heresy under the Christian emperors and of Christianity itself. Of course, both St. Augustine and Origen are at pains to demonstrate that Christianity is not destructive of the Roman state—and that the good Christian is the good citizen.

Delaisi makes the significant point that an attack on the dogmas of physical science at the time of Galileo constituted exactly this kind of inflexible myth with the equation: loyalty = orthodoxy. Social science tends to be bound by an analogous situation at the present time as progress in the social sciences is retarded by the taboos of the state. Delaisi claims that intolerance springs from the political function of myths:

> On the one hand, the myth endows the institution with its dogmatic fixity; on the other the state furnishes the myth with the power of its "secular arm" by which opposition is silenced. The maximum of resistance to every change is thereby attained.[56]

Barrows Dunham insists that not only does social myth tend to be conservative; it is also antidemocratic:

> Which is another way of saying that truth is on the side of democracy. Most social myths are aimed at freezing the status quo.[57]

Dunham points to racialism and various political injustices and demands a political *Entmythisierung: Ecrasez l'infame!* and meanwhile take the bishops to the lantern posts; destroy the *ancien régime!*

> Myths abound concerning the nature of society, and these myths will be found stretched screaming over many a long volume, in the very heart of the science itself. There can be few tasks more important than to remove these myths.[58]

In applied theory there is the racial myth of Hitler, Chamberlain, and deGobineau.[59] In pure theory there is the somewhat more obscure "general strike" of Georges Sorel.[60]

Myth is usually defined by social scientists in broad and sketchy terms. The most important error of the few political theorists who do consider myth is their persistence on its totalitarian nature. Myth has a tremendous capacity for human freedom. The search for a more complete political and co-organic meaning for myth is my principal purpose. The first stage will be an examination of mythopoeism, mythmaking, and a survey of materials which contribute to the understanding of myth in politics.[61]

Mythopoeism. The search for a structure of mythic reality has produced a wide range of theories. Most of these explanations suffer from a modern disease, a pernicious either-orism. Rahv suggests that our present day *mythomania* results from the fear of history.[62] Yet, interest in myth may be interest in history. The study of the process of mythopoeism has been burdened by these "derelict theories"—"conquered schools."[63] Each student of myth is only too much like the Reverend Casabon in Eliot's *Middlemarch;* he searches in mythology for the key to the universe.[64]

These examples are presented for three reasons: as a *caveat lector* to illustrate the pitfalls of myth interpretation, as a brief history of mythology as it approaches the political interpretation, and as a study of variant means of myth's development. The groupings of myth are: Euhemerism, linguistics, meteorology, psychology, anthropology, and philosophy. A co-organic system of myth attempts to synthesize these approaches.

In their simplest form, myths serve as explanations of material culture. Scott's antiquary, Monkbarns, discovers a stone inscribed A. D. L. L.. Desiring to substantiate the historical value of his property, he transforms the letters into *Agricola Dicavit Libens Lubens.* Next, he fabricates a tale of Agricola's conquest of the Picts, right on his own heath. Unfortunately, it is revealed that the initials stand for "Aiken Drum's Lang Ladle," and Aiken was "ane o' the best kale suppers o'Fife." (Many historical societies jealously superintend such treasures.) In Cooper's *The Prairie,* Dr. Bat transforms his own faithful donkey into a nightmarish mythical *Vespertilo horriblis* in a hilarious after-dark encounter.[65]

The real-life parallel occurs in New Guinea where the power pretensions of a native named Batari were recognized when boxes stenciled "Battery" began to arrive on the beach. The New Guinea cargo cults not too long ago centered on the arrival of Lyndon Johnson. Periodically archaeological *ignis fatui* flare up; a search for Noah's Ark was conducted while Soviet A-Bomb tests were being carried out in the Caucasus.[66]

Euhemerism

Of the three schools of myth-interpretation in Cicero's "On the Nature of the Gods," Euhemerism is perhaps the most interesting; this recurrent theory states that myths are true-to-life heroic stories. Euhemerus was criticized by Plutarch in "Why the Oracles Cease to Give Answers":

> This he did by describing all the received Gods under the style of generals, sea-captains, and kings, whom he makes to have lived in the remote and ancient time, and to be recorded in

> golden characters in a certain country called Panchon, with which notwithstanding never any man, either Barbarian or Grecian, had the good fortune to meet except Euhemerus alone.[67]

Euhemerism bolstered the self-apotheosis of Caesar and the deification of Alexander, both in the style of the Egyptian Pharoah. During the patristic period, the theories were seized upon by Clement of Alexandria and St. Augustine to explain the mortality of the pagan gods.[68] Seznec brilliantly traces the theme through the Middle Ages. Eusebius makes Baal the first king of the Assyrians; St. Isidore attempts to place the gods in a historical context as "founders of cities, discoverers of arts and skills."[69]

The Euhemerist compound of historicism, rationalism, and skepticism is traceable in Vico's *New Science,* where the theory is modified. The gods become men who have acquired fabulous qualities. In the Enlightenment it appears as the Abbé Banier's thesis that Jove smiting the Giants is a king suppressing sedition. In the nineteenth century, Herbert Spencer speaks of Aesculapius as a deified medicine man.[70] Brasseur de Bourborg, the interpreter of Mayan civilization, is also a thoroughgoing Euhemerist.[71]

Euhemerism was not vanquished by Plutarch, even less by recent attacks by Lord Raglan.[72] The desire to see the gods as historical figures is part of the Nietzsche syndrome—"If there were gods, how could I stand not to be one." Nietzsche couldn't stand it, and he is not alone among historical figures.

Linguistic Theories of Myth

Besides Euhemerism the linguistic approach to myth enjoys widespread popularity. In Socrates' dialogue with Hermogenes, the son of Hipponicus, myths are examined by etymology. According to this thesis, myths can be explained by cracking the names of the gods.[73]

During the 1800s Max Müller developed the theory that mythology resulted from a disease of language. Proto-Aryan man expressed himself in metaphoric poetry; later metaphor and reality were confused. Vedic myths were equated with Hellenic versions: *Dyaus-Pitar equals Zeus.* A major problem was the reconstruction of the original Sanscrit roots. As Lang pointed out with unconcealed glee, the etymological experts, Müller, Kuhn, Brown, and Preller completely disagreed on the root in *Chronos.*[74]

There is some evidence for the metaphoric degeneration process in myth formation. For example, the Hindu sun god appears literally golden-fingered as he is named. The work of the etymologists is simply the baroque overflow of a novel approach to myth.[75] The etymological tradition is continued by the poet-scholar Robert Graves. Linguistic analogies must be stamped "Use with Caution."

Meteorological Theories

Müller's linguistic derivations were based on solar metaphors. In fact, the proto-Aryans must have done little besides discuss the weather. The most extreme statement of the solar theory was in Cox's works, which even made black signify light and whiteness. Among historians, Hermann Schneider traced the solar hero through civilization.[76]

The Egyptian Osiris-Seth-Horus cycle represented a prototype of the solar hero story. The hymn of Ikhnaton placed the Pharoah in the solar pattern:

O sole god, like whom there is no other! Thou didst create the world according to thy desire . . . Since thou didst found the earth And raised them up for thy son Who came forth from thy body.[77]

Weather attributes, such as the lightning-bolt snake, were frequently associated with the pagan gods. It was natural to develop the theory that myths were the explanation of physical or natural phenomena. Such a theory was introduced into Rome by Ennius:

It brought welcome relief to many moderate minds who asked nothing better than some pretext for adhering to their old religion.[78]

The gods developed into cosmic symbols.

Passing over medieval astrology, the most important of the meteorological interpretations, the solar theory, was resurrected in 1795 with the publication of DuPuis' *L'origine de tous les cultes ou la religion universelle.* The author claimed that Christ, Osiris, Bacchus, and Mithra were solar personifications. This was an important step in the introduction of the comparative method in mythology.

There were a number of deviations from the solar theme. Preller insisted on the sky; Schwartz on the wind; Kuhn on the storm clouds; Nutall on the pole star. Fiske generalized the systems by making myths a primitive form of natural science.[79]

The critics of solar mythology were led by the anthropologist, Andrew Lang, who demonstrated that "Sing a Song of Six-Pence" could be converted into a solar myth. The most amusing refutation was attributed to the French ecclesiastic, Jean-Baptiste Pérès. Napoleon was a solar hero:

(a) Between the name Napoleon and Apollo or Apoleon, the god of the sun, there is but a trifling difference, indeed the seeming

> difference is lessened, if we take the spelling of his name from the column of the Place Vendôme where it stands Neapollo (Ne—an affirmative particle; Bonaparte "the good and luminous" as opposed to the moon). (b) Apollo and Napoleon were both born on islands. (c) According to Pausanias, Apollo was an Egyptian deity, and in the mythological history of the fabulous Napoleon, we find the hero in Egypt, regarded by the inhabitants with veneration. (d) The mother of Napoleon was said to be Letitia, which signifies joy . . . the Greek name for the mother of Apollo was Leto. From this the Romans made the name Latona. . . . But Laeto is the unused form of the verb *laetor*, and signified to inspire joy. (e) Napoleon's three sisters; the three Graces. (f) His four brothers were anthropomorphoses of the four seasons—all kings deriving their power from the sun except the fourth (winter) . . . who was invested with a vain principality, accorded to him *in the decline of the power of Napoleon* . . . that of Canino, a name derived from *cani*, or the whitened hairs of frozen old age. (g) Napoleon released France from the Hydra of Revolution. (h) Twelve marshals; the twelve signs of the zodiac. (i) His three months march into the boreal regions represented the annual course of the sun. (j) He rose in the East; he set in the West.[80]

Napoleon was a solar hero: *Q.E.D.* The solar theory has been largely 'eclipsed' by such attacks.

Anthropological Theories

Even before the solar myth was so devastatingly challenged, antiquarians had begun to collect primitive myths and arrange them into a comparative framework. Schoolcraft studied the myths of the Algonquins in his *Algic Researches.* Sir E. B. Tylor gathered a wide range of data into a synoptic view of primitive culture. Lang contributed some "flint-flakes from a Neolithic workshop" to counter Müller's "Chips."[81]

The high point of the anthropological study of myths was Sir James G. Frazer's *The Golden Bough.* Theodor Gaster recently edited a critical abridgment of Frazer's work. He wrote:

> *The Golden Bough* is a classic, but classics in the field of scholarship occupy a peculiar position. For while as literature they remain immortal and as cultural landmarks imperishable, the particular views they expound . . . tend in time to be superseded . . . they suffer the fate of Frazer's own King of the Wood and are obliged in due course to yield their authority to those who pluck the golden bough from the sacred tree . . . Frazer's interpretation of the priesthood at Aricia and of the rites which governed succession to it have been almost unanimously rejected by classical scholars.[82]

"The priest who slew the slayer and shall himself be slain," Macaulay's phrase, characterized Frazer's priest-king at Nemi. Frazer traced the origin of the Latin kingship to a ceremony in which the old king was challenged and killed by his successor.

> Moreover—he could fling his challenge only if he had first succeeded in plucking a golden bough from the tree which the priest was guarding . . . The post which was held by this precarious tenure carried with it the title of King of the Woods; but surely no crowned head ever lay uneasier . . .[83]

The bough was associated with that carried by Deiphobe in the *Aeneid* and with a cyclic vegetation cult. Eventually the king was able to consolidate sufficient power to arrange for a ritual substitute.

Frazer's source materials have been criticized; his theory of magic and religion attacked; his specimens of "primitive" culture questioned. Lang speaks derisively of the "Covent Gardens School." On the other hand, Frazer's work has served as a stimulus to anthropological research and the collection of myths. Source criticism creates an almost agonizing problem in the study of myths. But as Tylor asks in his *Primitive Culture:*

> A story by a bushranger in Australia may, perhaps, be objected to as a mistake or an invention, but did a Methodist minister in Guinea conspire with him to cheat the public by telling the same story there?[84]

One outgrowth of the "golden bough" is Malinowski's functionalism, another the myth and ritual approach.

The study of myth and ritual is based upon the Egyptian coronation-vegetation cult. Myth is treated as a ritual dramatization of a past event. Lord Raglan fuses myth and ritual, "sacred tradition and social structure."[85] Frankfort, however, has demonstrated that the myth-ritual theory of the kingship is largely limited to Egypt. Martin Foss takes the position that "Although the ritual receives all its life from myth, it nevertheless attempts to strangle the creative life of the myth and to enclose it in the reduced and fixed symbols of its typical repetitions."[86]

Theodor Gaster discusses the myth-ritual relationship:

> The function of myth . . . is to translate the real into terms of the durative and transcendental. This it does by projecting the procedures of ritual to the plane of ideal situations which they are taken to substantize and reproduce.[87]

Gaster maintains that many celebrations historicize agro-rituals; but the mock combats, commemorating the struggle between the Spaniards and the Indians, seem to have a core more historical than agricultural. Ritual may be associated with myth; it may at times be the source of myth, but myth, politics, and history are also sources for ritual.

Frazer's approach to myths has led others from the study into the "open air of the anthropological field." Malinowski's functionalism has placed myth in its appropriate social context. Gotesky, for example, summarizes several points which are fundamental to the study of political myths:

> Every culture will create and value its own myths, not because it may not be able to distinguish between truth and falsity, but because their function is to maintain and preserve culture against disruption and destruction. They serve to keep men going against defeat . . . and they preserve institutions . . .[88]

Although in general, anthropology has drifted away from the study of myth into material and demographic aspects of society, such contributions as content analysis and the psychocultural approach are important to mythology. Content analysis quantitatively examines the verbal content of myths, the number of power references, for example. Such information permits cross-cultural comparison of attitudes toward political power.[89]

David Bidney's psychocultural approach combines the studies of anthropology and psychology. Bidney uses a three-part classification of myths, similar to Comte's. Myth-making, however, never totally ceases from the precritical stage in which the emphasis is on magic and culture heroes to the scientific and secular myths of modern experience.[90]

Psychological Theory

After viewing some particularly grotesque mythological figures, Robert Burton came to regard mythology as a "diseased imagination."[91] Theophrastus much earlier sketched a cynical portrait of myth-haunted "superstitious man."[92] Modern melancholy anatomists in the guise of psychologists have built the

Oedipus complex, inherited from Vienna rather than Thebes, into the characters of primitive and modern man.

Based on a world of primitive dreams (stimulated by overindulging in Austrian tortes), the psychological interpretation of myths is exceptionally interesting qua interpretation. It also appears profitable to psychoanalyze the interpretations. Take, for example, the figure on a Cretan artifact described by Sir Arthur Evans—Hermann Schneider says it is a double-headed axe, a fertility symbol; Blinkenberg, a thunder symbol. Evans himself calls it a butterfly; that makes him normal for Rorschach.[93]

At times the psychological approach to myths is based on inadequate anthropology as Marcuse's observations on the "primal horde" in *Eros and Civilization.*[94] The wide variations, ranging from Jung's archetypes to Fromm's "forgotten language," usually converge on the dream experience.

Overemphasis on this experience characterizes the modern "psychologizing" of myths. Géza Róheim examines "The Meaning of Totemic Myth":

> I assume therefore as a working hypothesis that these myths arose in the dim past either on the basis of real history or of ontogenetic material of the original ancestor. This means simply that somebody in the past with an urge to communicate, first told a day-dream . . . Generations have been reelaborating this story in fantasy.[95]

Strehlow feels that among the once "model primitives," the Australian Arunta that *altjirama* (dream) is compounded from *altjira* (god?) and *rama* (to see); Róheim disagrees. Eliade distinguishes the dream as an extrication from a personal predicament and myth as a revelation of the universal.[96]

Dreams do meet myths on a common demonic or ecstatic ground. Among the Plains Indians the dream-experience is especially important. The fantastic trance-visions induced by narcotics as in the peyote cult result in myths. In the *Magliabecchiano Codex* a diabolic figure approaches a teonanacatl eater in a dreamy cloud; a similar figure dances on a plant in the *Florentine Codex.* The Dionysiac experience will be examined later.[97]

Totemism and taboo are important in cultural "psychodynamics." The exact connection of totemism and ancestor worship has been complicated by ritualistic and psychological interpretations. Lang indicates one problem:

> Should Müller's friend, Abeken, whose name means small ape, and who displays an ape in his coat of arms, be assigned the ape as his totem? It is true I never saw him eating an ape, but I feel certain this was not from any regard for his supposed ancestor.[98]

Of equal danger is the effort of some psychologists to establish a pattern of psychocultural evolution. Neumann, for example, attempts to apply Haeckel's "biological law," "ontogeny recapitulates phylogeny," to myths.[99] The psychological approach, the dream experience, and totemism-taboo must all be labeled "Dangerous."

Myth-Maker as Philosopher

As Aristotle tells us: "Even the lover of myths in a sense is a philosopher. For myth is a tissue of wonders."[100] The philosophic tradition in mythology treats myths as allegorical, poetic truths; symbolic, esthetic expressions; or etiological speculations of primitive man. The picture is indifferently that of Neanderthal contemplating a bust of Aristotle; or of Voltaire's Huron. Paul Radin's work emphasizes the existence of the creative, primitive intellectual. *Primitive Man as Philosopher* goes far to prove that the Winnebago and Maori are not "primitive," but the genealogy of this theory is rooted in Rousseau's "noble savage," with the overtones of Chateaubriand and Girodet. Tylor's supposition that primitive peoples necessarily represent early cultural stages has been sufficiently refuted.

The romantic notions of primitive intellectualism in mythology were countered by the equally questionable primitive ignorance of Fontenelle, and the pre-logical functions of Lévy-Bruhl.[101] But as Max Müller once said: "Early man not only did not think as we think, but did not think as we supposed he ought to have thought."[102]

The antecedents of modern philosophical interpretations of myth are varied. For example, there is the moral-allegorical tradition, which Rabelais cautions against:

> Do you honestly believe that Homer . . . had in mind the allegories which have been foisted off on him by Plutarch, Heraclides, Ponticus, Eustachius, and Phornutus and which Politian has purloined from them? If you do believe this, you are indeed far from my opinion, which is that Homer could no more have dreamed of anything of the sort than Ovid in his *Metamorphoses* could have been thinking of the Gospel Sacraments.[103]

In his *Confessions,* St. Augustine mentions the discovery of new allegorical meaning in the Scriptures; this approach to myth is found also in Philo and St. Ambrose. During the Middle Ages mythology tended in the direction of a moral philosophy in the *Moralia* of Gregory the Great and the *Mythologiae* of Fulgentius.

Francis Bacon differentiates a type called "poesy parabolic":

> for that tendeth to . . . illustrate that which is taught or delivered . . . that is when the secrets and mysteries of religion, policy, or parables.[104]

This kind of allegorizing emphasizes the close relationship of poetic truth, myth, and philosophy; it foreshadows romantic symbolism.

Symbolism was highlighted by the German interpreters of the nineteenth century. In his *Symbolik,* Creuzer derived Greek mythology from their scanty religious knowledge and the benevolent intent of Eastern priests. The *mythus* was "nothing more than a symbol expressed." Hermann spoke of the figurative representation of an idea, and Heyne of the *sermo symbolicus et mythicus.*

Voss in his *Anti-Symbolik* denied Creuzer's thesis. In returning to the skepticism of Vico and the Enlightenment, Voss claimed that myth was not emblematic but a rational product of reflection which gave meaning to ancestral ideas of virtue and honesty. Voss described Homer as "more god-like than his gods."[105]

Of course, symbolism flourished as a form of poetic expression. Novalis wrote: "Poetry is what is absolutely genuine and real. That is the kernel of my philosophy. The more poetic the more true."[106] Such sentiments have connected myth to philosophy; Maritain has spoken of "metaphysical myths" in this context.[107] Myth and philosophy have directed Eliade toward ontophany; Cassirer toward epistemology; Whitehead toward symbolic logic. The esthetic theory merits special attention. *La fonction fabulatrice* of Santayana and Bergson acts as a dramatic divining rod for the potentialities in human nature.[108] John Dewey describes myth:

> Myths were something other than intellectualistic essays of primitive man in science . . . Mythology is . . . an affair of psychology that generates art.[109]

Flinders-Petrie and Sorokin indicate parallels between the artistic remains of a culture and its political and moral condition; myths fit into the same pattern.[110]

A. H. Krappe's *La génèse des mythes* declares that myths are esthetic creations incorporated into sacred texts. Suzanne Langer's *Philosophy in a New Key* expands upon this theme.

> The great mythologies which have survived both the overgrowth of mystic fable and the corruption of popular tradition are those that have become fixed in national poems . . . This has given rise to the belief stated in somewhat doctrinaire and exaggerated terms by Krappe, that mythology is *essentially* the work of epic poets.[111]

NOTES TO CHAPTER I

1. Thomas Mann, cited in Mark Schorer's "The Necessity of Myth," *The Journal of American Folklore* (hereafter cited as *JAF*), "Myth: A Symposium" (1955), p. 360. This article originally appeared as a chapter in Schorer's book, *William Blake: The Politics of Vision* (New York: Henry Holt, 1946).

2. Ernst Cassirer, *The Myth of the State* (New Haven: Yale University Press, paperback ed., 1961), pp. 1, 263.

3. Jakob Grimm, cited in John Fiske's *Myth and Mythmakers* [Boston: Houghton Mifflin, 1892 (1872)], p. vi. The spirit behind the inquiry into political myths is the same which prompted Frazer to write: ". . . as the scholar of the Renaissance found not merely fresh food for thought but a new field of labour in the dusty and faded manuscripts of Greece and Rome, so in the mass of materials that is steadily pouring in from many sides—from buried cities of remotest antiquity . . . we of today must recognize a new province of knowledge which will task the energies of generations of students," *The Magic Art and the Evolution of Kings*, Vol. I, p. xxv, *The Golden Bough* (London: Macmillan & Co., 1911).

4. Friedrich Nietzsche, *Works* (New York: Tudor Publishing Company, 1931), pp. 326–27.

5. Valéry is cited in Harry Levin's "Some Meanings of Myth," *Daedalus*, "Journal of the American Academy of Arts and Science," Spring 1959, p. 223, reprinted in *Myth and Mythmaking*, Henry A. Murray, ed.

6. Richard Chase, *Quest for Myth* (Baton Rouge: Louisiana State University Press, 1949), p. 105.

7. Cp. Amos N. Wilder, "Myth and Symbol in the New Testament," in *Symbols and Values: An Initial Study*, Lyman Bryson, ed., Thirteenth Symposium of the Conference on Science, Philosophy, and Religion (New York: Harper's, 1954), p. 138.

8. C. Kerényi and C. G. Jung, *Introduction to a Science of Mythology*, "The Myth of the Divine Child and the Mysteries of Eleusis," trans. R. F. C. Hull (London: Routledge and Kegan Paul, 1951), p. 184; also in *Essays on a Science of Mythology*, Bollingen Series XXII (copyright © 1949, 1959, and 1963 by Bollingen Foundation), reprinted by permission of Princeton University Press.

9. Sir Walter Scott, cited in Chase, op. cit., pp. 76–77. The source is a footnote to "The Lady of the Lake."

Earl W. Court stresses the essential similarity of the types in "Myth as a World View: A Biosocial Synthesis," *Culture in History*, Stanley Diamond, ed., *Essays in Honor of Paul Radin* (New York: Columbia University Press, 1960), pp. 588–89.

10. Wundt's classification is sevenfold: mythological tale fables, pure fairy tales, biological tales and fables, pure animal tales, genealogical tales, joke tales and fables, moral fables. Cf. V. Propp, *Morphology of the Folktale*, "Biographical

and Special Series" (Philadelphia: American Folklore Society, 1958), Vol. 9, p. 6; Wilhelm Wundt, *Völkerpsychologie,* esp. II Teil: I: 507 (Leipzig, 1905–1909).

11. Bronislaw Malinowski, *Magic, Science, and Religion and Other Essays,* "Myth in Primitive Psychology," trade ed. (Boston: Beacon Press, 1948), p. 84; cf. T. A. Sebeok, ed., *Myth, a Symposium* (Philadelphia: American Folklore Society, 1955), Vol. V.

12. Schorer, *William Blake: the Politics of Vision.*

13. Robert Graves, The White Goddess, "A Historical Grammar of Poetic Myth" (New York: Creative Age Press, 1948), p. 7. Fromm is cited in Edward Bernays' "The Semantics of Symbols," Chap. XVI, *Symbols and Values: Symposium* (New York: Conference on Science, Philosophy and Religion in Relation to the Democratic Way of Life, 1954; distributed by Harper and Brothers), p. 229. Cp. Andrew Lang, *Custom and Myth* (New York: Harper and Brothers, 1885), p. 1. Max Müller, *Chips From a German Workshop,* "Essays on Mythology, Traditions and Customs" (New York: Charles Scribner's Sons, 1869).

14. Ernst Cassirer, *Language and Myth,* trans. Suzanne Langer (New York: Harper and Bros., 1946), p. 32.

15. This is Coleridge's phrase in the *Biographia Literaria.* Cp. *per contra,* Claude Lévi-Strauss, "The Structural Study of Myth," *JAF,* (1955), p. 430: "Poetry is a kind of speech which cannot be translated except at the cost of serious distortions; whereas the mythical value of myth remains preserved."

16. Cf. G. van der Leeuw, *Religion in Essence and Manifestation,* trans. J.E. Turner (London: George Allen and Unwin, 1938). Page 421 cites Preuss, *Religion und Mythologie der Uitoto* I, p. 26, 1921.

17. Henri Frankfort, *Kingship and the Gods,* "A Study of Ancient Near Eastern Religion as the Integration of Society and Nature," [Chicago: University of Chicago Press, 1955 (1948)], p. 27. Marduk is tested to see if he can rearticulate a fragmented body merely by "speaking it together." The word is given similar demiurgic power in Mayan, Maori, and Egyptian myths.

18. Daniel Brinton, *Myths of the New World,* "A Treatise on the Symbolism and Mythology of the Red Race of America," (New York: Leypoldt and Holt, 1868), p. 160. Hutton Webster, *Primitive Secret Societies,* "A Study in Early Politics and Religion" (New York: Macmillan Co., 1908), pp. 42–43.

19. Van der Leeuw, op. cit., p. 436, cites G. Roeder, *Altägyptische Erzählungen und Märchen* (1927), p. 145.

20. Graves, op. cit., p. 32, writes of the poem "The Battle of Achren": "There was a man in that battle, who, unless his name were known could not be overcome." Cp. S. Czarnowski, *Le Culte des Héros et ses Conditions Sociales,* Bibliotheque de Philosophie Contemporaine (Paris: Felix Alcan, 1919), p. 178.

To maintain that myth is essentially spoken is hardly to deny that it can be written down. This is the oral tradition of Grimm, Castren, and Boas. To record it may abstract myth from its social context. Cf. Melville Jacobs, *The Content and Style of an Oral Literature, Clackamas Chinook Myths and Tales,* Viking Fund Publications in Anthropology #26. (New York: Wenner-Gren Foundation for Anthropological Research, 1959). An anecdote on glossolalia is narrated by James Dalyell, *The Darker Superstitions of Scotland,* (Edinburgh: Waugh and Innes, 1834), p. 598.

21. Susan Feldmann, *African Myths and Tales,* Laurel Original (New York: Dell Publishing Co., 1963), p. 28.

22. Carl Otfried Müller, *Introduction to a Scientific System of Mythology,* trans. John Leitch (London: Longman, Brown, Green, and Longmans, 1844), p. 29. On the general problem of truth and myth, cf. *Truth, Myth, and Symbol,* ed. Thomas J. J. Altizer et al., Spectrum Book (Englewood Cliffs, N.J.: Prentice-Hall, 1962).

23. Cf. Lynn White, "Christian Myth and Christian History," *Journal of the History of Ideas* (1942), III:2, p. 155. Rudolph Bultmann, *Offenbarung und Heilsgeschehen* (Munich: A. Lempp, 1941); George Widengren, "Early Hebrew Myths and Their Interpretation," in *Myth, Ritual, and Kingship,* "Essays on the Theory and Practice of Kingship in the Ancient Near East and Israel," Samuel Hooke, ed. (Oxford: Clarendon Press, 1958), pp. 149–203. C. Koch, *Die römische Jupiter* (Frankfurt, 1937).

R. B. Ripley in *Harvard Politics* (1963), Vol. II, p. 2, cites the passage from Silone's *Bread and Wine* in which Spina discusses Church, myth, and revolution: "I have ceased trying to smother and repress my deepest impulses, solely because in my youth they had been bound up with religious symbols and practices. I tried . . . to substitute logic and intellectual ideas taken from the world of economics and politics for those deeper forces which I felt myself compelled to distrust . . . all that remained alive and indestructible of Christianity in me was revived: A Christianity denuded of all mythology."

24. Feldmann, op. cit., p. 12; cited from B. Cendrars, *Anthologie Nègre.* Some anthropologists have dismissed this question of truth as irrelevant. Coon and Chapple, *Principles of Anthropology* (New York: Henry Holt and Co., 1942), p. 602.

25. Random examples from *The American Scholar* (hardly a "popular" publication): Clarence A. Berdahl, "Myths About the Peace Treaties of 1919–1920" (1942) Vol. 11 No. 3, pp. 261–74; John Steadman, "The Myth of Asia" (1950), Vol. 25 No. 2, pp. 163–76. A more technical usage is that of H. Wentworth Eldridge in *The Second American Revolution* (New York: William Morrow and Co., 1964), p. 11: "The beloved sovereign state is the primordial myth which dominates our lives."

26. Littre's *Dictionary,* cited by Levin, *Daedalus,* (Spring 1959), p. 228.

27. S. H. Butcher, *Aristotle's Theory of Poetry and Fine Art,* 4th ed. (London: Macmillan & Co., 1923), pp. 163, 191.

28. Thomas Carlyle, *On Heroes, Hero-Worship and the Heroic in History* [New York: Charles Scribner's Sons, 1897 (1841)], p. 4. Many other authors agree: cf.

Ernst Cassirer, *Essay on Man* (New Haven: Yale University Press, 1944), p. 74: "Though myth is fictitious, it is an unconscious not a conscious fiction. The primitive mind was not aware of the meaning of its own creations." Vico treats myth in terms of poetic metaphor in *The New Science of Politics* and states that it was often glossed by the ancients as *vera narratio.*

J. O. Hall, *American Anthropologist* (1900), Vol. II, p. 290, writes of "volitional creation," which is Ruskin's opinion that the centaurs in Dante's *Inferno* actually trotted across the poet's brain in some shape.

29. Arnold Toynbee, *A Study of History,* abridgement, Vol. I-V, by D. C. Somervell (New York: Oxford University Press, 1947), p. 44. Cp. A. Sabatier, *Memoire sur la notion hébraïque de l'esprit* (Paris, 1879): "To create a myth, that is to say to catch a glimpse of a higher truth behind a palpable reality, is the most manifest sign of greatness of the human soul . . ." Cited by Count Goblet d'Aviella, *The Migration of Symbols* [New York: University Books, 1956 (1899)], p. 3.

Cp. Schelling's opinion, cited by Adolf Allwohn, "Der Mythos bei Schelling," *Kantstudien* No. 61 (Charlottenburg, Pan Verlag Heise, 1927), pp. 13, 16.

30. Frazer, op. cit., ed. T. Gaster, p. 96.

31. Joseph Campbell, *The Masks of God: Primitive Mythology* (New York: Viking Press, 1959), p. 117. *Marga,* "the path or the way to the discovery of the universal."

32. R.M. MacIver, *Symbols and Values: Symposium,* p. xi: "Foreword," "Through the visible symbol something invisible, something impossible to perceive and hard for the ordinary mind to conceive becomes an object of communication."

33. Yeats is cited in Levin, op. cit., *Daedalus,* p. 231. Cf. *Symbols and Values: Symposium:* Richard McKeon, "Symbols, Myths and Arguments," pp. 13–38; Lyman Bryson, "The Quest for Symbols," pp. 1–13.

34. Ilya Ehrenburg is cited in *Young Voices in Soviet Literature,* Independent Service for Information on the Vienna Youth Festival, (Cambridge, Mass., 1959), p. 7.

35. Nietzsche, cited in Chase, op. cit., p. 27; cf. George Sebba, "Symbol and Myth in Modern Rationalistic Societies," Altizer, ed., p. 141 ff. Tate's views appear in C.A. Ward's "Myths: Further Vanderbilt Agrarian Views," *University of Kansas City Review,* Vol. 25:1, p. 53: "Men who have lost both the higher myth of religion and the lower myth of historical dramatization have lost the forms of human action . . ."

36. Ward Pafford, "The Literary Uses of Myth and Symbol," pp. 129f. in Altizer, ed.; P. Walker, "Prophetic Myths in Zola," *Publications of the Modern Language Association* (1959), Vol. 74, p. 444f; W. W. Douglas, "Meanings of Myth in Modern Criticism," *Modern Philology* (1953), Vol. 50, pp. 232–42; Louise Brogan, "The Secular Hell," *Chimera,* "A Special Issue on Myth" (1946), Vol. IV # 3, pp. 19–32; Gilbert Highet, "Reinterpretation of the Myths," *Virginia*

Quarterly Review (1949), Vol. 25:1, pp. 99–115; Donald A. Stauffer, "The Modern Myth of Modern Myth," *English Institute Essays, 1947* (New York: Columbia University Press, 1948), pp. 23–50; C. Seidenspinner, "Mann and the Myth," *Christian Century,* April 13, 1938, Vol. 55, pp. 461–63.

37. Stevens is cited in Schorer, op. cit., p. 361.

38. Jung, op. cit., p. 227.

39. Mircea Eliade, *Myths, Dreams, and Mysteries:* "The Encounter Between Contemporary Faiths and Archaic Realities," trans. Philip Mairet, [London: Harvill Press, 1960 (1957)], p. 24.

40. Jerome S. Bruner, "Myth and Identity," *Daedalus,* p. 357.

41. The universal distribution of myth-themes presents a fascinating aspect of the study of comparative cultures and social experiences. In addition to the heroic pattern, including the flood story and the struggle with the serpent, which is analyzed in Chapter III, many themes are of wide occurrence: the earth-diver, the hare-marked moon, the night hatchet, and the chain of arrows.

A Shasta Indian tale and a Chinese myth both relate how a hero kills the nine suns which have been scorching the earth. Gudmund Hatt, *Asiatic Influences in American Folklore* (Copenhagen, 1949). "The Corn Mother in America and Indonesia," *Anthropos* (1951), Vol XLVI, pp. 853–914.

42. G. Elliott Smith, *The Evolution of the Dragon* (New York: Longmans, Green, and Co., 1919); Livingston Farrand, "The Significance of Mythology and Tradition," *JAF,* Vol. XVII, pp 14–22 (diffusion and independent development). H.R. Hays, *From Ape to Angel:* "An Informal History of Social Anthropology" (New York: Alfred A. Knopf, 1958), p. 284.

43. Julian Stewart, *Theory of Culture Change* (Urbana: University of Illinois Press, 1955). Johannes Maringer, *The Gods of Prehistoric Man,* trans. Mary Ilford [New York: Alfred A. Knopf, 1960 (bear cult)].

44. T. F. Crane, "The Diffusion of Popular Tales," *JAF* (1888), Vol. I:1, p. 12.

45. W. Y. Elliott, *The Pragmatic Revolt in Politics* (New York: Macmillan Co., 1928).

Many anthropologists and "political scientists" write of myth in organic terms without examining the ethical basis of myth.

W. G. Sumner writes of the "super-organic," *Folkways* (New York: Mentor Books, New American Library, 1960), p. vi. Cp. A. L. Kroeber's "The Super-Organic," *American Anthropologist* (1917), Vol. 19 No. 2, pp. 163–213.

"Organic patterns" is a more satisfying term than "law." There are "laws of the association of ideas," and "of imitation" (Tarde); "of sensibility" (Ribot); of "collective psychology, or the crowd" (Le Bon and Wundt).

Patterns in which myths react as organic are still hypothetical. Such phenomena as survivalism are well documented in J. C. Lawson's *Modern Greek Folklore and Ancient Greek Religion* (Cambridge: University Press, 1910). Jean Seznec, *The Survival of the Pagan Gods,* "The Mythological Tradition and Its Place in Renaissance Humanism and Art," Bollingen Series XXXVIII (New York: Pantheon Books, 1953).

46. Gaetano Mosca, *The Ruling Class,* trans. H. D. Kahn (New York: McGraw-Hill, 1939), pp. 62, 70–72. Barrington Moore, Jr., *Political Power and Social Theory* (Cambridge: Harvard University Press, 1958), pp. 10–16, 27–28, 79.

47. Edward Jenks, *Law and Politics in the Middle Ages* (London: William Clowes and Sons Ltd., 1912), Chap. I; from W. Y. Elliott and Neil A. McDonald, *Western Political Heritage* [Englewood Cliffs, N.J.: Prentice-Hall, 1961 (1949)], pp. 335–36.

48. George Sebba, "Symbol and Myth in Modern Rationalistic Societies," in Altizer ed., *Truth, Myth, and Symbol*, p. 165.

49. Lévi-Strauss, op. cit., p. 428.

50. Katherine Spencer, *Mythology and Values* (Philadelphia: American Folklore Society, 1957), p. 44, "An Analysis of Navaho Chantway Myths"; Malinowski, op. cit., p. 89. Cf. Ruth Benedict, *Patterns of Culture* (New York: Library of World Literature, 1946).

51. D. H. Munro, "Concept of Myth," *Sociological Review* (London, 1950), Vol. 42, pp. 115–32; Molly Francke, "The Socio-Economic Interpretation of Mythology," *Folklore* (1953), Vol. 54, pp. 369–78.

52. W. H. R. Rivers, "The Sociological Significance of Myth," *Folklore* (1912), Vol. 23, pp. 307–13.

53. John Dollard, *Caste and Class in a Southern Town* (New York: Doubleday, 1937), p. 263. Cited in Norman E. Whitten, Jr., "Contemporary Patterns of Malign Occultism Among Negroes in North Carolina" JAF (1962), p. 311.

54. Cf. Charles W. Lemmi, *The Classical Deities in Bacon*, "A Study in Mythological Symbolism" (Baltimore, Md.: Johns Hopkins University Press, 1933).

55. J. A. St. John, *The Philosophical Works of John Locke* (London: G. Bell and Sons, 1916), Vol. 1, p. 27.

56. Francis Delaisi, *Political Myths and Economic Realities* (New York: Viking Press, 1927), p. 38.

57. Barrows Dunham, *Man Against Myth* (Boston: Little, Brown and Co., 1947), p. 22.

58. Ibid., p. 22.

59. On the racial myth, cf. Boyd C. Shafer, *Nationalism: Myth and Reality* (New York: Harcourt Brace and Co., 1955), pp. 29–39; Paul Radin, *The Racial Myth* (New York: Whittlesey House, McGraw-Hill, 1934).

60. Georges Sorel, *Reflections on Violence,* trans. T. E. Hulme (New York: Peter Smith, 1941), p. 22; Richard Humphrey, *Georges Sorel,* "Prophet Without

Honor, A Study in Anti-Intellectualism" (Cambridge: Harvard University Press, 1951); Hans Barth, *Masse und Mythos* (Hamburg: Rowohlt, 1959); James H. Meisel, "Georges Sorel's Last Myth," *The Journal of Politics* (1950), pp. 52–65.

Eliade, op. cit., p. 25, writes of Sorel's "general strike" that it "might be an instrument of political combat, but it has no mythical precedents, and that alone is enough to exclude it from mythical status." The "general strike" is an antimyth. Cf. Ben Halpern, " 'Myth' and 'Ideology' in Modern Usage," *History and Theory* Vol. I: 2, pp. 129–49 (Sorel's "myth" and Mannheim's "ideology").

Halpern considers ideology to be the application of myth—"rational ordering of this material for communication and social control . . . An ideology arises when there is an attempt to reduce the pattern symbols of myth to the fixity of objective symbols; or, in other words, to convert the basic consensual values of society into a rational ideal system . . . establishing and governing social existence." "The Dynamics of Culture," *Ethics* (1955), Vol. 65, pp. 235–49.

61. There are no articles dealing directly with myth in the *American Political Science Review;* Ruth Benedict, "Myth," in *Encyclopedia of Social Sciences* (Washington, D.C.: Public Affairs Press, 1959), Vol. II, pp. 178–89; John T. Zadrozny, "Myth" in *Dictionary of Social Science.*

62. P. Rahv, "Myth and the Powerhouse," *Partisan Review* (1953), Vol. 20, p. 642; cf. A. M. Hocart, "Myths in the Making," *Folklore* (1922), Vol. 33, pp. 57–72; Hilaire Belloc, "On Myth: How a Myth Arises and Grows," *Commonweal,* Feb. 19, 1930, Vol. 11:450; P. Wheelwright, "Notes on Mythopoeia," *Sewanee Review* (1951), Vol. 59, pp. 574–92.

63. Arnold van Gennep, *La Formation des Légendes* (Paris: E. Flammarion, 1910); Lewis Spence, *The Outlines of Mythology,* Premier Book (Greenwich, Conn.: Fawcett Publications, 1963).

64. Cf. Albert J. Kuhn, "English Deism and the Development of Romantic Mythological Syncretism," *Publications of the Modern Language Association* (1956), Vol. 71, pp. 1099–1116. Kuhn traces the deistic search for a key myth through such works as Jacob Bryant's *A New System, or an Analysis of Ancient Mythology* (1774–76) and Godfrey Higgins' *Anacalypses* (1836).

65. Sir Walter Scott, *The Antiquary* (Edinburgh: T. A. Constable, 1901, Vol. I, pp. 47–51. A prototype occurs in Voltaire's French peasant d'Aoudri.

On the silent Harpocrates, cf. M. Clermont-Ganneau, *Mythologie Iconographique* (Paris: E. Leroux, 1878), p. 85.

A further example of myth-making from material culture is the unfortunate legend of St. Ursula, as told by Sabine Baring-Gould in *Curious Myths of the Middle Ages* (London: Rivington's, 1868), pp. 61–62. This story was used to explain the excavated remains of the Roman cemetery of Cologne by the visionary Elizabeth of Schonau. It was revealed to her that these were St. Ursula's remains. When men's bones were uncovered among the virgins, she had another revelation which brought the Pope and half of his cardinals to Germany. The children's remains were explained by a Praemonstratine monk after Elizabeth's death.

D. S. Lamb, "Mythical Monsters", *JAF,* Vol. II, pp. 277–91.

66. Batari's tale is in Peter Worsley's *The Trumpet Shall Sound,* "A Study of the 'Cargo Cults' in Melanesia" (London: MacGibbon and Kee, 1957); reprinted by permission of Schocken Books, Inc., copyright © 1968 by Peter Worsley). Rupert Furneaux, *Myth and Mystery* (London: Allan Wingate, 1955).

67. Plutarch, *Miscellaneous Essays* (Boston: Little, Brown and Co., 1888), Vol. IV, p. 84.

68. Hugh Farmer, *The General Prevalence of the Worship of Human Spirits in the Ancient Heathen Nations* (London: Galabin and Baker, 1783), pp. 219–24. Seznec, op. cit., pp. 12–13.

69. Seznec, op. cit., pp. 14–15, 22.

70. C. O. Müller, op. cit., p. 256. Spencer's Euhemerism also assumes the simpler form of ancestor worship: *Principles of Sociology* (New York: D. Appleton Company, 1923), I, p. 404. E. B. Tylor, *Primitive Culture,* "Researches into the Development of Mythology, . . ." (London: John Murray, 1920), p. 279 (Banier's *La Mythologie et les Fables expliquées par l'Histoire,* Paris, 1738).

71. Adrian Recinos, trans., *Popul Vuh: The Sacred Book of the Ancient Quiche Maya* (Norman, Okla.: University of Oklahoma Press, 1950), pp. 53, 93. Ximenez's servants of Lucifer become de Bourborg's primitive kings. Rafael Girard, *El Popol Vuh* (Guatemala, C. A.: Fuente Historica I, Editorial del Ministerio de Educación Publica, 1952).

72. Lord Raglan, *The Hero,* "A Study in Tradition, Myth, and Drama" (London: Methuen and Co., Ltd., 1936).

73. Plato, "Cratylus," *The Dialogues of Plato,* Jowett, ed. (Scribner, Armstrong and Co., 1874), Vol. I, p. 589ff. Cp. Propertius on Jupiter Feretrius IV:10, L.R. Lind, ed., *Latin Poetry in Verse Translation* (Boston: Houghton Mifflin, 1957).

74. Lang, *Custom and Myth,* p. 57.

75. Seznec, op. cit., p. 182. A. LePlongeon, *Queen Moo and the Egyptian Sphinx* (New York: published by the author, 1896). (The Greek alphabet is a Mayan epic on the destruction of the Continent Mu; there is an amazing correspondence with the twelfth letter.) Harold Bayley, *The Lost Language of Symbolism* (London: Wingate and Norgate, 1912), 2 vols. (M'Lud is a solar oblation.)

Cf. Graves' *White Goddess,* in which the ogams are converted into a hymn dedicated to Dionysus, the *Boibel-Loth.* With the slightest dash of metathesis and phonetic juggling it can be converted into a beautiful Sanscrit poetic image of the sacrifice of the Soma priest to the Cosmic Serpent.

76. Richard M. Dorson, "The Eclipse of Solar Mythology," *JAF,* pp. 393–416, "Myth: A Symposium," 1955; Andrew Lang, "Max Müller," *Contemporary Review* (1900), Vol. 77, p. 785. Cox is cited from his *The Mythology of the Aryan Nations,* I:145; cf. George Cox, *An Introduction to the Science of Comparative Mythology and Folklore* (New York: Henry Holt, 1881).

Hermann Schneider, *The History of World Civilization,* 2 vols. (London: George Routledge, 1931).

77. William C. McDermott and W. E. Caldwell, *Readings in the History of the Ancient World* (New York: Rinehart and Co., 1951), pp. 90–92, from James B. Pritchard, *Ancient Near Eastern Texts Relating to the Old Testament*, trans. E. A. Speiser (Princeton, N. J.: Princeton University Press, 1930), p. 93.

78. Seznec, op. cit., p. 37 (Ennius and Cicero).

79. Cf. S. G. F. Brandon, "The Myth and Ritual Position Critically Considered," Hooke, ed., p. 261. Mrs. Zelia Nutall, *The Fundamental Principles of Old and New World Civilization,* "Peabody Museum Archaeological and Ethnological Papers" (Cambridge, 1901), Vol. II; Fiske, op. cit., p. 21.

80. Albert L. Guérard, *Reflections on the Napoleonic Legend* (New York: Charles Scribner's Sons, 1924), pp. 19–20.

81. Lafiteau's *Moeurs des sauvages Americaines comparées aux moeurs des premiers temps* (1724) is an early example. Cf. Robert H. Lowie, *The History of Ethnological Theory* (New York: Rinehart and Co., 1937). Lang, *Custom and Myth,* p. 9.

82. Theodor H. Gaster, ed., *The New Golden Bough* by Sir J. G. Frazer (New York: S. G. Phillips, Inc., 1959), p. xiii. Mannhardt's work in some respects anticipates Frazer's.

83. Frazer, op. cit., p. xix.

84. Tylor, op. cit., Vol. I, p. 9.

85. Lord Raglan, op. cit., p. 130. For criticisms of Frazer, cf. Chase, op. cit., p. 68. On myth and ritual: Clyde Kluckhohn, "Myth and Rituals, A General Theory," *Harvard Theological Review* (1942), Vol. 35, pp. 45–81; William Bascom, "The Myth-Ritual Theory," *JAF,* Vol. 70, pp. 103–12. Lord Raglan, Stanley E. Hyman, "The Ritual View of Myth and Mythic," *JAF,* Vol. 68, pp. 462–72; Stanley E. Hyman, "Myth, Ritual, and Nonsense," *Kenyon Review* (1949), Vol. 11 No. 3, pp. 455–75.

86. Martin Foss, *Symbol and Metaphor in Human Experience* (Princeton, N. J.: Princeton University Press, 1949), p. 93.

87. Theodor Gaster, *Thespis: Ritual, Myth, and Drama in the Ancient Near East* [Garden City, N.Y.: Anchor Book, Doubleday and Co., 1961 (1950)], p. 24.

88. R. Gotesky, "The Nature of Myth and Society," *The American Anthropologist* (1952), Vol. LIV, p. 530.

89. Bernard Berelson, "Content Analysis," *Handbook of Social Psychology,* G. Lindzey, ed. (Reading, Mass.: Addison-Wesley Publishing Co., 1954), p. 489.

90. David Bidney, "The Concept of Myth and the Problem of Psychocultural Evolution," *The American Anthropologist,* Vol. 52 No. 1, pp. 16–26.

91. Seznec, op. cit., p. 313.

92. W. R. Halliday, "The Superstitious Man of Theophrastus," *JAF* (1930), Vol. 41, pp. 121–54.

93. Sir Arthur Evans, *The Earlier Religion of Greece in the Light of Cretan Discoveries* (London: Macmillan & Co., 1931), pp. 37–41. Toynbee, op cit., p. 97; Smith, op cit., p. 10.

94. Herbert Marcuse, *Eros and Civilization,* "A Philosophical Inquiry into Freud" (Boston: The Beacon Press, 1955), pp. 15, 58ff., 159–71 ("The Images of Orpheus and Narcissus").

95. Géza Róheim, *The Eternal Ones of the Dream* (New York: International Universities Press, 1955), p. 7.

96. Ibid, p. 210; Eliade, op. cit., p. 17.

97. Harvard Museum Display. Cf. Karl A. Bell, *Dreams and Myths,* "Nervous and Mental Diseases Monograph Series," #15, 1914. Irving Hallowell, "Myth, Culture, and Personality," *AA* (1947), Vol. 47, pp. 544–56. Sigmund Freud, *Totem and Taboo,* "Some Points of Agreement between the Mental Lives of Savages and Neurotics" (London: Routledge and Paul, 1950).

98. Lang, cited in Dorson, op. cit., p. 402; Richard N. Dorson, "Theories of Myth and the Folklorist," *Daedalus* (1959), pp. 284–85.

99. Erich Neumann, *Origins of the History of Consciousness,* Bollingen Series #42 (New York: Pantheon Books, 1954), p. xvi.

100. Alexander Eliot cites this phrase, "When the Gods Talked," *Saturday Evening Post,* October 27, 1962, p. 66.

101. L. Lévy-Bruhl, *Les Fonctions Mentales dans les Sociétés Inférieures* (Paris: F. Alcan, 1910). J. R. Carrie, ed., Fontenelle's "De l'Origine des Fables" (1724) (Paris: Librairie F. Alcan, 1932).

102. Müller, cited in Spence, op. cit., p. 18

103. Cited by Seznec, op. cit., "Gargantua's Prologue," p. 95.

104. Cited by McKeon, *Symposium,* p. 33; Francis Bacon, "Of the Proficience of Learning Human and Divine," Book II, *The Works of Francis Bacon,* J. Spedding, ed. (London: Longmans, 1857), p. 344. Ihab Hassan writes in terms of transcendental myth themes "Towards a Method in Myth," *JAF* (1952), Vol. 65, p. 206. Just because some myths are treated as containing allegorical truths does not make every myth a condensation of *Pilgrim's Progress.* What is perhaps most important are the variant allegorical meanings which have been read into myths. For example, Marx views Prometheus as the proletariat. This is context analysis.

105. O. Müller, op. cit., pp. 259, 299; Friedrich Creuzer, *Symbolik und Mythologie der alten Völker,* four parts (Leipzig and Darmstadt, 1842).

106. Novalis, cited by Cassirer, *The Myth of the State,* p. 5.

107. Jacques Maritain, cited by F. Fergusson, "Myth and Literary Scruple," *Sewanee Review* (1956) Vol. 64, p. 178.

108. A. N. Whitehead, *Symbolism, Its Meaning and Effect* (Cambridge University Press, 1928). G. Santayana, *The Idea of Christ in the Gospels* (New York: Charles Scribner's Sons, 1946), p. 178.

109. John Dewey, *Art as Experience* (New York, 1934), p. 30.

110. W. M. Flinders-Petrie, *The Revolutions of Civilization,* 2nd ed. (New York: Harper's, 1912); Pitrim Sorokin, *Social and Cultural Dynamics* (New York: American Book Co., 1937–41)—"sensate and ideational culture." For example, examine the Byzantine coinages in the series from Arcadius to Justinian. The earlier emperors look like emperors; the later ones, like dry-docked codfish. Cf. Count Ivan Tolstoy, *Byzantine Coinage,* n.p. Arnold Hauser, *The Social History of Art,* trans. by author and Stanley Godman, 2 vols. (New York: Alfred A. Knopf, 1951).

111. Suzanne K. Langer *Philosophy in a New Key,* Mentor Books [New York: New American Library, 1948 (1942)], p. 169. A. H. Krappe, *La génése des mythes* (Paris: Payot, 1938). Langer finds the source of myth in fantasy and not necessarily primitive. Cf. L. E. Loemker, "Symbol and Myth in Philosophy," *Truth, Myth, and Symbol,* pp. 109–127.

II. THE POLITICAL MEANING OF EPIC

• • •

Epics are systems of political myths. Epics are the cultural Weltanschauung—in Herder's phrase, "the folk spirit speaking." To understand the epic is to understand the growth of political and social consciousness. Some epics, as the *Nibelungenlied,* express a cultural catastrophism; others, as the *Aeneid,* a political messianism. My study focuses first on the social myths of the epics and then on the epic hero.

The epic hero is a political animal; his antithesis is Polyphemus-like "clanless, lawless, and hearthless," a social outcast, an *idiot.* Philoctetes' isolation during the Trojan Wars expresses the asocial human predicament.

Myths from the epic cycles perform significant political functions. There is, for example, the theme of justice and retribution in the *Oresteia.* This trilogy is inseparable from the Athenian constitutional crisis of the period, for Athena herself legitimizes the Areopagus. From the time of Peisistratus and the collection of the Homeric poems, epics have stimulated an ethnic or patriotic loyalty.

Epics contain the animating principles of society: *Virtus, Pietas, Humanitas,* in the *Aeneid;* duty in the *Ramayana;* toleration in the *Henriade.* These ideas are not necessarily conscious creations of the poet, as LeBossu suggests.[1] These are spontaneous outpourings from the cultural matrix. Epics make "discordant elements . . . cling together in one society." They serve to prevent the anarchic, Yeatsian state in which "things fall apart." Epics generate social cohesion and moral consensus by providing educational models.

A central concern of the epic is the ideal of freedom. Voltaire notes the lack of liberty in France and associates it with the lack of a great French epic. The struggle for freedom from tyranny occurs in such epics as Lucan's *Pharsalia* and Ercilla's *La Araucana.*

At the center of the configuration of social values stands the archetype of virtue, the epic hero. Through a queer political synecdoche the hero comes to represent the entire community. The individual member participates empathetically in his exploits, in his tests. The hero becomes superorganic. His search projects the wish fulfillments of a nation. His forms are Protean, from the poet Wainamoinen to the trickster Reynard.

Often the hero is plagued by a very human sense of loss; he must search; he must suffer. Frequently he is searching for his weird, his *alter ego.* In the political context, he searches for security, for power, for legitimacy, or for knowledge. He struggles with the demonic, driven *"wie von unsichtbaren Geistern gepeitscht,"* and from the irrational he establishes society, ancestor worship, or a cult.

Remarkably, the epic conventions vary only slightly from culture to culture. The Polynesian Maui cycle has much the same leitmotif as the propagandized exploits of Stalin, who expropriates a capitalist dragon in Tiflis. These are protoepic forms.

Grousset's analysis of Chinese culture challenges the epicless nature of China and places Far Eastern art and literature in the perspective of political myth. Grousset gives epic a connotation of *grandeur,* a sense of chivalry. The cavalcades and processions of the Han Dynasty manifest an epic power: "Who ever said the Chinese was not epically minded? T'ai-tsung the

Great wished to sleep his last sleep with his battle horses."[2]

During the San-kuo (Three Kingdoms), the epic and heroic drama stresses the opposition between the virtuous Kuan Yü and Chang Fei and the usurper Ts'ao Ts'ao. The story is cast in the traditional heroic mold. The struggle with the barbarians during the Six Dynasties is depicted in an epic ballad, "The Poem of Mu-lan," in which the heroine disguises herself as a man to fight in the Tartar Wars.[3] Chinese poets, however, suffer less from the Western "epic-anxiety"—having their long narrative poems classified as "epics."

Epic ideals have not vanished in the modern world. Epics have been fragmented into their component political myths and incorporated into ideologies. My study will explore the great epic themes in their political context. The analysis aims at establishing the intimate relation between politics and literature. Many a line like that of Ennius, which "tramps so heavily across the stage," is omitted—but the "realms of gold" are as inexhaustible as those encountered by Voltaire's hero.

Gilgamesh[4]

The tablets which narrate the epic of the Sumerian Noah, Gilgamesh, were excavated from the library of Assurbanipal. The fatalistic theme marks a continuity in Assyro-Babylonian civilization. The kingship and political phenomena are preordained; humanity is limited. Gilgamesh attempts to escape from fate and seeks eternal life.

Political decisions are made by the heavenly council which ordains the kingship. This reflects Chaldean astrological determinism. "Casting the fates" had a crucial political importance. The priesthood was in a position to make certain that the decree of heaven came true. The state of Sumer resembles modern totalitarian forms:

> All human beings and animals, as well as inanimate objects, natural phenomena, and even abstract ideas constituted the state. Difficult as it is to grasp the Sumerian conception of the state, it becomes clearer when we recall that early man considered inanimate substances . . . as being full of life.[5]

In spite of this absolutism there are possibly some traces of primitive democracy in the Gilgamesh story. A related inscription contains an invocation against tyranny.[6] As Frankfort notes, Gilgamesh does consult a popular assembly as well as the elders before he engages in war:

> Such a relationship, if it existed in reality, would have presented a most precarious balance of power . . . which would have been upset if the war leader were at all inclined to dominate. This is exactly the situation which we find described in the Babylonian *Epic of Creation,* which tells how the gods, threatened by the powers of Chaos, appealed to Marduk . . . to be their leader against the host of Tiamat . . .[7]

Marduk accepts on one realistic condition—that the other gods cede absolute power to him.[7] Political absolutism in Gilgamesh is supported by fatalism:

> As for mankind, their days are numbered,
> Whatever they do is but wind
> Already thou art afraid of death
> What has become of thy heroic power?[8]

Such reflections lead Gilgamesh to his quest for immortality. He passes through the country of the scorpion-people and visits the Adamic Utnapishtim. He finally obtains the rejuvenating plant, only to have it swallowed by the serpent.

The flood story parallels that of the Bible. The motive of the Sumerian gods is not retribution for sin—in the Atarhasis fragment mankind's major fault is that he is too noisy. Such an explanation is inconsistent with Utnapishtim's highly ethical warning to Gilgamesh:

Man of Shurupak, son of Ubar-tutu,
Tear down this house, build a ship!
Give up possessions, seek thou life.
Despise property and keep the soul alive!
Aboard the ship take the seed of all living things.[9]

Historical pessimism, divinely instituted authority, and absolute government are the forms which substantiate society. The striving to break through human limitations and the immortality search are universal themes. Gilgamesh is Nimrod-like and a warrior hero; yet parts of the epic have the spirit of Bernard of Morlas' *De Contemptu Mundi.*

The Iliad[10]

Recall Rembrandt's much-publicized canvas of Aristotle contemplating a bust of Homer. The Homeric epics have served as inspirations in poetry and models in philosophy and education. Plato protests the use of unexpurgated Homer, but Horace describes Homer's poem as an *exemplar utile.*[11] Through the Middle Ages, authors such as Politian eulogize Homer; archaic Greece is the idealized "golden age." The Wolfian criticism comes to marvel at the panoramic view of society and objects that it could not be the work of a single poet.[12] Troy becomes an ahistorical myth.

But the Homeric poems possess a certain *élan vital* that shakes the dust off calfskin bindings. Such a force prompts the visit of Alexander to the tomb of Achilles. Such is the force felt by Keats in Chapman's translation; it directs Schliemann to the ruins near Hissarlik and causes Keller to restore Homeric society.[13]

The cyclic forces of the *Iliad* cause the wrath of Achilles; cause Aias to be torn by inward Furies; cause Paris to choose Helen's beauty over power or renown in war. When Paris rejects the traditional values of society, the whole of archaic Greece is plunged into war—if Homer's catalogue of ships and ancestors is to be credited. The forces unleashed are dreadfully elemental: *hybris, ate, aristeia, arete, dike,* to name a few. These are the controlling heroic principles. The power of Agamemnon and the renown in war of Achilles are fated to punish the Trojans.

The profusion of human forces breaks through social boundaries, confuses political power, and instigates the war. There is a series of political crises which the system attempts to absorb. The king is supposed to act as Zeus and impartially balance the golden scales, but when even the gods are partisans, who can expect men to do better?[14] Agamemnon is challenged in his authority; he justifies his position with an absolutist political philosophy:

> Lordship for many is no good thing. Let there be one ruler one king to whom the son of devious-devising Kronos gives the sceptre and the right of judgment, to watch over his people.[15]

Lattimore draws a political moral from Agamemnon's behavior:

> That tyranny corrupts character, so breeds tragedy, becomes a commonplace for Herodotus and the tragic poets. Sophocles' Kreon is the clearest case: a good man, inadequate to monarchy, whose disqualification ruins him and others. Kreon and Agamemnon alike make one rash statement, after which their rebellious opponents give them no chance to escape.[16]

The political ideal of Homer is summarized in the epithet, "shepherd of his people," which frequently refers to the leaders. Such a condition is echoed in the pastoral similes which contrast with the violent action. Homer's own inclination is pacific—"Yet why must the Argives fight with the Trojans? . . . I wish that strife would vanish away from among gods and mortals."[17]

Homer's similes reveal the life of the common people: "even as the scales which a careful widow holds, taking it by the balance beam and weighs her wool evenly . . ." *Hoi polloi* rarely appear in the epics, but this particular portrait reminds me of the statue, *An Old Market Woman* in the Metropolitan Museum of Art. It is Homer's social realism which vitalizes his epics. Homer's minor characters, like Scott's, seem sketched from life. There is the aged Nestor and the Trojan Polydamas, who alone "looked before and after," and the dream-interpreter Eurydamas. There is Merops of Perkote, who senses the impending deaths of his warrior sons, and also Thersites, who provides comic relief as a scapegoat.

The Homeric social experience is summarized on "the shield of Achilles"—the beseiged city, the wedding feast, the argument over the blood price, the reapers of the king, the vineyard, cattle and herdsmen, and the dancing floor. The scenes are encircled by cosmic bodies and the River Ocean.

The ethical code of the *Iliad* moves between the barbarism of the dragging of Hector's body, an act unsanctioned by the gods, and the high ideals of the exchange between Diomedes and Sarpedon and the reception of Priam as a suppliant. The highest value is placed upon martial heroism, which becomes the sole virtue, or *arete,* yet Homer points to the additional need for self-containment. There is the terrifying valor of Hector as a warrior and the ideal of *aristeia.* Homer's lines, "He has no dishonor when he dies defending," anticipate Horace's *dulce et decorum* and Simonides' war poems. Homer makes Hector a worthy opponent for Achilles—"single man against single man, in bitter combat."

When the heroes abandon the boundaries of *arete,* they may challenge the gods themselves, as when Diomedes wounds Aphrodite. This is an act of *hybris,* and Homer reminds his hearers "how that man who fights the immortal lives for no long time." *Hybris* is punished by divine wrath and ruin, *ate:* "Ruin is strong and sound on her feet, and therefore far outruns all prayers, and runs into every country to force men astray . . ." (IX:505-507) *Ate,* with *moira, nemesis,* and *thanatos* gives the *Iliad* its patina of pessimism as the heroes move along their "paths of glory."

These concepts provide the leitmotifs of the Homeric *Antike,* the epic consciousness and the mythic experience which structures Greek civilization and are emulated in later times. Behind *hybris* is man's urge to equal god-in-power. This is the moral of Grimm's tale of "The Fisherman and his Wife," in which a grateful fish grants all the wife's desires: riches, nobility, royalty, to be Pope. She is still discontent and demands to be God. The fish tells the fisherman: "Go back, and you will find her in her hovel." So it is with the Tibetan tale of King Mandhatar. Dissatisfied with only half of the throne of Sakra, the king of the thirty-three gods:

> . . . came to the conclusion that he must expel the king of the gods . . . from his throne, and take into his own hands the government of both gods and men. As soon as he had conceived this idea, the great king Mandhatar came to the end of his good fortune.[18]

The social principles, the genre portraits, and the models of character make the *Iliad* an epic of the people. Realists can admire its true-to-life quality—*wie ganz anders, anders war es da.*

The Odyssey

I cannot rest from travel: I will drink
Life to the lees . . .
Much have I seen and known; cities of men
And manners, climates, councils, governments . . .
I am a part of all that I have met;
Yet all experience is an arch wherethro'
Gleams that untravell'd world, whose margin fades
Forever and forever when I move.[19]

Thus, Tennyson's Ulysses expresses the ever-popular literary theme. From "Telemaque" to *Ulysses* the figure of the wanderer has appealed to various periods of civilization.

The political content of the myths of the *Odyssey* is akin to that of the *Iliad.* Mentor's speech establishes the archaic kingship—"kindness, generosity, and justice." There are several structuring elements in the political mythology: the character of the hero, the rejection of Utopia and antinomy, and Odysseus' pressing desire to return home.

Pragmatically, Odysseus *is* the sole survivor among the returning Ithacans. His character is a model—"For of all the Achaeans who toiled at Troy it was Odysseus who toiled the hardest and undertook the most."[20] He becomes the prototype of the clever hero in Western literature. In the test of the bow, the emphasis is upon his physical prowess; in the story of Nemo and Polyphemus, his resourcefulness. His concern for his men inspires the faithfulness of Eumaeus. At times the ideal of Propertius, *mens sana in corpore sano,* is approached—at times the Aristotelean ideal of moderation.[21]

One of Odysseus' salient characteristics is his rejection of the Utopian ideal—consequently his political realism. The lotuseaters, for example, reflect an "escape from freedom"; he will have none of it. Calypso entertains in a style which would have pleased the Cavalier poets; he will have none of it; nor of Circe. The overriding concern is the emotional drive to return to the fatherland, which is an element in modern nationalism. The consultation of the spirits of Teiresias, the heroes, and his ancestors, which anticipates the search and descent of later heroes, has an intensely practical motive—how to get home.[22]

Order is another ideal of the *Odyssey.* The despised *anomie* of the Cyclops has already been noted—he has "no assemblies for making laws." There is also the antinomy of the suitors. Odysseus addresses Amphinomus:

> There was a time when I was marked out to be one of the lucky ones, yet what must I do but let my own strength run away with me and take to a life of lawless violence under the delusion that my father and my brothers would stand by me? Let that be a lesson to every man never to disregard the laws of god. . . . The lawlessness I see here is a case in point.[23]

The relation of the suitors to the political order raises the issue of the succession to the kingship. Marriage to Penelope is obviously important. Like Oedipus' marriage to Jocasta, it is an affair of state,—a question of power, not of love. On the other hand, Telemachus appears to have hereditary claims, and the assembly holds some powers. The ambiguity may mark a transition away from *Mutterrecht;* however, this is doubtful, as Penelope is the daughter of a Spartan, King Icarius; and Odysseus has claims through his father, Laertes.[24]

The feud with the suitors becomes a blood feud, and Eupeithes calls for revenge. Zeus himself restores the political balance:

> . . . let them make a treaty of peace to establish him as king in perpetuity, with an act of oblivion, on our part, for the slaughter

of their sons and brothers. Let the mutual goodwill of the old days be restored, and let peace and plenty prevail.[25]

The restoration of the Hesiodic golden age is hardly successful; the *Odyssey* ends on the same restless, wandering note on which it begins. In both Homeric epics the myths serve as vehicles for the political ideals.

The Aeneid

Thumb through the pages of the *Aeneid;* lay your finger on a passage; Vergil's words will tell your fortune. This was a mystic formula of the Middle Ages in which Vergil was substituted for the *sortes evangelicae,* which used the Bible. The term *fidus Achates* became proverbial; Vergil served as Dante's guide through *The Inferno.*

Many medieval power claims were supported by the Brut cycle in England and the Francus story in France. Charles IX commissioned and personally supervised Ronsard's *Franciade.* Even the "Younger Edda" is concerned with connecting the Norse gods and the Trojans. Gildus, Nennius, and Geoffrey of Monmouth chronicled the wanderings of Brut. This oracle is given by the statue of Leogecia according to Geoffrey:

Brutus! there lies beyond the Gallic bounds
An island which the Western sea surrounds,
By giants once possessed; now few remain
To bar thy entrance, or obstruct thy reign.
To reach that happy shore thy sails employ;
There fate decrees to raise a second Troy,
And found an empire in thy royal line,
Which time shall ne'er destroy, nor bounds confine.[26]

Likewise, the English poets, full of dynastic or national pride, take up the Trojan theme.[27]

Perhaps the *Aeneid* stimulates so many political myths because the epic itself incorporates many myths, revealing Roman values, Roman mores. The moving principles are the imitation of Hellenic ideals, *Virtus, Pietas, Humanitas,* legitimation and messianism, the *pax Romana,* patriotism and anti-Punic propaganda.

Museums are crowded with Roman copies of Greek statuary; Polybius preached mixed constitutionalism to Rome; Catullus imitated Sappho. Propertius boasted:

> I am the first, priestlike to appear from a clear spring,
> Uniting with Greek music the mysteries of Italy.[28]

Propertius captured the epic theme of Aeneas only momentarily:

> All that you see here stranger, where Rome now stands,
> Was once, before Phrygian Aeneas came, native bill and turf . . .
>
> I may say "Troy thou shalt fall, Rome thou shalt rise."[29]

It was for Vergil to produce the continuation of the *Iliad.* His lack of originality is offset by the poetic framework. The *Aeneid* illustrates the unity of Graeco-Roman culture.[30]

The linchpin of this culture from a political standpoint is "Book VI." The visit to Anchises is associated with Roman ancestor-worship, the lares and penates, the Elysian Fields. As in the "Fourth Eclogue," there is the promise of a political messiah:

> And to another Troy
> The great Achilles shall again be sent.[31]

As in Horace there is the promise of Rome's future greatness:

> Jupiter set apart these shores for a pious people,
> when he debased the golden age with brass; with brass,
> then with iron, he hardened the ages; from which there
> shall be a happy escape for the good . . .[32]

Tu regere imperios populos Romane echoes the prophecy of millennial resurrection and messianism. There is a clear resemblance to modern nationalistic cults. Turnus must die because he opposes the birth of Rome. In "Book I" there is a prophecy of Caesar:

> And from this great line
> Will come a Trojan Caesar, to establish
> The limit of his empire at the ocean
> His glory at the stars, a man called Julius
> . . . Welcome awaits
> For him in heaven, all the spoils of Asia
> Will weigh him down, and prayer to be made before him.[33]

The deification of the leader, *das Führer Prinzip,* "the cult of the individual," all are fused into the Roman patriotic myth. It is hardly surprising to see a pronounced Roman "racialism" in other passages:

> Some day, to overthrow the Tyrian towers,
> A race would come, imperious people, proud
> In war, with wide dominion, bringing doom for Libya . . .
> And so they wandered over many an ocean.
> Through many a year, fate-hounded. Such a struggle
> It was to found the race of Rome![34]

Dido and the Carthaginians are distinctly *other* than the future Romans. In *La Araucana,* Ercilla goes to great lengths to refute Vergil's picture of Dido. Vergil's anti-Punic feeling is heightened by Dido's curse:

No love, no peace, between these nations, ever!
Rise from my bones, O great unknown avenger . . .[35]

The cult of the Cumaean sybil is closely associated with these mystic prophecies. Vergil establishes the legitimacy of the cult in these "eternal voices prophesying war":

You will come to a town called Cumae, haunted lakes
And a forest called Avernus, where the leaves
Rustle and stir in the great woods and there
You will find a priestess, in her wilderness singing
. . . . She will predict the wars to come, the nations
Of Italy . . .[36]

The political vision of the *Aeneid* is a stereoscopic scene which blends a utopian vision of the future with Roman historical consciousness and the return of the Saturnian Age. The historic patriotism is embossed on the shield of Aeneas, the founding of Rome, the expulsion of the Tarquins, the triumphs, Horatius and Manlius.

Vergil's political myth creates a peaceful society, the *pax Romana:*

Then wars will cease, and a rough age grow gentler
While Faith and Vesta, Romulus and Remus,
Give law to nations. War's grim gate will close,
Tight shut with bars of iron, and inside them
The wickedness of war sit bound and silent . . .[37]

There is an absolute ideal of order, embodied in the well-known passage describing Neptune and beginning *Quos ego:*

Sometimes in a great nation, there are riots
With the rabble out of hand, and firebrands fly
And cobblestones; whatever they lay their hands on
Is a weapon for their fury, but should they see
One man of noble presence, they fall silent.[38]

Aeneas himself focuses the cultural ideals which are to bring order and peace to the Roman community. Aeneas as a great mythic man serves as a folk leader, subordinating his private desires to his people's needs. *Virtus, Pietas, Humanitas*—manly courage, duty, brotherhood inadequately translate these concepts. There is also much Stoicism in Aeneas, but the hero abandons the Stoic ideal in shedding the *lacrimae rerum* as he views the frieze which depicts the Trojan War. Aeneas is a Roman—"A man renowned for goodness . . . for nerve in battle" —"so known for goodness, for devotion.[39]

Lucan's Pharsalia

Critics have sustained Quintilian's verdict that Lucan's rhetoric sometimes burns out his poetry. Voltaire describes Lucan as "with all his political notions . . . but a declamatory Gazeteer." Shelley, however, preferred Lucan to Vergil.[40]

As an exposition of political myths, the *Pharsalia* ranks as a major epic: first, because of Lucan's intimate association with his uncle Seneca and also the Emperor Nero; second, because the *Pharsalia* deals with historical events; third, because of Lucan's republicanism which idealizes Freedom and Cato.

Freedom animates the *Pharsalia.* Freedom is endangered by the struggle between Pompey and Caesar. Cato, who embodies the old Roman virtues, states the issue in his reply to Brutus:

> Though no enemy today of either Caesar or Pompey, I shall wait until the fighting is done and then declare against whichever emerges victorious . . . No man will ever prevent me from embracing for the last time the cold corpse of Rome, whose other name was Freedom.[41]

The freedom motif occurs in Pompey's exhortation to his soldiers on the battlefield:

> Imagine that every Roman alive today, and every one who shall be born hereafter, is joining in her prayer (the Goddess of Rome against Caesar's tyranny)—the former begging to die free; the latter to be born free.[42]

For Lucan, the struggle for freedom is a continuing struggle. The epic contains an undercurrent of criticism against Nero in the passages ostensibly directed against the King of Parthia and Romulus. The cry *O tempora, o mores* is muted but nonetheless present. The *Pharsalia* contains a warning theory of revolutions:

> Revolutions are caused only by hunger, and a government prepared to feed the easy-going masses can count on their loyalty. Starve the mob and it grows restless.[43]

Lucan was implicated in the conspiracy of Piso and was executed by Nero's order.

Except for the outburst of Stoic philosophy and possibly the increased role of Fortuna, the guiding principles of the *Pharsalia* are those of the *Aeneid.* The Trojans are mentioned; the battles are gory; the folk superstitions are authentic. In fact, the Thessalian witch, Erichtho, resembles a modern sorceress reported by Lawson. Political polemic, rhetoric, the struggle against Caesardom are perhaps more believable because less perfect. Lucan's own opinion of his epic is somewhat higher than that of other critics.

> Yet Caesar need not have felt jealous of the heroes commemorated by Homer, because if Latin poetry has any future at all, this poem of mine will be remembered as long as Homer's . . .[44]

The Ramayana

As a didactic myth the *Ramayana* is unequaled in epic literature. The central theme is man's duties, his domestic duty, his social duty, the duties of monarchy, the duties of friendship. The *Ramayana* is a textbook for moral education. The episodes and aphorisms are quoted by the Hindus as we might cite the *Bible.* To study the *Ramayana* is, as Dutt comments, "to trace the influence of the Indian epics on the life and civilization of the nation . . . to comprehend the real history of the people."[45]

The epic recalls the golden age of Hindu life and ideas:

> Neighbor loved his righteous neighbor and the people
> loved their lord . . .
> Loom and anvil gave their produce . . .
> and the nation lived rejoicing in their old ancestral soil.[46]

The setting of the epic's first part is Ayodhya, the Righteous City, a Zion-like Utopia. The ruler is Dasa-ratha, Rama's father, who is a paternal monarch:

> Truth and Justice swayed each action and each baser
> motive quelled.
> People's Love and Monarch's Duty every thought and deed
> impelled.

Galling penury and famine in Ayodhya had no hold . . .
Kshatras bowed to holy Brahmas, Vaisyas to Kshatras bowed,
Toiling Sudras lived by labour and their honest duty proud.[47]

Rama is the Hindu paragon of virtue; he is a true "Aryan," a man of honor:

Truth impels his thought and action. Truth inspires
his soul with grace,
And his virtue fills the wide earth and exalts his
ancient race.[48]

The first test of duty comes with the order of banishment by the king. Rama exemplifies perfect obedience:

In his father's sacred mandate still his noblest Duty saw,
In the weal of subject nations recognized his foremost Law.[49]

Dasa-ratha is bound to keep his oath in spite of the circumstances.

Rama—"true to law and true to scripture, true to woman's plighted love"—begins his exile with his wife Sita and his loyal brother Lakshman. Lakshman personifies fraternal duty: "Go my son, the voice of Duty bids my gallant Lakshman go."[50]

On his wanderings Rama crosses the Ganges and the Jumna; he meets the aged poet, Valmiki, reputed to be the epic's author. Each station is retraced by modern Hindu pilgrims. At every point there is an exemplary act of devotion or a conflict of duties.

Rama encounters his brother, Bharat, who comes into the wilderness to resign the throne:

For our ancient Law ordaineth and thy duty makes it plain,
Eldest-born succeeds his father as the king of earth and main.[51]

Rama, however, places obedience to Dasa-ratha's oath above the kingship itself—"That a righteous father's mandate, duteous son may not recall."[52] He lectures Bharat on the duties of kingship:

For the monarch's highest duty is to serve his people's weal,
And the ruler's richest glory is to labour and to heal!

Guard thy forts with sleepless caution . . .
Guard Kosala's royal treasure . . .
Render justice, pure and spotless . . . Fruitful be thy
lore of Veda.[53]

Rama's wanderings constantly test his perseverance and devotion. He meets the sophist-skeptic Jabali who admonishes him:

As I weep for erring mortals who on erring duty bent
Sacrifice their dear enjoyment till their barren life
is spent.[54]

Rama reaffirms his duty and continues wandering along the Godavari and into the Deccan. He meets with St. Agastya who, according to legend, opened India to Aryan colonization. Like many other myths, this journey may contain recollections of prehistoric migrations. Dharma is appealed to as a protector of human duty and righteousness.

Suddenly a new element disturbs the peacefulness of the epic. When Lakshman is caught in a conflict between his brother's orders and the fear that Rama is endangered, Prince Ravan steals Sita. Ravan is a Raksha, a demonic, malicious, and inferior race who inhabit Ceylon and are capable of transforming themselves into animal forms.

Rama begins his quest after Sita in an attempt to heal the

traumatic sense of loss. He allies himself with the aboriginal bear and monkey people, whom he holds in contempt. However, he is bound by the duties of friendship to overthrow the usurper who is oppressing them.

Hanuman, the monkey-god, penetrates into the Raksha's territory; this threat forces a meeting of the Raksha's council. (The council scene is a standard epic element; even the most despotic monarch, Satan in Pandemonium, has an advisory group.) The problem faced by the Raksha's council is curiously like that faced by the Trojans. Sita has been seized; is the seizure legitimate? The opinions range from censures of Ravan's actions to the sentiment: "True to brother and to monarch, be he right or be he wrong."[55]

The battle scenes which follow also parallel the *Iliad.* There is divine intervention, with the heroes protected by magic mists; there is valorous single combat. The real ending of the poem comes with the victory of Rama and the return of Sita:

> And the earth by ocean girdled with its wealth of teeming life
> Witnessed deed of dauntless duty of a true and stainless wife.[56]

However, in an epilogue, Sita's virtue is challenged; the tests purify her by fire. There is also a list of Rama's descendants including Taksha-sila (Greek, Taxila, fourth century B.C.) and Lava, who ruled Sravasti in the fifth to sixth century B.C. Such genealogical tables customarily serve as part of a legitimizing myth.[57]

The themes of duty, which are the framework of the *Ramayana,* also are an idealized model for Hindu society, a textbook of political action and personal virtue. Many passages have almost the value of legal precedent in establishing orthodox patterns of behavior.

The Mahabharata

Myths frequently arise during periods of conflict; they may express tensions or escape from tensions. The usual form of the struggle pits "the children of light" against "the children of darkness." In Hindu theology, however, good and evil are not absolute concepts; in this case the warring parties are cousins. The *Mahabharata* narrates the Kuru-Panchala War in the thirteenth or fourteenth century B.C. The epic ideals conveyed by political myths are military valor, truth, and virtue.

A great many disparate elements compose the *Mahabharata;* there are interpolations on law, religion, and legendary figures. Dutt describes this epic:

> Every generation of poets had something to add; every distant nation in Northern India was anxious to interpolate some account of its deeds in the old record of the international war; every preacher of a new creed desired to have in the old Epic some sanction for the new truths he inculcated. . . . If the religious works of Hooker and Jeremy Taylor, the philosophy of Hobbes and Locke, the commentaries of Blackstone and the ballads of Percy . . . were thrown into blank verse and incorporated with the *Paradise Lost,* the reader would scarcely be much to blame if he failed to appreciate that delectable compound.[58]

Such would be an English *Mahabharata.* The epic serves as an ordering basis for Hindu society and is influential as a moral educator in national life:

> The almost illiterate oil manufacturer of Bengal spells out some modern translation of the *Maha-bharata* . . . no work in Europe is the national property of the nations to the same extent as the epics of India.[59]

Early in the epic, the Kurus hold a tournament; Karna arrives. He is reputedly a chariot driver's son; his father is actually Surya, the sun. The theme of the "young stranger" is a major messianic, political myth. Another version is the great conflict of political orders, Apollonian and Dionysian, in Euripides' *Bacchae.* During the Alexandrian period, the Hindu Shiva is equated with Dionysus.[60]

Duryodhan welcomes Karna. His speech emphasizing "natural aristocracy" as opposed to the caste system is intriguing, but he is the "villain":

> "Prince we reckon," cried Duryodhan, "not the man of birth alone,
> Warlike leader of his forces as a prince and chief we own! . . .
> Proudest chief may fight the humblest, for like river's noble course,
> Noble deeds proclaim the warrior, and we question not the source . . .
> Arjun is the gallant victor! Valiant Karna's won the day!
> Prince Duryodhan is the winner! Various thus the people say."[61]

Yudishthir becomes heir apparent; Duryodhan attempts to slay his cousins, but the plot fails. The cousins flee to the Panchala kingdom, where Yudishthir wins the hand of Princess Draupadi through the customary bridal tests such as archery. The list of the great princes at the feast establishes their divinity:

> All these kings were gods incarnate, portions of Celestial Light,
> And he saw in them embodied beings of the upper sky,
> And in lotus-eyed Krishna saw the Highest of the High,
> Saw the ancient World's Preserver, great Creation's Primal Cause,

Who had sent the gods as monarchs to uphold his righteous laws,
Battle for the cause of virtue, perish in a deadly war . . .[62]

King of men! with sleepless watching ever guard thy
kingdom fair,
Like a father tend thy subjects with a father's love
and care.[63]

The unfolding drama reveals the *hamartia* of Yudishthir; he is a gambler and loses his kingdom to a loaded dice expert. He and his brothers are banished:

It is a trial and *samadhi*, for it chastens but to heal,
Reft of all save native virtue, clad in native inborn might.[64]

Before the outbreak of the war, there is a moralistic digression which recalls the Alcestis-Admetus theme. It is the allegory of a true woman's love. The passage on duties is especially significant:

Fourfold are our human duties, first to study holy lore,
Then to live as good householders, feed the hungry at our
door,
Then to pass our days in penance, last to fix our thoughts
above,
But the final goal of virtue, it is Truth and deathless Love! . . .
For a woman's troth abideth longer than the fleeting breath,
And a woman's love abideth higher than the doom of death.[65]

Stratagems and single combat, culminating in the final struggle between Karna and Arjun, mark the *Mahabharata*'s great battle scenes. The repeated theme is the eventual triumph of Virtue: *Yato dharma stato jayah!* (Triumph doth on virtue wait!)[66] *Recht* decisively defeats *Macht:*

They must win, who, strong in virtue, fight for virtue's
stainless laws,

Doubly armed the stalwart warrior who is armed in righteous cause.[67]

The Kalevala

Rugged individualism and self-reliance keep society unsettled in the land of the heroes, Kalevala. The "evil" Lapps constantly threaten the Finnish community. The epic myths are elemental; the politics basic, but there is considerable syncretism. The story of the Virgin Mariatta indicates Christian influences, but the prevailing tones are pagan. The paganism is that of the sacred birch groves.[68] The mood is also fatalistic:

All this life is cold and dreary,
Painful here is every motion . . .
Thus to struggle for existence . . .
'Tis not well to sing too early
Time enough for songs of joyance
When we see our homeland mansions,
When our journeyings have ended . . .[69]

Some scenes such as the theft of the sun and the fire-fish are part of the *Kalevala*'s rough-hewn structure. The theft of the fire marks a major civilizing influence in a world inhabited by frost-fiends, sorcerers, and witches. The domestic duties, song contests, rain prayers, beer-brewing, barley sowing and bridal theft depict society in its first stages of rationalization. There is an agrarian ideal of plenty, produced by the magic Sampo, which resembles the Celtic Undry, the Roman Cornucopia, and the Ashanti "Fill-Up-Some-And-Eat."[70]

In addition to the practical arts, the epic accords magic an important role. Inserted in the text are remnants of a primitive pharmacopoeia. There are incantations which give the origin of iron, of serpents, and of the nine diseases. The primitive instruction for treatment applies the remedy to the cause or origin rather than to the effect. The blood-oozing hairbrush exemplifies contagious magic.[71]

Aside from magic, the epic's guiding philosophy is simple: "Evil only comes from evil."[72] The moral code establishes a series of prohibitions on individual action:

Every child of Northland, listen:
If thou wishest joy eternal,
Never disobey thy parents,
Never evil treat the guiltless,
Never wrong the feeble-minded,
Never harm thy weakest fellow,
Never stain thy lips with falsehood,
Never cheat thy trusting neighbor,
Never injure thy companion,
Lest thou surely payest penance
In the kingdom of Tuoni,
In the prison of Manala.[73]

The figure who typifies this ethical system is the aged *Meistersinger,* Wainamoinen; he resembles Orpheus. His role is the preservation of the traditions of the community; the hero is myth-preserver. Another hero is Ilmarinen, the blacksmith, who forges the magic Sampo; he is the Vulcan, the practical inventor. Another is Lemminkainen, the reckless warrior, whose fate is like that of Osiris. There is also Kullervo, the "Child of Evil."

Both war and peace are epic ideals. Iron soliloquizes on the advantages of being a "plough-share" or "pruning hook" rather than a "sword." Other passages have a Teutonic atmosphere:

Bravely will I fall in battle,
Fall upon the field of glory,
Beautiful to die in armor,

Mid the clang and clash of armies
Beautiful the strife for conquest.[74]

The political myths which substantiate society in the *Kalevala* are formative and primeval; the source of power is magic; the customs, archaic. The Finnish national epic is a great social encyclopedia.

The Shahnama

The *Shahnama* shares with the *Kalevala* the distinction of having served as material for Soviet propaganda. In order to establish their claims to Karelia the Russians cited the *Kalevala.* The agitation of the Tadzhiks against the Germans used the *Shahnama.*[75] This modern application of the epics demonstrates their political vitality.

Whereas the action of the *Iliad* transpires in a fraction of a year, the *Shahnama* spans 3874 years—from the pseudohistorical Pishdadian Dynasty to 1010 A.D. Warner describes the historical process:

> (T)he mythical demigods of the Zandavasta came to be regarded in Sassanian times as the historic Shahs of the Iranian race. These and what was recorded of them . . . formed a convenient epic framework whereon to hang legends of Assyrian oppression, Arab raids, Turanian invasions, wars with the West, the deeds of national or local heroes.[76]

The epic summarizes the transition from barbarism to civilization, the social progress, the cultural crises, and the dynastic power struggles. Such a historic diorama. There are several motive forces in the epic: justice, fatalism, and moral dualism.

These principles, presented in mythic form, structure Near and Middle Eastern society.

The *Shahnama* expounds a very Platonic theory of Justice, founded in the division of labor. Faridun expresses this principle:

> Ye citizens possessed of Grace and wisdom
> Disarm and follow but one path to fame,
> For citizens and soldiers may not seek
> A common excellence; this hath his craft,
> And that his mace; their spheres are evident,
> And if confounded, earth will be so too . . .[77]

Faridun parcels out the earth to his three sons: Salm, Tur, and Iraj. But the just "balance of power," in which each keeps to his own "sphere of influence," proves unsatisfactory, as per usual. Iraj goes to the extreme of epic heroism in his self-denial and "abnegation of power"; he is killed. The murder of Iraj unleashes an interracial cycle of blood feud and revenge.

There is an intense moral dualism in the continuous struggle. On the highest plane, it reflects the Zoroastrian conflict between Ormuzd and Ahriman. The antagonism between Iranian and Turanian repeats the theme. There is never a synthesis from the dialectic; only a repetition of the old feud with new actors. Minuchihr revenges Iraj; Faridun and Kawa the Smith overthrow Zahhak; Afrasiyab revenges Tur—"Speed and incarnadine the streams with blood." Afrasiyab's tyranny is an ideal condition for myth-formation:

> It is because unjust kings rule the world
> That good of every kind is vanishing
> No onagers are breeding in their season . . .
> And population faileth everywhere.[78]

Liberation from this oppression and the epic's vicious circle requires a *deus ex machina* in the form of the messianic Siyawush and his son Kai Khursrau:

And there will come a savior from Iran,
One with his loins gird up by God's command,
Who will convey thee and thy son in haste
Toward the Jihun . . .[79]

Historical parallels for the messiah story from Herodotus are: Kai Khursrau, Cyrus; Siyawush, Cambyses; Afrasiyab, Astyages.[80]

The notion of a higher law and the legitimizing Grace justify a new political order. The "spirit of the law" of Antigone's speech to Creon assumes the form of "God's word" in the *Shahnama:*

The Shah's command
Is higher than the sun and moon to me,
Yet none from straws to elephants and lions
May brave God's word, and he that disobeyeth
Hath troubled wits and is beside himself . . .[81]

The divine Grace, like the "mandate of heaven," legitimizes the kingship. The Grace abandons the culture-hero Jamshid when he arrogates divine honors to himself. It abandons Kai Kaus when he attempts to fly to heaven. When even the monarch attempts to break through the divinely appointed boundaries, he is punished by loss of authority. By analogy, the principle of justice is established for commoners.

Fatalism dominates the epic and the Grace itself. Kai Kaus is rescued from his eagle throne only because he contains the *fravashi,* or immortal principle, of the future messiah. There is the tragic *pathei mathos*—"he will grow wise through suffering." There is also the combat of Sohrab and Rustum, well-known from Matthew Arnold's poem.

> Thus was it written down for us by fate
> And by decree of fate the sequel came;
> E'en world-consuming lions and fierce dragons
> Escape not from the net of destiny.[82]

The myths of the *Shahnama* are frequently political moralizations:

> All have gone sweeping in the garth of lore,
> And what I tell has all been told before . . .
> Deem not these legends lying fantasy,
> For most accord with sense, or anyway contain a moral.[83]

The Nibelungenlied

The myth of cultural catastrophe is the leitmotif of the great Germanic epic. The final holocaust of the blood feud, the slaughter in Etzel's hall, echoes the themes of fate and pessimism—*sollst Europa stehen in Flammen.* The *Nibelungenlied* has also been adapted to modern political mythology, from Wagner's *Ring* cycle to Hitler's Bayreuth.

The sense of inevitable doom occurs in the versions of the Siegfried myth which date to the fifth century A.D. The epic itself contains many anachronisms. There is a veneer of feudalism; behind the facade is the society of Tacitus' *Germania.*

The final scene of the epic covers an interesting nationalistic myth. The factual basis appears to be the defeat of Gundicarus by Attila in Burgundy, 437 A.D.:

> This disaster preceded, and perhaps gave the most powerful impulse to, that general break-up of the old Germanic settle-

> ments, and the period of stormy wanderings and wars . . . known as the Migration of the Peoples.[84]

Such a period is a hothouse, a "garden of Adonis," for political myths. The interesting feature is the transposition of the action to Hunland, which salvages German *amour propre* by having the defeat occur on distant soil.

The final episode plunges society back into the utter disorder of barbarism. In some respects this scene is the exact opposite of Siegfried's great *Kampf um Drache.* The death of the dragon is the defeat of the demonic and irrational; the event releases the people from fear; it marks the cultural crisis which permits the growth of civilization.

Siegfried's virtues as a knight overshadow his heroic individualism as a culture hero. He undertakes the quest to secure Brunhilde and is victimized by the jealous status-struggle of the queens. His cultural role appears clearest in the pattern of the young stranger. He is also cast as a popular protector:

> But he yearned in his fearless spirit to break the
> oppressor's yoke,
> And to rid of the fear of the spoiler the hearth of
> the lowly folk.[85]

Rüdiger of Bechlaren partially assumes Siegfried's virtuous role, but as Way notes:

> The other champions are fully conscious of the inequity of those whose cause they support; their merit is that which in those times covered a multitude of sins . . . unflinching bravery and fidelity to their cause and to each other.[86]

The murder of Siegfried by Hagen of Troneg is "the beginning of the end." A legal myth and a rather primitive theory of magic and justice prove Hagen's guilt:

When the slayer murder-polluted is seen by the dead-man's side,
The wounds bleed in witness against him: so did it now befall,
And thereby was the guilt of Hagen made manifest to all.[87]

A murder trial in Wilmington, North Carolina, applied this "bier-right" in 1875.[88] This belief is part of an ingenious series of superstitions for determining guilt. Such beliefs merge with the "trial by ordeal" in the Christianizing orthodoxy of medieval myth and epic.

Medieval Myths and Epics

Feudalism and the relationship between paganism and Christianity repeatedly concern the medieval epics. Hierarchic order and peace mortise medieval politics to religion; but the gargoyle of political myth projects between other-worldliness and the search for daily bread.

Beowulf describes an embryonic feudal society, touched with Christianity but with an admixture of paganism. Such a condition recalls the stories of St. Boniface and St. Hubert in the *Urwald.* The fusion of myths accepts the saints but replaces Tubal Cain with Weland the Smith. Goodrich's claims are rather extravagant:

> Without this poem the modern world would be at a loss to explain the institution of feudalism that suddenly confronted classical tradition and Roman law with a way of life often in complete variance with . . . Roman ideas.[89]

In the Crusades and Tasso's *Jerusalem Delivered*, the great quest legends of the Grail, of Galahad and Perceval, of Longinus, there is a transition to a militant religious spirit. Myths themselves preach with as much fervor as Peter the Hermit.

A myth recounts the deliverance of Rome from the barbarians by an iron-clad pilgrim in the Ragnar Lodbrok Saga. The Cid routs the Moors from their holdings in Spain, and St. James of Compostella appears to succor the faithful. Roland expounds Christianity to the Giant Ferracute and kills him when he refuses to accept the Trinity. Huon of Bordeaux pursues his quest to the Near East, where he is to cut off the pasha's head and marry the sultan's daughter. Stories of pilgrimages, martyrs, miracles, and the advent of the millennium and the anti-Christ occur in profusion, indicating the immediacy of the religious experience.[90]

Tasso's poem reflects the militant temperament with the martyrdom of Sophronia and Olindo. In Tasso, piety assumes its religious connotation of duty to God. The poet sings a new song:

> The pious arms and pious chief I sing,
> Who the great sepulchre of Jesus freed.

In the background of the epic is the feudal greatness of the House of Este, associated with Rinaldo's heroism.[91]

The ideal of Christian knighthood inspires the allegorical figures of Spenser's *Faerie Queene.* Spenser uses the Pauline imagery of the "arming of the Christian hero" to illustrate the virtues of Gloriana's knights.

Some of the religious legends conceal a political content. The Grail quests, although apparently stressing monastic asceticism, bolster the power of the Knights Templar. Parzifal's stepbrother weds Repanse de Joie; from this union comes the founder of the knights.[92] The monks of Glastonbury claim Joseph of Arimathea. Henry II fosters this myth in his struggle against the authority of Rome and St. David's. In 1189 the tombs of Arthur, Guenevere, and Gwalchmei are uncovered at

Glastonbury; this discovery seems calculated to discourage Welsh pretensions. Henry VII and the Tudors cultivate a healthy interest in King Arthur, discoverer and colonizer of Greenland and perhaps Newfoundland.[93]

The political myth of the returning king is also part of the Arthurian legend. As late as the coronation of Queen Mary, Philip of Spain had to guarantee that he would vacate the throne should "the once and future king" reappear.[94] The well-chronicled variants of this myth include: Holger Danske, Barbarossa, Owain Lawgoch, and Sebastian of Portugal.[95] In his preface to *Waverly,* Scott describes the typical legend, the story of Thomas of Hersildoune:

> This personage, the Merlin of Scotland . . . was, as is well known, a magician, as well as a poet and prophet. He is alleged still to live . . . and is expected to return at some great convulsion of society . . .[96]

The stories of the *parousia* are prototypes of messianic nationalism. The essential question is Ruodi's in Schiller's *Wilhelm Tell: "Wann wird der Retter kommen diesem Land?"*[97] The second coming of the hero is frequently tied to the struggle for freedom. The popular theme also occurs in the tales of Robin Hood in his perennial defeat of the Sheriff of Nottingham.

Medieval myths and epic cycles almost always depict the ideal feudal court. The zodiacal douzepers are the flower of Christian chivalry. The political theorist, Carlyle, uses the *chanson de geste,* "Raoul de Cambrai," to illustrate the complexities of feudalism. The poem expresses the conception of personal loyalty and devotion of the vassal to the liege lord. There is, however, a profound contempt for the overlord. Medieval heroes swear by oaths of fealty to protect orphans and widows and to fulfill certain contractual obligations.

Many insights into the operation of feudalism may be culled

from the epics. Popular ballads, commemorating the struggle of Charles the Bald with his feudatories, may be the source of the sons of Aymon cycle. The *Nibelungenlied* mentions a coronation oath, binding on Siegfried as well as on an advisory council. The *Cid* offers a glimpse of the marriage contract with the Counts of Carrion, the conflict of feudal duties, and the church-state controversy between Henry III and Ferdinand.

There are also the judicial problems of feudalism. Lohengrin champions the cause of Elsa of Brabant in a trial by combat. There is also the trial of Ganelon in the *Chanson de Roland.* Ganelon's treachery, like Sinon's before and Vuk Brancovic's after, runs completely against the grain of the cultural ideal.[98]

The best synoptic view of the common people in feudal society is the popular *Reynard the Fox.* Reynard is a very specialized type of epic hero, the trickster, who crashes through the limitations of legal and social taboos.[99] His first cousins are Coyote and B'rer Fox. Such a mythic figure serves as a social cathartic by releasing social tensions. In the Reynard story the Machiavellian politics of "fox and lion" mix with the Aesopian animal fable.

Among the episodes which contribute to medieval political mythology is the testimony of Henning the Cock that Reynard, disguised in a monk's habit, has robbed the hen-house. Here the myth functions as social, anticlerical satire. Renyard also claims that he must visit Rome to seek absolution; his state *ex gratia* contaminates the court. He also maintains like a true Augustinian that King Nobel is nothing but a big-time robber. If there were really any justice, Reynard himself would be king as the clever thieves of Egyptian and Tibetan popular tales.

Notorious as a lawbreaker, Reynard also concerns himself with the intricate workings of the feudal judicial system. He slyly takes advantage of all the complex legal forms. To ingratiate himself at court, he uncovers a false conspiracy. John of Salisbury is little more effective in exposing the foibles of the courtiers. Reynard also gets involved in a fish-stealing case. At one point he declares an equitable judgment which is closely paralleled in a Hottentot fable.

> A Dutchman was walking by himself and saw a snake lying under a large stone. The snake implored his help, but when she had become free, said, "Now I shall eat you." The man answered "That is not right. Let us . . . go to Jackal." The Jackal answered very slowly . . . doubting the whole affair, and demanding to see first the place, and whether the man was able to lift the stone. The snake lay down, and the man to prove the truth of his account put the stone over her. When she was fast, the Jackal said, "Now let her stay there."[100]

Through Boiardo, Ariosto, Pulci and Trissino, the ideals of knighthood appear in the epics; romance alternates with a preoccupation with power and religion. The later medieval epics are part of the great Quixotesque library consigned to the padre's fire. The myths decay and become increasingly florid and imitative. The Sangreal finally disappears, and the Faustian search for immortality begins.

Divine Comedy

The transition from Cimabue to Giotto in Italian art freed the artist from Byzantine formalism. Likewise Dante's epic escaped from the classical patterns. In a sense, Dante's synthesis of Aristotelean ideals and Christianity was a secular Thomism. His use of the Italian vernacular paved the way for modern nationalism. The red, green, and white fireworks patriotically displayed in every Italian piazza were Beatrice's tricolor. These colors which embellished the Bargello portrait of Dante were painted over in chocolate in 1850 because they symbolized the Sardinian liberation movement.[101]

On a broader basis the *Divine Comedy* was a pivotal point in intellectual history. The epic established the articles of faith for the later Middle Ages: peace, justice, and hierarchy. As apocalypse cum mystery play, Dante's epic in triptych summarized the religious art forms of his age.

The student of politics is possessed of somewhat more than a lingering desire to embroil the entire poem in the controversies of Guelph and Ghibbeline, Neri and Bianchi, Cerchi and Donati. Symonds describes Rossetti as "perverted by the desire to find political allegories in everything connected with Dante."[102] To the litterateur, the politics of the *Divine Comedy* appears as a *trompe d'oeil* backdrop. Politics is not illusory but the living matrix of the epic myths. The political interpretation of the epic fuses the "literal, anagogical, moral, and allegorical." If the subject of the epic is Man, the hero is nonetheless Political Man.

Of course, the *Inferno* is more than a rogue's gallery—as it is indeed seen by Boccaccio:

> Boccaccio, staring at this mighty pile, when its masonry was new and its frescoes still unfaded, pronounced that Dante had erected it solely as a gallows for the better gibbeting of his political antagonists.[103]

Frequently a turbulent political environment serves to stimulate mythopoeism; such is the condition of Dante's Italy:

> The *Selva Selvaggia*—that wild, and rough, and stubborn wood, whose bitterness was scarce less terrible than death—in the midst of which Dante found himself at the beginning of his journey, is a true metaphor, not only for the trouble of the poet's

> soul, but also for the civil and political confusion of his nation. . . . His purpose was both moral and political.[104]

Out of the factional corruption came Dante's cry for a messiah, be he Can Grande, Henry, or Uguccione. Out of the political persecutions, the battles of Benevento and Montaperti, came the vision—*beata pacifici*—of world government and peaceful order.

The ideals of peace and freedom pervade the epic. Dante idealizes the peace of Rome, of Augustus, of Justinian, a peace for humanity to realize its full potential. In the tract *On Monarchy*, he writes:

> Mankind is at its best when it is most free. This will be clear if we grasp the principle of liberty. We must realize that the basic principle of our freedom is our freedom to choose . . . liberty is God's greatest gift to human nature.[105]

The emphasis on man's free will departs radically from the fatalism of the earlier epic myths. The epic search is a search for freedom. The corruption and confusion of church and state cause the absence of freedom and peace. The final paragraph of *On Monarchy* summarizes Dante's position:

> It is now clear that the authority for temporal world-government must come directly, without intermediary, from the universal Fount of authority, which, though it flows pure from a single spring, spills over into many channels . . . the truth concerning this last question must not be interpreted so strictly as to imply that the Roman government is in no way subject to the Roman pontificate . . . Caesar . . . owes to Peter the piety which a first-born son owes to his father. And so, in the light of paternal grace, this government will better enlighten our globe, over which it rules through Him alone who is the ruler of all things spiritual and temporal.[106]

The Stoic cosmopolis anticipates the theme of world government, the *Respublica Christiana,* which develops in the writings of Engelbert of Admont.

The Earthly Paradise of the *Divine Comedy* is deserted because Church and State have been untrue to their mission. This is a crime against Aristotle's teleology. Dante indicts Boniface VIII more specifically with corruption and neglect of duty. St. Peter himself fulminates against Boniface, and the unfortunate papal victim of Dante's ire is consigned to an awkward position in the Inferno. Dante hurls epithets against Boniface accusing him of being corrupt, failing to recover the Holy Land, and abusing the "Donation of Constantine." The dialogue with Marco Lombardo and Peter Damian's speech voice typical criticisms:

> Say henceforth that the Church of Rome by confounding two powers in herself, falls in the mire, and fouls herself and her burden. . . . Therefore it is the Gospel and the great Doctors are deserted, and only the Decretals are so studied, as may be seen upon their margins.[107]

Dante does not spare secular rulers who have destroyed the peace. Philip of France is a frequent target. Many passages attack tyranny in general—"For the cities of Italy are all full of tyrants and every clown that comes to play the partisan becomes a Marcellus."[108] Dante immerses tyrants in a bloody river in the *Inferno.*

Tyrannicide, preached by John of Salisbury and practiced by Jean Petit, forms an interesting sidelight in Dante. Brutus' disloyalty to Caesar places him in one of the deepest circles, but Brutus who expelled the Tarquins is in one of the outermost.

Dante raises a voice of social protest and reform against the social crimes, barratry and counterfeiting. He attacks the immorality of Genoa, the vanity of Siena, and the corruption of

Lucca and Pistoia. Dante opposes the social disorder with the ideal of peaceful, hierarchic order, precise as pseudo-Dionysius. He idealizes the Roman law and the maxim of retributive justice—"Wherewithal a man sinneth by the same also shall he be punished." The hierarchy of virtue structures the *Divine Comedy* and the ideal society.[109]

An oriflamme surrounds the epic as the incarnation of the spiritual ideals of the Middle Ages. Inspired in the fashion of Isaiah, the entire plan is prophetic and providential. The political allegory is like Lorenzetti's mural, *Good Civic Government*, in the Palazzo Publico at Siena. Dante's epic compounds the satire of Juvenal with the *tristia* of Ovid, the "human interest" of Francesca and La Pia with the scholastic questions of Averroism. The epic demonstrates the close relationship between politics and poetics and reveals the poet-politician as mythmaker.

The Araucana and The Lusiads

Blood or life is paltry payment
For your sword's eterne remembrance!
Let our ancient laws dishonored
Be restored by free men's power!
Let all dwellers 'neath the starlight
Live as equals under heaven.[110]

This is the speech of Caupolican, chief of the Araucana. The plea for the restoration of freedom and equality is the unifying theme of Ercilla's epic. The author is the "unquiet soul," the apologist of the Spanish conquest of Peru. The political myths of the epic arise from the tensions between might and right, rational and demoniac, civilization and barbarism, conquistador and Indian.

Camoëns' objective is to magnify the greatness of Portugal by narrating da Gama's exploration of India. His is a righteous cause, following in the footsteps of St. Thomas and combating the "lies and superstitions of paganism"—to the greater glory of Portugal. His Christianizing cause urgently pleads for a spiritually united Europe.

These Iberian epics contain the myths which activated "The Age of Exploration and Discovery." In the *Lusiads* there is the search for a passage to India, the fabled realms of Prester John, and the pagans eagerly awaiting salvation. In the *Araucana,* there is the search for Quivira, the invulnerable conquerors, the "noble savages." Such Spanish myths, a specialized type of propaganda, aided the Conquest. Elsewhere the myths are: Quetzalcoatl and Viracocha, the muskets' powdered thunder, and the invulnerability which necessitated the clandestine burial of DeSoto. Latin American folklore still preserves such myths.[111]

Ercilla's epic is inherently an apologia for the Conquest—the victory of civilization over heroic barbarism and the struggle for liberty. Freedom is also important to Camoëns—"for the rising sun, as it vanquishes the darkness, frees men's minds too from the grip of fear."[112] Salvation is the source of freedom; the Portuguese empire is the savior.

In the *Lusiads,* da Gama and the navigators are the heroes; the Mohammedans are the villains. Ercilla's epic breaks the conventional dualism; both the conquistadores and the Indians are heroic. The autochthonous race, although characterized as "godless, lawless, nought respecting," possesses a code of individual liberty and a pantheon of gods, albeit demonic gods. The Araucana resemble the inhabitants of Melville's Marquesas. The conquistadores, jaundiced by gold fever, contaminate the Indians. El Capitán Valdivia is like Midas and Crassus.

Ercilla's dual heroism does more than secure the patronage of the Spanish court for his epic—although it does that too. It points to the essential ethical problem of freedom in the epic.

In Ercilla's favorite metaphor, in the struggle between *toro* and *torero,* there is ample opportunity for bravery, but the matador must win.

Ercilla's description of "trial by combat" covertly parallels the struggle between Might and Right in the Conquest:

Christian princes ne'er should favor
Nor should authorize contention
Arms condemned that strike for hatred,
Vengeful lust, or competition
Nor should causes be decided
By decrees of might, for often
By mysterious chance the guilty
Wins and washes clean his stigma.[113]

The digressions on Dido's escape from tyranny and the battles of Lepanto and St. Quentin contain the same moral. Significantly, both of Camoëns' insertions, the sad tale of Inés de Castro and the "Twelve of England," also deal with power and justice.

Both poets compose their works in the war-correspondent's style of Lucan. W. H. Prescott calls the *Araucana* "a military journal done in rhyme."[114] Camoëns is a geographer; his most original creation is Adamastor, "The Spirit of the Cape." He is shown the world by the ocean goddess, Tethys. Likewise Ercilla views the Hispanic Empire from the cave of Fiton the Sorcerer. The adventuresome spirit of exploration parallels the *Argonautica* of Apollonius Rhodius and Sinbad's Voyages.

Camoëns and Ercilla both employ realistic descriptive language. The *Araucana* captures the arrival at Concepción:

Milling groups of wild-eyed travellers
Jostled, elbowed, tripped each other,
One man moaned a last confession

Publicly for past transgressions,
Some swore oaths and others vowing,
Bade farewell to absent mothers
Panic swelled the plangent chorus
To a solem miserere.[114]

The epic's realistic description of the struggle for freedom is a landmark in the progress of political myths dealing with the idea of freedom.

Paradise Lost and Paradise Regained

The idea of freedom in the epic and political myth further matures in Milton's *Paradise Lost.* Milton quotes from Euripides' *Suppliants* on the title page of the *Areopagitica:*

This is true Liberty when free born men
Having to advise the public, may speak free,
Which he who can, and will, deserves high praise,
Who neither can nor will, may hold his peace;
What can be juster in a State than this?[115]

In a troubled age, and most myth-bearing ages are troubled, Milton approaches the problem of order and disobedience to constituted authority: the problem of freedom defined as perfect obedience to perfect law; the problem of rebellion, *non serviam.* Milton does far more than project Cromwell's England into a planetarium. He penetrates into the problems of political and social theory. These he projects through the *camera obscura* of his mind into *Paradise Lost.*[116]

Milton's epic contains a synthetic philosophy, conjoining the ethics of Aristotle with the heresy of Boehme, the Christology of the medieval church epic with the writings of Hooker, Bonaventura, and Aquinas. The inspiring structure contrasts with Bunyan's plodding Puritanism. In Milton's epic the myth appears as theodicy, "justify(ing) the ways of God to man."

There is a fundamental dictum in Milton's epic: freedom is commensurate with obedience. Freedom equates with Cicero's *recta ratio,* right reason. Freedom is associated with Thomistic free will; freedom is freedom to choose the good. Hence, rebellion is an escape from freedom, or "a reflex of the will upon the understanding."

Adam's sin is the perversion of right reason, a denial of freedom, a denial of submission, the Baconian "first act of the rational mind." The Tree is the traumatic point of separation, the point which fractures reason from imagination. The Tree is the tragic point of the act of disobedience, which gives birth to the existential "sense of loss," the breakdown of communication between God and Man. The Fall, however, paves the way for the Advent. There is an interesting passage in the Hindu *Upanishad* on the Creation: "He caused that self to fall *(pat)* into two pieces. Therefrom arose a husband *(pati)* and a wife *(patni).*"[117]

The Tree appears as a key mythological symbol as early as the tree-spirit seal reported by Sir John Marshall at Mohenjo-Daro.[118] There are the Norse Yggdrasill, the Oriental "Tree of Heaven," the tent pole of the Buriat shaman, the sacred pole of the Plains Indians, the *axis mundi.* In the Mayan sacred book, *The Popol Vuh:*

> The head of Hunhun-Apu was, however, suspended from a tree, upon the branches of which grew a crop of gourds. . . . The fiat went forth that no one in Xibalba must eat of the fruit of that tree. But the Lords of Xibalba had reckoned without feminine curiosity and its unconquerable love of the forbidden.[119]

Among the Blackfoot there is a story of Pöia, who eats the sacred Turnip; when she has completely uprooted it, she falls through the hole to the earth. The classical parallel is Pandora; there is also the Celtic tale of "disobedience and the fruit," Grainne and the rowan berries. In the African Efe version, God tells Ba-atsi that he must impress upon the children that prohibition: "Of all the trees of the forest you may eat, but of the Tahu tree you may not eat."[120]

Paradise Lost is a study in the psychology of free choice, which is associated with the world-tree myth and the resulting human predicaments. Man desires to be like God, having knowledge of good and evil. He is punished. He is redeemed. Through knowledge of evil he attains a more complete recognition of the good; this is St. Augustine's doctrine of the *felix culpa.*

Milton's Adam is a denial of Calvinist predestination and an affirmation of prevenient grace:

> I made him just and right,
> Sufficient to have stood, though free to fall . . .
> Freely we serve,
> Because we freely love. (III: 98–99; V:539)

On the Calvinist doctrine of election, Milton wavers, but there is a latent antidemocratic element:

> Some I have chosen of peculiar grace
> Elect above the rest. (III: 262)

To the Calvinist, Satan's plight resembles that of Oedipus. Oedipus, who knows, refuses to submit to his fate. Oedipus fancies that he has free will, yet he is in the condition of Browning's "Andrea del Sarto"—"so free we seem; so fettered fast we are." Milton's theological framework is basically Arminian.

Satan is the antitype of epic heroism. He searches for an illusory type of freedom in the futilitarian structure of Pandemonium. First, he desperately attempts to be God; then, to be utterly evil. In an Augustinian universe where to be is to be in some degree good, to be evil is to non-exist. Satan gets stuck in a Xenonian paradox and becomes insane. He preaches egalitarianism and the destruction of the *ancien régime;* he practices slavery. Satan, although he lacks real foresight, tries to act like Prometheus; his hypocrisy in this role even deceives some critics. Satan then pleads "reasons of state" in a much quoted passage:

> Yet public reason just,
> Honor and Empire with revenge enlarg'd
> By conquering this new world, compels me now
> To do what else though damn'd I should abhor—
> So spake the Fiend and with necessity,
> The Tyrant's plea, excus'd his devilish deeds. (IV: 389–394)

Hughes glosses Milton's views on rational liberty, Adam's sin, and the loss of liberty:

> (Milton's) politics stemmed equally from Plato's *Republic* and its echoes in definitions of "true libertie" such as Castiglione's view of it . . . as not living "as a man will," but rather as living "according to good lawes."[121]

Paradise Lost is a poetic dramatization of freedom. Freedom as obedience is the precondition of man's being. Here Milton's ontology comes to the fore. Man, in spite of his infinite aspirations and limited capacity, is part of the "great chain of being."[122] Here the myth appears as metaphysics.

Christ's realization of his being as a result of Satan's temptation is the irony of *Paradise Regained.* Satan repeatedly challenges Christ to assert his divinity. Christ replies: "(C)anst thou not remember *Quintius, Fabricius, Curius, Regulus?"* (III:446) Hughes reminds his readers of Tasso's essay, "Del Poema Eroico":

> . . . the working ideal of heroic magnanimity seems almost like a design for Milton's Christ. . . . The finest earthly honor, he thought, belonged to the Curii, Decii, and Marcelli, . . . but their heroic spirit seemed to Tasso to be "a mere shadow and figure" of the divine love which Christ brought into the world.[123]

In "The Laws" Cicero describes Gaius Fabricius and Curius Dentatus as paragons of Roman honor. Fabricius arranges the Samnite Peace terms and refuses the bribes of King Pyrrhus. Regulus was an heroic prisoner of the First Punic War; A. Quintius Cincinnatus "left the plow." They appear as model heroes in Dante, Lucan, and Vergil. Milton takes these figures as Christ in poverty and Christ in peace. Milton exemplifies Christian principles with pagan myths and heroes. The Antaeus myth is emblematic of the victory of truth over falsehood and spirit over flesh.

The deeper significance of the lines, "(C)anst thou not remember *Quintius, Fabricius, Curius, Regulus?"* is the Latin meaning suggested by the words, for it is "Who (Qui); Makes; Priest; King." It is the revelation of Christ's divine identity. Such is the *eneirgia* of Milton's poetry, the quality which in a blinding flash pierces the *gutta serena* and produces literature more real than life.

The Henriade

Voltaire's epic of the Enlightenment, *The Henriade*, idealizes toleration and the opportunity for rational freedom. The historical background is the French Civil Wars, St. Bartholomew's Day, the struggles between Guise and Bourbon, the siege of Paris, the assassination of the Duke of Guise at Blors, the realignment of Henry III and Henry of Navarre, and the regicide of Henry III by James Clement, a young Dominican monk.

Voltaire's epic attacks the religious fanaticism which led to the *auto-da-fé* as well as the death of Servetus. As Voltaire wrote "On Toleration":

> Not only is it cruel to persecute, in this brief life, those who differ from us, but I am not sure if it is not too bold to declare that they are damned eternally. . . . Are you sure that our Creator will say to . . . virtuous Confucius. . . . Go monster . . . and you, my beloved Cartouche . . . come and share my empire and felicity forever.[124]

Voltaire defends "the right to be wrong." He directs his caustic verses against both papism and Calvinism:

> Religion was it whose inhuman zeal
> The war-steel put in every Frenchman's hand
> Rome and Geneva, I do not decide
> Between them . . .
> Both parties then are equally unjust,
> Alike in blindness and alike in crime.[125]

The *Henriade* preaches the universality of salvation as a tenet of rational religion. This egalitarian doctrine removes the necessity for Christianity according to Voltaire:

> There at his feet, a Judge corruptless calls
> That inf'nite being whom we serve nor know
> Him, under diff'rent names, the world adores.
> She (Death) brings, at once, the Bramin, and the Bonze.[126]

In the epic there is a nostalgia for the Age of St. Louis:

O days! O manners! times of deathless fame!
Blest was the realm, the king with glory crown'd;
All tasted of the fruits of his mild laws
Blest times return, another Louis bring.[127]

St. Louis, incidentally, serves in a traditional epic role, that of conducting Henry IV through Heaven and Hell. He foretells the destiny of France and of Henry's posterity.

Voltaire also reflects the pronounced Anglophilism of Montesquieu and other French political theorists of his epoch. He praises Elizabeth and the laws of England. The rule of law and presence of freedom in England contrasts with the absence of freedom in France:

Upon an iron altar, there, a book
Inexplicable, of the future dread
Th' irrevocable history contains . . .
There, is seen Liberty, that haughty slave,
Bound in those places, but by unseen ties;
Under a yoke unknown that naught can break.[128]

The vision of chained Liberty recalls the words of Rousseau and Lammenais, the revolutionary spirit, the statue by Bartholdi itself. It recalls the motto over Voltaire's cortege on the way to the Pantheon:

He gave wings to the human mind,
He prepared us to be free.[129]

Notes to Chapter II

1. Francis D. White, ed., "Voltaire's Essay on Epic Poetry," (Albany: Brandow Printing Co., 1915). Cf. Addison cited at p. 94 n. 1 in LeBossu's *Traité du pöem épique.*

2. René Grousset, *Chinese Art and Culture* (Orion Press, n. d.), pp. 194-95.

3. Ibid., pp. 108-15.

4. Alexander Heidel, *The Gilgamesh Epic and Old Testament Parallels* (Chicago: University of Chicago Press, 1946). *Ancient Near Eastern Texts* (Princeton, N.J.: Princeton University Press, 1950), pp. 93-95 (Xisuthros fragment). A. H. Sayce, *The Ancient Empires of the Near East* (New York: Charles Scribner's Sons, 1902), pp. 106–8. S. H. Hooke, "Some Parallels with the Gilgamesh Story," *Folklore* (1934), Vol. 45, pp. 195-215.

5. C. A. Robinson, *Ancient History* (New York: Macmillan Co., 1951), p. 37.

6. Heidel, op. cit., p. 5.

7. Frankfort, *Kingship and the Gods,* p. 220; Thorkild Jacobsen, "Primitive Democracy in Ancient Mesopotamia," *Journal of Near Eastern Studies* (Chicago, 1943), II, pp. 159–72.

8. Heidel, op. cit., p. 36.

9. McDermott and Caldwell, op. cit., p. 38; from Pritchard, *Ancient Near Eastern Texts,* trans. John A. Wilson, pp. 370–71.

10. Homer, *The Iliad,* trans. Richard Lattimore (Chicago: University of Chicago Press, 1951).

11. Herbert Musurillo, *Symbol and Myth in Ancient Poetry* (Bronx, N.Y.: Fordham University Press, 1961).

12. F. B. Jevons, *A History of Greek Literature* (New York: Charles Scribner's Sons, 1897), pp. 7–17.

13. A. G. Keller, *Homeric Society,* "A Sociological Study of the *Iliad* and the *Odyssey*" (New York: Longmans, Green, 1902). Gilbert Murray, *Five Stages of Greek Religion* (Garden City, N. Y.: Anchor Books, Doubleday & Co., 1951). C. M. Gayley, *Classic Myths in English Literature* (Boston: Ginn and Co., 1900), pp. 277–302. C. W. Ceram, *Gods, Graves, and Scholars* (New York: Alfred A. Knopf, 1951), pp. 29–55 (on Schliemann).

14. Robert J. Bonner and Gertrude Smith, *The Administration of Justice from Homer to Aristotle* (Chicago: University of Chicago Press, Chicago, 1930), esp. Vol. I, pp. 1–50.

15. *Iliad,* II: 204–6, p. 81.

16. Lattimore, op. cit., p. 49 note 1.

17. *Iliad* IX:337; XVIII: 107; XI: 506 (Paris).

18. F. Anton von Schiefner, *Tibetan Tales Derived from Indian Sources* (Kah-Gyur), English trans. W. R. S. Ralston (Boston: James R. Osgood, 1882), p. xxxvi.

19. Bayley, op. cit., pp. 335–36.

20. *The Odyssey,* trans. E. V. Rieu (Baltimore, Md.: Penguin Books, 1946), pp. 53, 67.

21. Ibid., pp. 124, 142. This idealized Odysseus is not in accord with Sophocles' or Dante's tradition. Cf. the Dolon episode in the *Iliad,* X: 313–464.

22. Ibid., pp. 168–71.

23. Ibid., pp. 142, 279–80. *Tyche* (luck) is an important ordering principle; there are many others. Cf. G. Lowes Dickinson, *The Greek View of Life* (New York: Doubleday, 1909).

24. Ibid., pp. 35, 38, 304, 329. Sir Henry Maine, *Ancient Law* (London: J. M. Dent, 1917), p. 141.

25. Ibid., p. 363.

26. Seznec, op. cit., p. 24; Geoffrey of Monmouth, cited in H.A. Guerber, *Legends of the Middle Ages,* p. 308.

27. Wace's "Brut," Shakespeare and Chaucer, the Troilus and Cressida theme, Spenser, Drayton's "Polyalbion."

28. Lind, *Latin Poetry,* p. 188; Propertius III:1, F. Fletcher, trans.

29. Ibid., Propertius IV:1, pp. 194–95.

30. Cf. Robert Seymour Conway, "Vergil as a Student of Homer," John Rylands Library *Bulletin* (Manchester, 1929), Vol. 13, pp. 272–92. Conway analyzes many similarities between the *Iliad* and the last half of the *Aeneid.*

31. J. A. Wilstach, ed., *The Works of Vergil* (Boston: Houghton Mifflin, 1884), Vol. I, p. 158. Cf. H. Jeanmaire, *Le Messianisme de Vergile* (Paris: J. Vrin, 1930). Tasso refers to the prophecy in Canto XV of *Jerusalem Delivered.* Dante's Statius credits his conversion to Christianity to the poem.

32. Horace, "Epode XVI: To the Roman People," *The Works of Horace,* C. Smart, ed. (Philadelphia: Uriah Hunt, n.d.), pp. 147–48.

33. *The Aeneid of Virgil,* trans. Rolfe Humphries (New York: Charles Scribner's Sons, 1951), p. 13.

34. Ibid., p. 4.

35. Ibid., p. 109. "Racialism" is not intended in an anthropological sense.

36. Ibid., pp 76–77.

37. Ibid., p. 13.

38. Ibid., p. 5.

39. Ibid., pp. 3, 23, 157; Lind, op. cit., p. 59.

40. Quintilian is cited by J. W. Mackail, *Latin Literature* (New York: Charles Scribner's Sons, 1900), p. 178. Voltaire, op. cit., p. 99; other Latin epics are Statius' *Thebaid* and Italicus' *Punica.*

41. Lucan, *Pharsalia,* trans. Robert Graves (London: Penguin Books, 1956), p. 19.

42. Ibid., p. 160.

43. Ibid., p. 68. The Trojan Capys founds Capua, p. 58; Caesar visits Achilles' shrines in Asia Minor, pp. 220–21; the people of Auvergne falsely claim Trojan descent and therefore kinship with the Romans, p. 38.

44. Ibid., pp. 185, 220–21.

45. C. Romesh Dutt, trans., *The Ramayana and the Mahabharata* (London and Toronto: J.M. Dent, 1910); U. Fausbøll, *Indian Mythology, According to the Mahabharata in Outline,* Oriental Religions Series (London: Luzac and Co., 1903); Dutt, op. cit., p. 192.

46. Ibid., p. 169.

47. Ibid., pp. 2–3.

48. Ibid., p. 22.

49. Ibid., p. 68. Because the content of the *Ramayana* is somewhat less familiar than that of the other epics, a brief synopsis of the early action is required. Two peoples are involved, the Kosalas and the Videhas. Rama goes to marry Sita, the Videha princess. He is tested by the bending of the great bow and wins Sita. He is appointed regent, but *Kabale und Liebe* intervene as Bharat's mother uses her charms to get Dasa-ratha to promise the throne to her son. Later it is related that Rama's suffering is a retribution and atonement for an early wrong done by the King. Rama is banished; the remainder of the epic details his wanderings.

50. Ibid., p. 46.

51. Ibid., p. 68.

52. Ibid., p. 70.

53. Ibid., p. 67.

54. Ibid., p. 71.

55. Ibid., pp. 128–31.

56. Ibid., p. 163.

57. Ibid., p. 179.

58. Ibid., pp. 370–72.

59. Ibid., p. 381. Pandu and Dhrita-rasha were brothers. Pandu died young. His brother became king of the Kurus and raised Dhrita-rasha's sons: Yudishthir, whose major virtue is truth and piety; Bhima, military valor; Arjun, skill in arms; Nakula and Sahadeva, the twins. Duryodhan's jealousy of his cousins destroys the harmony of the kingdom. These are the leading *dramatis personae* of the epic. Karna is introduced in the text.

60. Heinrich Zimmer, *Myths and Symbols in Indian Art and Civilization,* Bollingen Series VI (Washington, D.C.: Pantheon Books, 1946), p. 186 note.

61. *Mahabharata,* pp. 206–9.

62. Ibid., p. 232.

63. Ibid., p. 237.

64. Ibid., p. 247; *samadhi,* religious austerity.

65. Ibid., p. 264. There is another curious passage on duty in the epic in which Krishna explains the doctrines of the *Bhagavad-Gita* on duty. One authority feels that there may be a reversion to the doctrine that regardless of caste the zealous performance of duty is of utmost importance. (Ibid., p. 296, Prof. Garbe.)

66. Ibid., p. 351.

67. Ibid., p. 309; cf. pp. 302–3 on Arjun.

68. John M. Crawford, trans., *The Kalevala,* pp. 724–29; cf. River Jordan on p. 254.

69. Ibid., pp. 5, 620.

70. Charles Squire, *Celtic Myth and Legend* (London: Gresham Publishing Co., c. 1910).

71. *The Kalevala,* pp. 106, 201, 414, 654.

72. Ibid., p. 435.

73. Ibid., p. 237.

74. Ibid., p. 553.

75. Walter Kolarz, *Russia and Her Colonies* (New York: Praeger, 1952), pp. 103, 286.

76. Arthur G. Warner, trans. *The Shahnama of Firdausi,* 9 vols. (London: Kegan Paul, Trench, Trübner and Co., 1905), Vol. I, pp. 65–66.

77. Ibid., Vol. I, p. 168.

78. Ibid., Vol. II, p. 236.

79. Ibid, Vol. II, p. 311. Emil Abegg, *Der Messiaglaube in Indien und Iran auf Grund der Quellen dargestellt* (Berlin, Leipzig: W. de Gruyter, 1928).

80. *Shahnama,* Vol. II, p. 188f.

81. Ibid., Vol. II, p. 251. Kai is the Kavi of the Vedas and connotes a priest inspired by the Soma, Vol. II, p. 8.

82. Ibid., Vol. I, p. 209.

83. Ibid., Vol. I, p. 108.

84. Arthur S. Way, trans., *The Lay of the Nibelung Men* (Cambridge University Press, 1911), p. xi.

85. Ibid., p. 3.

86. Ibid., p. xv.

87. Ibid., p. 142.

88. Newman White, gen. ed., *Popular Beliefs and Superstitions from North Carolina,* #3695 (Durham, N.C.: Duke University Press, 1961).

89. Norma L. Goodrich, *The Medieval Myths,* Mentor Book (New York: New American Library, 1961), p. 16.

90. Hélène A. Guerber, *Legends of the Middle Ages,* pp. 162–99, 215–41, 327. Archer M. Huntington, trans., *Poem of the Cid* (The Hispanic Society of America, 1901, 1908), Vol. II.

91. Torquato Tasso, *Jerusalem Delivered* (London: Kegan Paul, Trench and Co., London, 1884). Cf. p. 146.

92. Guerber, op. cit., pp. 241–73.

93. John Rhys, *Studies in the Arthurian Legend* (Oxford: Clarendon Press, 1891), pp. 171, 331. E. M. W. Tillyard, *Myth and the English Mind* (New York: Collier Books, 1962), p. 48.

94. Guerber, op. cit., p. 309.

95. Lord Raglan, op. cit., p. 42; Hans Kohn, *The Idea of Nationalism* (New York: Macmillan Co., 1944), p. 494.

96. Sir Walter Scott, *Waverly* (New York: Harper's, 1901), Vol. I, p. 50.

97. Schiller, *Wilhelm Tell,* Deering, ed. (Boston: Heath and Co., 1898), Act I:182. E. L. Rochholz, *Tell und Gessler in Sage und Geschichte* (Heilbron, Verlag von Henniger, 1877). The Tell theme was particularly popular during the *Schweizerbegeisterung* from 1750–1815.

98. Goodrich, op. cit., pp. 98–99. Brancovic deserts on the battlefield at Kosovo in the Serbian epic.

99. Paul Radin, *The Trickster,* "A Study in American Indian Mythology" (London: Routledge and Kegan Paul, 1956).

100. W. H. I. Bleek, *Reynard the Fox in Africa,* or *Hottentot Fables and Tales* (London: Trübner and Co., 1864), p. 13.

101. Mary Innes, *Schools of Painting,* Charles DeKay, ed. (New York: G. P. Putnam's, 1911), pp. 54–55.

102. John Addington Symonds, *An Introduction to the Study of Dante,* 4th ed. (London: Adam and Charles Black, 1899), pp. 19, 40, 55; cf. J. A. Symonds, *A Short History of the Renaissance in Italy* (New York: Henry Holt, 1893), pp. 122, 134.

103. J. A. Symonds, *An Introduction to the Study of Dante,* p. 100.

104. Ibid., pp. 31, 110.

105. Dante, *On World Government,* or *De Monarchia,* trans. H. W. Schneider (New York: Liberal Arts Press, 1949), pp. 6, 16; reprinted by permission of the publisher, The Bobbs Merrill Company, Inc.

106. *De Monarchia,* pp. 79–80; cp. Charles H. McIlwain, *The Growth of Political Thought in the West* (New York: Macmillan Co., 1932), pp. 275–76. This is, of course, a problem passage in Dante; the *De Monarchia* remained on the *Index* until the 1800s.

107. *Divine Comedy,* pp. 286, 458.

108. Ibid., p. 226.

109. Ibid., pp. 242, 518, 573. For additional material on the classical and medieval epics, cf. H. V. Routh, *God, Man and Epic Poetry,* "A Study in Comparative Literature," 2 vols. (New York: Cambridge University Press, 1927).

110. C. Maxwell and Paul T. Lancaster, trans., *The Araucaniad* (Nashville, Tenn: Vanderbilt University Press, 1945); Alonzo de Ercilla y Zuniaga, *La Araucana* (Santiago, Chile: Editorial Nascimento, 1933). *Araucana,* pp. 163–64; Luis Vaz de Camoëns, *The Lusiads,* trans. William C. Atkinson (Baltimore, Md.: Penguin Books, 1952); H. H. Hart, *Luis de Camoëns and the Epic of the Lusiads* (Norman, Okla.: University of Oklahoma Press, 1962).

111. Cf. Alexandre de Humboldt, *Examen Critique de l'Histoire du Nouveau Continent* (Paris: Librairie de Gide, 1837), Vol. II, p. 264.

112. *Lusiads,* p. 162.

113. *Araucana,* p. 320.

114. Ibid., p. 159.

115. Merritt Y. Hughes, ed., *John Milton, Complete Poems and Major Prose* (New York: Odyssey Press, 1957), p. 717; reprinted by permission of the publisher, The Bobbs Merrill Company, Inc.

116. Ibid., p. 57, "De Idea Platonica Quemadmodum Aristoteles Intellexit"—*Non, cui profundum caecitas lumen dedit, Dircaeus augur vidit hunc alto sinu.*

117. Cited by Neumann, op. cit., p. 9.

118. Sir John Marshall, *Mohenjo-Daro and the Indus Civilization* (London: Arthur Probsthain, 1931), p. 64.

119. Cited by Lewis Spence, *The Myths of Mexico and Peru* (London: George H. Harrap and Co., 1912), p. 221.

120. Feldmann, op. cit., #10, 46, 47, pp. 24, 43, 118–119; cf. Squire, *Celtic Myth and Legend,* pp. 55, 218. Campbell, op. cit., p. 388 (extremely primitive Papuan version of loss of immortality.)

121. Merritt Y. Hughes, ed., op. cit., p. 456.

122. Ibid., p. 314; A. O. Lovejoy, *The Great Chain of Being* (Cambridge: Harvard University Press, 1953).

123. Ibid., p. 477.

124. Voltaire, *Toleration and Other Essays,* Joseph McCabe, trans. (New York: Putnam's, 1912), pp. 85–87.

125. Voltaire, *The Henriade,* trans. C. L. S. Jones, (Mobile, Ala., 1834), p. 59.

126. Ibid., pp. 149–50; Voltaire's remarks on Druids and Arch-Druids in *Candide* are apropos.

127. Ibid., p. 156.

128. Ibid., p. 157.

129. D. C. Peattie, "Voltaire: Spark of Liberty," *Reader's Digest,* February 1949, p. 131.

III. THE POLITICS OF EPIC HEROISM

• • •

> Each . . . is a refutation to the despondency and cowardice of our political theorists. (Possessing a) wild courage, a stoicism not of the schools but of the blood . . . we need books of this tart cathartic virtue more than books of political science.
>
> —Emerson's "Heroism"[1]

Politics and the Epic Hero

Epic is the monstrance in which the myth is displayed to the believers. It is the ciborium, the sacred covering, which contains the symbolic message of heroism. The hero is hierophant, connecting humanity with the divine mysteries, establishing sacrament and ritual. The hero is also man searching for power, legitimacy, security, knowledge, or immortality. The heroic quest is concerned with the ultimate questions of human existence. The social mission of the hero is to give moral purpose to the community, thereby extricating humanity from the shadows of the Cave. In a Tennysonian phrase he becomes "ideal manhood closed in real man."

Epic is the response to the "cry of the times."[2] It expresses the prevailing social predicament. This conception of epic and myths serves as the basis for the systematic theory of myth and society, formulated in the next chapter. The story of the *Kulturheld* is the story of the parturition of civilization. The myth recounts the psychological coming into being, the social *rites de passage,* the meteorological cycles. The myth of the hero traces the genesis of history and the etiology of things.

The hero is the conqueror of the demoniac, the savior of his people, the exorciser of the energumen, the shaman, the politician. The heroic epiphany is a series of dramatic episodes which live in the public memory. The heroic struggles embody the human struggles. As in Tasso's *Jerusalem Delivered,* the hero often fights with phantasmagoria produced by his own mind. He alone can be translated up to the *fata morgana.* The mythic protagonist is frequently the Shekinah, but it is not the semidivine or shamanistic quality alone which makes the hero believable. It is his humanity, manifested in the excruciating heroic agony, which evokes our sympathy—*eli, eli lama sabachthani.*

The heroic story has a symbolic composition like a Van Eyck altarpiece; here a trefoil, there a lily or a forget-me-not. Such significant attributes as triskelion and trident Dr. Elliott terms epic symbols.[3] Such symbols have a peculiarly universal appeal. The triskelion, for example, is on the Manx coat-of-arms, the Myrmidons' shields, shell gorgets from Tennessee, or more recently the Fugitives' publication. Neptune and Shiva both carry tridents. The *uroboros,* the self-consuming serpent, appears on the Mexican calendar stone, a brass shield of the Nigerian Benin, and a Mandaean bowl of the sixth century A.D.[4]

Together with the heroic personification symbols, the epic symbols interact to construct the myth. As iconographs, the epic symbols evoke the myth; the personification symbols then connect the hero to communal values. The epic hero fuses the human and the divine. He reflects the divinity and participates in the divine nature of the universe. In a way the hero is an affirmation of ethics and philosophy. As Dr. Elliott suggests, the heroic myth contains an epistemological verification of ontology. He fuses the organic processes with the moral purpose of the community.

The divinely guided hero discovers the "Way," then communicates it symbolically. Such symbolization allows Raphael to expound the "ways of God" to Adam:

> . . . what surmounts the reach
> Of human sense, I shall delineate so,
> By lik'ning spiritual to corporal forms,
> As may express them best, though what if Earth
> Be but the shadow of Heav'n and things therein
> Each to other like, more than on earth is thought.[5]

The heroic outlook occurs most strongly in the formative stages of society. T. E. Lawrence tells of Auda, an Arab chieftain:

> He saw life as a saga. All the events in it were significant; all personages in contact with him heroic. His mind was storied with poems of old raids and epic tales of fights, and he overflowed with them on the nearest listener.[6]

Here are the remnants of the heroic age, the time of the folk epic and the cycles of epic heroism. The folk epic is like the stirring paddle of the Shintoist gods which brings order to chaos. The struggle between hero and demoniac results in the coalescence of society.

With varying degrees of success the literary epic attempts to restore this lost condition. The epic formula substitutes changing heroic names. Thus, in translating Boethius, King Alfred replaces Fabricius with the meaningful Weyland Smith. Such a change personalizes the myth. Only the content of epic heroism varies; the form remains constant. The proud warrior Achilles differs from the dutiful Aeneas; the wily self-sufficient Odysseus from the chivalrous Roland. The epic myth is as constant as society itself. Changes in the content of epic heroism reflect changes in social evolution.[7]

The political figure enjoys being cast in the heroic role. Such is our legacy of marmoreal statues, laurel-wreathed and Benthamite that we can hardly doubt it. For every General Nicholson, who finds it deucedly inconvenient to be incorporated into the Hindu pantheon before the gates of Delhi as Nikal-sen, there is a Sikander (Alexander), who is moderately flattered by the idea of appearing on coins in a Herculean lion outfit.

The great man qua hero accumulates the characteristic anecdotes of his predecessors. The story of the conqueror who slips in getting off the boat and then embraces the land is told of Napoleon, William the Conqueror, Junius Brutus, and King Olaf Harald of Norway.

The Siamese venerate great men, *paraks,* as models of virtue. Chinese and Japanese differ on the exaltation of the scholar or the warrior, but hero worship still obtains. The Hopi have their *kachinas,* or heroic clan ancestors.[8] The stations of the *Heldenleben* epitomize the social myths—legitimacy, establishment, messianism. The hero is the eponymous hero, the name-giving culture hero, the paragon, the link between social microcosm and celestial macrocosm. The hero anthropomorphizes the nation. As Nehru states:

> It is curious how one cannot resist the tendency to give an anthropomorphic form to a country. Such is the force of habit and early associations, India becomes *Bharat Mata,* Mother India . . .[9]

The hero is a colossal figure capable of inspiring either an *Eroica* or a nationalistic movement—*Wer ein Volk retten will kann nur heroisch denken. Der arme Hermann* unites the German peasantry in kinship. The "one-gallus" genealogist of Cash's South connects himself with the Lees, with Brian Boru, with Robert Bruce, and William the Conqueror.[10] The hero himself, as Sidney Hook shows, is at the center of historical consciousness because in times of crisis he is the decision-making leader.[11]

The Monomyth

The heroic monomyth, as James Joyce terms it, is the key to political mythology.[12] In order to view the political, epic hero in proper perspective, it is necessary to summarize briefly the studies of the monomyth. The leitmotifs of epic heroism reduce to these categories: the birth-death of the hero, tested heroism, the struggle with the demoniac, the descent into the underworld, and the anti-heroic types, trickster, unpromising hero, and punished wanderer.

The diagram below presents the hypothesis of this chapter in outline form.

Political Myth Type	*Epic Hero*	*Typical Episodes*
Civilizing; Rational vs. Demoniac; Humanity	Beowulf	The hero in society; the fight with the dragon; heroic agony
Messianism	Dionysus	Rescue of the people; arrival of the young stranger
Cultural Catastrophism	Siegfried	Death of the hero; sense of loss
Legitimizing	Aeneas	Tested heroism; descent to the dead; receipt of power-talisman

Social Establishment	Hun-Apu	Elite birth of the hero; class establishment or punishment
Legality	Hiawatha	Ethical exemplification or receipt of laws
Paideia; Moral Purpose	Roland	The point of honor, the heroic disagreement; the ideal of virtue; hero as myth-preserver
Power	Achilles	Invulnerability; hero-shamanism; excess of power; combats; power quest
Historic Myths	Cid	Generations of the hero; fatalism; determinism; transformations; weird
Bipolarity National-Racial	Afrasiyab	Racial stereotypes; hero conqueror; enslaves inferiors
Freedom or Escape	Prometheus	Miraculous rescue; search for immortality; magic flight
Anti-Heroic Functions		
Iconoclasm; Antilegality	Satan Wandering Jew	Rebellion; nihilism; destruction of power; attempts to destroy hero; punished wanderer
Social Satire; Catharsis; Scapegoats	Reynard	Broken taboos; tricksters; pleas of insanity; stratagem relief from tensions; witch hunting; disgrace

This diagram attempts to show how the psychological and anthropological functions of heroism are associated in a political framework. *The epic hero is a political hero. The epic myth is socially limited.*

Modern attempts to study the monomyth have emphasized the many parallelisms in the heroic stories. There have been two key problems—one of repetition, the other of retention. Why are the morphae of myths more consistent than the patterns of history, when history is limited by human experience but myth by human imagination? Why is humanity so mimetic that certain mythic themes are habitually retained?

In answering these questions regarding myth many authors have stressed either the external impositions of cosmology or the life-cycle or the internal *ananke* of the psyche. The alternative solution makes myth an intermediary between the individual and the universe. The location of society is also at this point. The myth, therefore, serves as the bonding unit between man and the state. Since the number of forms of acceptable social action are limited, the bonding relationships are also limited.

Recent examinations of the monomyth are traceable to the work of Bishop Huet in the eighteenth century. Bishop Huet compares Moses, Osiris, and Perseus.[13] In his *Manual of Mythology,* Cox makes some generalized comparisons of heroic traits; there are also the studies in gray and black of Carlyle's *Heroes and Hero Worship.*

Plutarch's method of comparison comes to light in the work of Hermann Schneider. Schneider's religious history traces the heroic myth from its Neolithic origins into all Near Eastern cultures. The model of the myth includes the victory of the sun hero over his dark brother; the sun hero's death through treachery, and the repetition of the cycle with the heroic revenge. The solar *mythos* is evident in Enkidu as well as Gilgamesh, Min of Coptos, Osiris, Horus, Tammuz, Min of Crete, Hercules and other heroes of the same area. Schneider concludes from the evidence:

> . . . man realized more and more profoundly that the sun's course is eternally the same . . . myths were permeated by the influence of political conditions to the new settled life. Solar mythology progressed side by side with the advancing organization of the state and the family.[14]

According to Schneider, the death-resurrection cycle is the basis of a fundamental analogy. The sun enters the mountain-side and reemerges; the hero's tomb is a mountain cave from which he will reemerge. It is possible that this "pre-logical" line of thought persists in modern funerals.

It is unnecessary to accept the minor premises of Schneider's solarium; for example, that trepanation and quoit-throwing represent the sun's flight. However, the evidence forces agreement that the growth of eponymous heroism parallels political development. Apollo, the Delphic Oracle, and the fundamental idea of an amphictyony are inseparable from the consolidation of early Greek alliances. The Roman Jupiter personifies centralized imperial power. Schneider correlates the Spartan policies of peace or force and the Dionysian solar *mythos.* The heroic cults catalyze loyalty to the *polis.* The folk hero or totemic hero, as a personification symbol, involves the tribe in a system of obligations and responsibilities.

Schneider's work, unfortunately, represents only one part of the multicornered tug of war over the epic hero. Psychologists, literary critics, and students of religion have all claimed the hero for their own. Raglan's *The Hero* belongs to the myth-ritual school; Rank's *The Birth of the Hero* and Campbell's *The Hero with a Thousand Faces* are psychoanalytic; Propp's viewpoint is that of the folklorist.

Lord Raglan offers a framework with which to examine the recurrent elements of the monomyth. The episodes are these:

(1) The hero's mother is a royal virgin, (2) his father is a king and, (3) often a near relative of his mother, but (4) the circumstances of his conception are unusual and (5) he is also reputed to be the son of a god. (6) At birth an attempt is made, usually by his father or maternal grandfather to kill him. (7) He is spirited away and (8) reared by foster parents in a far country. (9) We are told nothing of his childhood, but (10) on reaching manhood he returns or goes to his future kingdom. (11) After a victory over the king or a great dragon or a wild beast, (12) he marries a princess, often the daughter of his predecessor, (13) becomes king. (14) For a time he reigns uneventfully and (15) prescribes laws, but (16) later he loses favor with the gods and/or his subjects and (17) is driven from the throne and city after which (18) he meets with a mysterious death (19) often at the top of a hill. (20) His children, if any, do not succeed him. (21) His body is not buried, but nevertheless (22) he has one or more sepulchres.[15]

Raglan then correlates these episodes in the careers of a representative group of heroes. Unfortunately he omits such specific motifs as the descent into the underworld. The results of his examination are:

Oedipus–21	Theseus–20	Moses–20
Dionysios–19	Arthur–19	Romulus–18
Perseus–18	Watu Gunung–18	Heracles–17
Llew Llawgyffes–17	Bellerophon–16	Jason–15
Zeus–15	Nyikang,–14	Pelops–13
Robin Hood–13	Joseph–12	Asclepius–12
Apollo–11		Sigurd–11

On this scaling system Alexander the Great receives about 7.

Raglan's quantitative analysis of epic heroism is open to a wide range of criticism. I will attempt to reduce the pattern to its important elements: Raglan's first three points are not too significant.

(a) The *hero is of royal birth.* This is eugenically quite logical and meshes well with an elitist myth. Possibly the nearness of relation is unusual but not in the light of intradynastic marriages. (1–3).

(b) The hero is the *son of a god.* This simply associates the concepts of divinity and royalty. It is important in the question of legitimacy. Gods and mortals do not miscegenate normally anyway. (4–5) He himself is deified. (21–22)

(c) An *attempt* is made *to kill the hero,* but he is not killed. (That would quite ruin the story; and as it is inconvenient to bring him up in the palace, he has to be reared elsewhere.) I do not accept Raglan's ninth point at all; Hercules, Romulus, and Llew Llawgyffes have important childhoods which often presage later events. (6–9)[16]

(d) He returns to his future kingdom and *fights with the dragon.* This is the only point where the theme of tested heroism enters into Raglan's analysis. (10–11)

(e) The hero *marries a princess* and becomes king; his children, if any, do not succeed him. This seems to be a reminiscence of matrilineal succession. Marriage of a princess is therefore tantamount to becoming a king. The failure of his children to succeed him is of somewhat less significance in this light. His uneventful reign does not distinguish the hero from some very unheroic rulers. (12–13–14–20)

(f) The *hero is a lawgiver.* Although this is significant as a political myth of legality, it is the natural result of the other characteristics that the hero should determine the laws and customs. (15)

(g) He dies a mysterious death, often on a hilltop. Frankly, hilltops are pretty mysterious places to die; there is no reason for separation. The mysterious death as we shall see simply parallels the mysterious birth—just as a normal death sometimes is preceded by a normal birth. (18–19)

Scored against this condensation, all of Raglan's heroes fall into a six to eight range. Elijah receives a two. Alexander the Great scores within the mythic range. After Raglan is completely simplified, the striking fact remains that *the hero is a divine priest or king.* Most of the attributes of Raglan's hero are common to royalty or divinity. The most interesting factors are the loss of popular favor and the assassination attempt. What Raglan really leaves us with is possibly more historical than mythical.

Turning from the myth-ritual theory of Lord Raglan to the folklorist work of Vladimir Propp, we find a complex analysis of the *Morphology of the Folktale.* Propp differentiates a large number of persistent "story radicals" in the heroic story. These are Veselovsky's motifs and Bédier's elements. Propp states his theory in four parts:

> 1. Functions serve as stable, constant elements in folktales, independent of who performs them, and how they are fulfilled by the *dramatis personae.* They constitute the components of a folktale. 2. The number of functions known in the fairy tale is limited. 3. The sequence of functions is always identical. 4. All fairy tales, by their structure, belong to one and the same type.[17]

Propp studied a relatively limited body of material, Russian fairy tales. His approach is understandably orthodox and formal, as the literature is highly stylized. The only objection is that the limitation of the sample tends to emphasize the shamanistic hero to the detriment of the human hero. A wider study should also show the association of seeker with victim-hero, which Propp is unable to find in the fairy tales. The heroic functions are:

> a. Initial situation; b. Absence; g. Interdiction; d. Violation; e. Villain's reconnaissance; z. Delivery; e. Fraud or Deception; th. Complicity, hero agrees or reacts; 1. preliminary misfortune. A. Villainy . . . B. Misfortune or shortage is made known, mediation, connective, brings hero into play, victim-heroes or seekers; C. Beginning counter-action, and departure of the hero. D. Func-

tion of the donor; first magical agent to hero. D-1 tests of hero by the donor; D-2 greeting or interrogation, a weaker form of testing; D-3 A dying request; D-4 Prisoner asks for freedom; D-4 Preliminary imprisonment; D-5 Request for mercy; D-6 Request for property division; D-7 Other requests; D-8 Hostile creature or D-9 Combats the hero; D-10 Hero shown a magical agent; E. Hero's reaction as ordeal or shows mercy; apportionment, services; F. Receipt of magical agent; G. Spatial translocation; H. Struggle between hero and villain; J. Branding or wounding of hero; burning star on forehead; small mark; I. Victory; K. Initial misfortune liquidated; L. Return; Pr. Pursuit; Rs. Rescue (may repeat A-G); O. Unrecognized arrival; M. Difficult task; N. Accomplished; Q. Recognition; Ex Exposure of villain; T. Transfiguration of the hero; V. Punishment of the villain; W. Wedding; X. Close, other actions.[18]

The folklorist may also single out certain areas of social concern which give rise to recurrent elements in the heroic story. Spencer mentions the hero's vindication and reconciliation among the Navaho. The important areas are health, knowledge, power, proper family relations, self-assertion and responsibility.[19]

The psychological approach to the epic hero stresses the family relations, the heroic traumas, the psychological complexes. Oedipus undergoes transformation into the ideal mythic hero. This may or may not be convenient for the psychoanalyst, but it certainly is not for the student of comparative mythology. As Dr. Elliott has described this approach: "The psychiatrists of politics like to pull men and movements to pieces, as if they were clocks with wheels, or patients under the most cruel of all dissecting scalpels."[20]

In the *Hero with a Thousand Faces,* Campbell takes a psychological approach. However, major concerns are the *rites de passage,* the theme of tested heroism, and the hero's social context. His view of the monomyth is relatively simple and hence valuable from the political standpoint. Campbell's hero develops through three stages:

(a) *Separation or Departure:* the call to adventure; refusal of the call; supernatural aid; the crossing of the first threshold; the belly of the whale.
(b) *Trials and Victories of Initiation:* the road of trials; the meeting with the goddess; woman as temptress; at-one-ment with the father; apotheosis; the ultimate boon.
(c) *Return and Reintegration* with society; refusal of return; the magic flight; rescue from without; the crossing of the return threshold; master of two worlds; freedom to live.[21]

Campbell's progressive analysis is important, but the predominant concern is to unravel Ariadne's thread which leads through the labyrinthine psychology of the heroic mind. Campbell makes the significant point that when Minos prays for a bull from the sea and promises to sacrifice it to the gods he breaks the promise. He decides to keep the bull for his own herd, his own economic benefit. He lays the welfare of his people aside. The result is the Minotaur, which the hero must kill.

Rank's *The Birth of the Hero* contains another psychological approach. Rank reduces the heroic legend to these terms:

The hero is the child of most distinguished parents, usually the son of a king. His origin is preceded by difficulties. . . . During or before the pregnancy, there is a prophecy . . . cautioning against his birth and usually threatening danger to his father . . . As a rule, he is surrendered to the water in a box. He is then saved by a humble woman . . . he finds his distinguished parents in a highly versatile fashion . . . takes revenge on his father . . . finally achieves rank and honor.[22]

The Birth of the Hero

Myths of epic heroism begin with the birth of the hero. The heroic birth condenses into a single, meteoric moment the pattern of the hero's later development. The heroic birth myth couples the romantic notion of a "sleeping and a forgetting" with the Darwinian struggle for survival. The heroic birth is always a dramatic *tour de force.* Associated with the heroic birth myths is a configuration of themes: emergence, elitism, the significant myth setting, the hero's preliminary testing, the repetitions of the heroic theme, and the birth-death cycle.

The emergence theme plays a prominent role in the heroic myth. There is a demiurgic repetition which makes the emergence of the hero identical with the emergence of the psyche, the emergence of the earth, and the emergence of society. Because the widespread flood stories deal with a reemergence of humanity through the mediation of the hero, they, too, are connected to the heroic birth. It is little wonder that the Biblical text calls both the bulrush boat of Moses and Noah's Ark, *tebah.*

Customarily the hero is well-born; this is the elitist myth. The hero, however, always fuses a natural ability with an aristocratic birth. He is the legitimizer, tacit or otherwise, of the class into which he is born.

The class setting is part of the initial setting of the heroic birth stories. The scenario is of immense significance because it is a time of troubles. The people, starving and oppressed, await the arrival of the hero as messiah. Portents of fire, disaster, and fearful cataclysm frequently accompany the heroic birth.

At the outset, society rejects the hero; he is despised. Bulfinch narrates a typical situation in the *Legends of Charlemagne:*

> Milone, a knight of great family and distantly related to Charlemagne, having secretly married Bertha, the Emperor's sister, was banished from France and excommunicated by the Pope.

> After a long and miserable wandering on foot as mendicants, Milone and his wife arrived at Sutri, where they took refuge in a cave and in that cave Orlando was born. There his mother continued, deriving a scanty support from the compassion of the neighboring peasants.[23]

Often he is set adrift in a coracle or exposed. This rejection places the hero outside society; yet his triumphal advent is much-anticipated. This rejection occasions the next important stage in the heroic birth or childhood, his preliminary testing. This pits the hero against the forces of nature. His is a crucial struggle for human existence; his only resource is self-reliance. The hero's very identity is at stake. He is the homunculus which paradoxically contains all the future promise of civilization. His baptism is by fire or sword, by the waters of the Styx or the dragon's blood.

The hero must foil all efforts to destroy him. In this situation, the Indo-Tibetan hero Suryanemi flees from his father's mercenaries, who try unsuccessfully to prevent the fulfillment of the prophecy that he will take the king's life and usurp the royal power.[24]

Rejected by human society, the hero finds theriomorphic parents. In this manner the Simurg (Roc) nourishes Minuchihr, exposed on Mt. Alburz. Similar stories relate to Romulus and Remus, and Wolfdietrich, not to mention Edgar Rice Burroughs' hero! A shepherd or gardener may rescue the hero as in the case of Oedipus on the Cithaeron. He often substitutes an animal's heart for the hero's.

Dr. Elliott notes the curious parallelisms in the heroic birth myths. The diffusion and interaction of these polyphonic themes begins in an ancient text on King Sargon of Agade:

> Sargon the mighty king, King of Agade, am I. My mother was a vestal, while my father I knew not. . . . In a hidden place she brought me forth. She laid me in a vessel made of reeds, closed

> my door with pitch, and dropped me down into the river . . . (which) carried me to Akki, the water carrier . . . who made of me his gardener.[25]

The myth next appears in a Near Eastern environment; it is the well-known Mosaic version. There are similar elements in the stories of Cyrus and Osiris. According to Pausanias, Bacchus, set adrift in the Nile, escapes the persecution of the king. A *liknos,* or osier basket, is associated with the Eleusinian mysteries. It seems possible that the popularization of the "great Dionysiak myth" led to a second diffusion of the heroic birth motif. In the much later tale in the *Legenda Aurea,* the anti-hero, Judas Iscariot, is exposed. This is an interesting parody of the heroic story.[26]

Evidence from *Beowulf* shows the story's penetration into Europe. The poem calls the hero's father Scyld the Scefung because as a young boy "he was cast ashore as a stranger, asleep in a boat on a sheaf of grain."[27] Kullervo, "the child of evil," of the *Kalevala* is another example:

> He was placed within a basket
> And with willows firmly fastened,
> Taken to the reeds and rushes,
> Lowered to the deepest waters
> In his basket there to perish.[28]

A shepherd rescues Kullervo and sells him to Ilmarinen as a slave.

A more distant echo of the birth theme occurs in the story of the Celtic hero Gwion, or Taliesin, who stirs the cauldron of knowledge for Cardiwen. He tastes some of the liquor and learns of his impending murder. To escape he finally transforms himself into a grain of wheat, but Cardiwen in the form of a hen swallows him. He is then reborn and cast into the sea in a leather bag.[29]

The motif also diffuses southward and eastward; it enters India and China. King Chandragupta of the fourth century B.C., abandoned in an earthen jar, recalls to Campbell the Pueblo story of "water-jar boy." In another Indian variant, reciting the birth of Karna, this passage occurs:

> Then my nurse and I made a large basket of rushes, placed a lid thereon, and I lined it with wax, into this basket I laid the boy and carried him down to the River Acva.[30]

In the Chinese story, Hsüan Chuang, the Master drifts on a plank. A monk discovers him and renames him "Waif of the River." At the birth of the Iroquois law-giver Deganawida there is a prophecy that his birth will indirectly cause the ruin of his people. The tribe exposes the child in an ice hole, but he repeatedly returns unharmed.[31]

The Polynesian story of Maui, although ethnically altered, seems to belong to the same class of heroic narratives. Maui searches for his parents.

> I did not think I was your child . . . because I knew I was born at the side of the sea, and was thrown by you into the foam of the surf after you had wrapped me into a tuft of your hair . . . then the seaweed formed and fashioned me.[32]

This myth evokes a poetic analogy to Botticelli's Cythaerean Venus.

In association with the birth of the hero are other stereotyped events. The hero's conception is frequently unusual. The Aztec Huitzilpochtli is conceived by a feather ball. Zeus comes to Danaë's tower in a shower of gold and begets Perseus. In the Phaeton-like story of the northwestern Indians, Mink is conceived by the sun's rays. Gogzalhamo, the mother of the Tibetan hero, Kesar of Ling, conceives not only him but also the sun and moon.[33]

The hero often performs prodigious feats of strength at birth. William Crooke comments on the birth of Krishna:

> Like that of so many . . . the birth of Krishna was in wondrous wise. A supernatural voice, what the Greeks would have called a *Pheme*, announces to the usurper Kamsa that his slayer would be born in the eighth son of his kinsman Vasudeva and Devaki . . .[34]

Kamsa unsuccessfully attempts to thwart the prophecy and prevent the heroic birth. Crooke continues:

> All the fateful children of the folktales have miraculous powers at birth . . . Otus and Ephialtes . . . were born of monstrous size; the new-born Apollo, who in the Homeric hymn, when he tastes the nectar and ambrosia, leaps from his swaddling clothes, begins to speak, and wanders through the land; Vali, in the Norse tale, when one night old, sallies out to avenge the death of Balder, and Magni, the son of Thor . . . when three months old flings off the giant's foot with which the monster would have crushed his father. So the Dayaks have a like marvellous child in Seragunting . . . As St. Benedict sang Eucharistic hymns before he was born, so in the Zulu folktale there is a child who speaks in the womb . . .

Bowra describes the heroic birth complex in the heroic poetry of the peoples of Central Asia:

> Asiatic heroes are often born in strange circumstances. The Nart Uryzmag is born at the bottom of the sea, while Batrazd is born from a woman who was kept a virgin in a high tower . . . A particularly elaborate case of this (birth in direct response to a prayer) is the Canaanite Aqhat, whose father conducts a watch of seven days and seven nights in the sanctuary of Baal . . . Helgi Hundingsbane is born in full mail . . .[35]

Likewise Athena springs forth fully armed.

It seems apropos to conclude with the birth and childhood of Merlin. Vortigern, the Prime Minister, deserts King Constans and his sons, who have driven Hengist from England. Vortigern attempts to build a great fortress on Salisbury plains, but the walls will not stand. He is informed that they will never stand until the blood of a virgin-born child waters the earth. This element combines parthenogenesis with building-sacrifice—still found in "shadow-traders." Satan's demon child is to be Merlin. His mother averts the evil by consulting the Holy Man, Blaise.[36]

In all of these heroic myths the community segregates the hero. Because the myth-maker possesses a fine sense of repetition, he scores the heroic story *da capo.* Such a device makes the first scene of *Macbeth* acceptable as the final scene. The death of the hero returns to the birth theme. The mysterious barge arrives to carry Arthur to Avalon; a serpent raft wafts the aged Quetzalcoatl away. Balder and Beowulf are also set to sea. Sometimes the hero ascends in a fiery chariot.[37]

In a coronach or elegy the myth reverts to the beginning. The community poignantly feels the loss because it throws society back to the chaotic barbarism from which the hero rescued it —"So on the floor lay Balder dead . . ."[38]

Because the epic hero is the bonding unit of society, the hero's death causes hysteria. The Shilluks deny the death of Nyikang; if the hero dies, his people die. Such is the death of Hector, even the temporary withdrawal of Achilles. Disaster accompanies the wrathful departure of the Hittite hero Telipinu; both men and gods are near starvation.[39] Because the hero provides the boundaries of discipline and order, his absence signals a dissolution, a chaotic situation such as Shakespeare describes in *Troilus and Cressida:*

Take but degree away, untune that string,
And hark! What discord follows . . .
Then everything includes itself in power,
Power into will, will into appetite . . .[40]

Shakespeare's perceptive treatment of hero and myth in passages such as this one merits the adjective "epic" applied to his plays by A. W. Schlegel. The same theme, the collapse of the unifying center, occurs in *The Tempest* with the political chaos which results from the withdrawal of Prospero.

Tested Heroism

The process by which the heroic consciousness becomes the moral consciousness of the community is the process of tested heroism. Tested heroism includes the labors of the hero; the encounter with the demoniac, and the descent to the Underworld. The essential problem of tested heroism is to establish the identity of the hero beyond dispute and thereby to legitimize the hero and his descendants. Tests cover perseverance, loyalty, honesty, courage, and power. The tests therefore determine social values. Stoic testing, *exercitatio*, strengthens heroic character according to the maxim that "practice of virtue leads to perfection of virtue." The individual tests are legion, from the temptations of St. Anthony to Oedipus and the Sphinx.

Tested heroism provides awesome models of virtue. The emulation of tested heroism is the better part of military martyrdom, itself a kind of sacrifice urged on by mythic commitment to a "cause." Heroism teaches self-discipline and subordination to authority. Job, who suffers much for the Lord and yet sits before the gates meting out impartial justice, is probably the greatest of tested heroes. The *Book of Job* is the great Hebraic epic. *Maccabees* and Fox's *Book* testify to the viability of the image of Job-tested.

Celtic and Polynesian myths of tested heroism furnish models for initiation rites. The novice must reenact the tasks of the eponymous hero. Such tests prove him ready for admission into society.[41]

Often testing occurs at great assemblies, the Greek funeral games, the Astra-Darsana of the *Mahabharata*, the Arthurian jousts. Frequently the objective is winning a bride. In many Oriental tales it is "off with his head" if the hero fails. In other cases, the hero undertakes a difficult quest or mission in search of a talisman. The hero's success assures his status, and he and his bride "live happily ever after."

There is an exception to this pattern in the Nyasaland myth of coney. The hero decides to take a human wife; first, he must pass a test of hunting ability. Instead, he eats millet from the family's field, which leads to his detection. In his second test he is to rout the wildcats from the fruit trees. He succeeds in this by using poison, but the bride's family denies his reward, and he commits suicide.[42]

The totemic ancestor often aids the eponymous hero in the performance of his tasks. This occurs in the African story of Crocodile which resembles Cadmus and the dragon's teeth.

> A crocodile came to the cave and spoke to the fugitive
> saying,
> "Hail chief!"
> He replied, "I am no chief, I am an empty-handed wanderer.
> I came here to die with my friends!"
> "Hoe a garden and put pumpkin seed in it," said the
> crocodile, and departed.[43]

Out of the pumpkin seed comes a leopard which destroys the old chief; from that time the tribe holds Crocodile sacred.

Perhaps the best-known labors are those of Hercules: the Nemean lion (Hercules clad in a skin which makes him invulnerable); the Lernean Water-snake; Boar of Erymanthus; Deer of Ceryneia; Stymphalian Birds; Augean Stables; Cretan Bull; Diomedean Horses (Hercules swallowed by a sea monster which had come to devour Hesione); Queen of the Amazon's Girdle; Geryon's Cattle; Apples of the Hesperides and Cereberus. Rhys places the Labors *vis à vis* those of the Celtic heroes, Cuchulainn and Peredur. The parallels are quite close.[44]

The importance of the Herculean Labors can hardly be overestimated. For example, in Spanish medieval chronicles the episode of Geryon's Cattle highlights the legitimacy problem of the Spanish monarchy. Foreign relations with Italy can be plotted against the hero's exploits. In the chronicle of Ximenez de Rada, Archbishop of Toledo (thirteenth century), and of Afonso the Wise, the Argive Hercules arrives in Spain to rescue the people from Geryon's tyranny. The hero is not a conqueror, but *un sabio,* a wise man.[45]

In the fifteenth century a reaction sets in among Spanish historians. For Margarit, Geryon becomes the cattle's legal guardian. Hercules is nothing less than a member of the Italian *banditti.* The myth now reflects the Spanish rejection of Italian cultural supremacy. By 1498, Spanish influence begins to rise in Italy; the *Commentaria* of Annius of Viterbo propagates a new version of the Hercules myth. The hero is now the son of Osiris, giving the Spanish monarchy a connection to the Pharoahs. The myth of Geryon appears again in Spenser. Prince Arthur fights "Gerioneos Seneschall" for Belge (V:x).

More striking even than the parallels cited by Rhys are the Celtic labors of the sons of Turenn. The tasks comprise an elaborate *wergeld,* assessed for the death of Cian, Lugh's father. The required items include: the apples of the Hesperides, the magic pigskin of King Tuis of Greece, the magic spear of the King of Persia, the hound of the King of Iorusidhe, three shouts from a hill north of Lochlann, where the guardians kill anyone who shouts. The sons of Turenn are to collect the amphibious horse of Dobhan, King of Sicily, and the cooking spits of the women of Fianchueve at the bottom of the sea. Even after they complete these deeds, Lugh is merciless.[46]

The heroes of the *Kalevala* perform similar feats: catching the magic reindeer, bridling the flaming horse of Hisi, and killing the swan of Tuoni. Thor is known for his struggle with the old hag, Death, and his attempt to drink the Ocean from the bottomless horn. The Scottish story of "Nicht, Nought, Nothing" tells:

> I cleaned the stable, I laved the loch, and I clamb the tree and all for the love of thee.[47]

Jason, of course, seeks the golden fleece, drives a furrow with firebreathing oxen, defeats the dragon-teeth's children and the guardian serpent.

Tested heroism recurs in the flood myths. Here the test determines the survival of human culture. In the *Zatapatha Brahmana,* Manu and seven *rishis* survive. Since the heroes are cultural survivors, they must restore the severed relationship with heaven. For example, in Gippsland the cause of the flood is that women have been permitted to see the bull-roarer. The hero must rectify this situation by reestablishing the mysteries.

The Sauk-Fox variant makes the flood part of a primordial power struggle and the effort of the manitous to slay the culture-hero Wisaka:

> In their anger they howled and wailed, and the tramp of their feet was so heavy that the whole earth shook beneath them. They hurled fire into all the places where they thought Wisaka might be hiding. After the fire, came the rain. It pursued wherever he fled . . . it pursued him up a lofty pine to the very tip of

> the topmost branch. And as the water was about to lay hold on him, Wisaka called to the pine for help. And lo, a canoe slid off from the top of the pine where he was standing. The canoe floated upon the water.[48]

At times the heroic tasks are a penance. Thus, Admetus imposes certain duties on Apollo. Mercury appears as a servant in a parable of Eirenaeus Philalethea.[49] In the Polynesian tale of Tawhaki the hero disguises himself as an ugly old man. In this guise his in-laws, who are canoe builders, enslave him. Each evening Tawhaki secretly finishes off the work with a single adze-stroke. Grey points to the humor of a situation of a paramount chief who is treated as a servant. Tawhaki seeks revenge against the brothers who attempt to kill him. He is closely associated with the deluge-rainbow myth and resembles the Biblical Joseph with his rainbow-colored coat.[50]

Myths which make the hero play the servant are part of the heroic epiphany. The menial tasks contrast sharply with the future glory. Jung discusses this myth with reference to the *Magnum Opus:*

> The figure of the thrall generally leads up to the real epiphany of the semi-divine hero. Oddly enough, we have a similar modulation of themes in alchemy—in the synonyms of the *lapis.* As the *materia prima,* it is the *lapis exilis et vilis.* As a substance in the process of transmutation, it is *servus rubeus* or *fugitivus,* and finally, in its true apotheosis, it attains the dignity of a *filius sapientiae* or *deus terrenus,* a "light above all lights," a power that contains in itself all the powers of the upper and nether regions. It becomes a *corpus glorificatum,* which enjoys everlasting incorruptibility and is therefore a panacea.[51]

The Fight with a Monster

The final stage of transmutation frequently brings the hero into contact with the demoniac. Usually his opponents are the dragons or giants, which overpopulate the heroic world. Among the inferior specimens the Chinese *Shan hai ching* catalogues the one-eyed, six-toed, and three-headed.[52] Chinese apothecary shops preserved their relics, especially dragon's skin, giant's teeth, and unicorns' horns, well into the present century. Likewise, medieval romances abound in Ferracutes and Angoulaffres.

A prototype of the heroic struggle is the fight between Hercules and Cacus, studied by Michel Bréal.[53] The salient theme, running through Gilgamesh and Humbaba to Jack the Giant Killer, is the conquest of civilization over barbarism. In the *Popol Vuh,* the heavenly twins curb the pride of the earth-giants. When the heroes come into contact with the giants, as David does with Goliath, we instinctively feel our sameness with the hero. The theme of human survival comes to the fore, bridging all gaps between the hero's self-sufficiency and the reader's insufficiency. The hero's problems become our problems.

A variant myth replaces the giant with a dragon or another monster. The Dietrich von Bern cycle combines the traditions. Dietrich fights the giants Hilde and Grim, who like the classical hydra, keep regenerating. The precocious Basuto hero, Dit-ao-lane, slays the "swallowing monster," a "huge shapeless thing." In slaying the monster he accidentally slashes a man inside. His people salute him as hero, deliverer, and chief, but the wounded man never forgives him. Finally he tires of eluding the efforts to kill him, and resigns himself docilely to death.[54] The dragon or monster may symbolize almost any negative quality.

The English *Gesta Stephani* refers to the king as combating the hydra of rebellion.[55] The Medieval Church attacked the dragon of heresy, and diabolism produced an infinite supply of Behemoths, Astaroths, and Beelzebubs for the hero to conquer. Among the Celts the red dragon is a symbol of sovereignty, presumably wrested from the dragon. Gaster offers the insight that the problem of sovereignty is present in all the dragon combats. For example, in the Canaanite version Baal acquires this attribute on conquering Prince Sea. Although Gaster does not develop this thesis, the problem of sovereignty is as crucial as the seasonal cult ritual.[56] The dragon-slaying episode is an essential of tested heroism. Thurman Arnold has suggested in *The Folklore of Capitalism,* "Coupled with the national hero in every institutional mythology is the national devil."[57]

The fight with the dragon may also have psychological, demiurgic, or messianic significance. Plutarch discusses the psychological connotation of the story:

> The passionate, Titanic, irrational, and brutal part of the soul is Typhon and the name of Seth, by which they call Typhon, declares as much for it denotes a domineering and compelling power.[58]

The myth commemorates a traumatic conflict within the hero, the struggle between the rational, self-regulating, self-disciplining and the demoniac; between white and black horses of the "Phaedrus," between *thumos* and *sophrosyne.* The familiar struggle between the hero and his wicked brother, his other self, reiterates the theme.

The attack on the heroic alter ego occurs in many ancient traditions. The Onondaga twins, Yoskeha and Tawiscara, engage in a prenatal fight. An African variant, the Mande creation myth, stresses the *animus dominandi,* the desire to dominate. Two pairs of twins are born in the cosmic world-egg. Pemba in lust for power and domination breaks out prematurely; the result is the impurity of the red earth. The other male twin is Faro:

> In order to atone for Pemba's sin and purify the earth, Faro was sacrificed in heaven and his body . . . was scattered through space. . . . God then brought Faro back to life in heaven and, giving him human shape, sent him down to earth in an ark. . . . In the ark were also all animals and plants. . . . Emerging from the ark they watched for the first time the rising sun.[59]

The schizoid tendency of epic heroism intensifies the struggle with the demoniac by making it fraternal—it is the terrible isomerism of Jekyll and Hyde. The Symplegades, the clashing rocks, express the same theme.

Jung also analyzes the dragon-slaying myth in psychological terms:

> More especially the threat to one's inmost self coming from dragons and serpents points to the danger of the newly acquired consciousness being swallowed up again by the instinctive psyche, the unconscious. The lower vertebrates have from earliest times been favorite symbols of the collective psychic substratum.[60]

In addition to the psychological interpretation, the myth may contain a *demiurgic*, recreation theme. This variant occurs in the archaic struggle between Marduk and Tiamat, between Thor and the Midgard Serpent. In the Hindu myth, Sarpa-Rajni may symbolize the earth's condensation from cosmic dust in serpentine form.[61]

The encounter with the serpent may also have a meteorological meaning. In Chinese myths the dragons can be benevolent rain gods. However, when an evil dragon refuses to release the waters, there is a drought. Such is the Indian story of the conquest of Ahi by Indra. The serpent king Muchalinda protects the Buddha from the elements.

Fewkes records this Amerindian myth:

> . . . at one time the Great Serpent rose in the middle . . . of an ancient village until his head projected to the clouds. As this monster emerged from the earth he drew after him an overflow of water that covered the whole land and drove the inhabitants to the mountains. When a flood covered the earth, the chief of the village, speaking to the serpent, whose head was in the zenith, said, "Why do you thus destroy my people?" The snake replied, "You have a bad man, or wizard, in your number who bewitches you. I will not return to earth until you sacrifice to me your son." Sorrowfully the chief followed this demand for the relief of his people and threw his son into the water, and the serpent sank into the earth, dragging after him the flood.[62]

The myth's political content relates to its messianism. Perseus and St. George both rescue oppressed peoples from a tyrant-monster. In Ariosto's poem, Rogero delivers Angelica from the Orc. In *Beowulf* there are two such mythic combats. The first is Beowulf's fight with Grendel and Grendel's mother. Here the young stranger arrives to save the people. In the second episode, the aged king fights the fire-drake to preserve their welfare.

In the *Thebaid,* Statius uses the serpent theme as a propaganda-myth: Apollo, after killing the Python, has gone to the Court of Crotopus of Argos and had a child by the king's daughter, Psamathe. Wild beasts destroy the child, which has been entrusted to a shepherd. In revenge Apollo creates an Egyptian monster:

> He sends a monster, horrible and fell,
> Begot by furies in the depths of hell.

> The pest a virgin's face and bosom bears;
> High on a crown a rising snake appears.[63]

The encounter with the serpent may be a meeting with the Mother Goddess, the Cretan snake-encircled charmer, the Magna Mater, the Aztec Earth-Mother, Coatlicue.[64] The *Arabian Nights* recounts the strange adventure of Hasib Kerimeddin in encountering the Queen of the Serpents:

> He came to a gallery and then to an iron door fastened with a silver padlock in which was a golden key . . . which he turned; and he walked till he came to a great pond, full of something glistening like water. Nearby was a mound of green jasper, supporting a throne of gold . . . what he had thought was water, moreover, was a mass of serpents. Then one as high as a mule came bearing on its back a charger of gold, whereon was another serpent, shining like crystal, with a woman's face. . . . She greeted Hasib in fluent Arabic. Have no fear of us, O youth, I am the Queen of the Serpents.[65]

The myth may assume the form of a struggle between a bird and a serpent. In the Aztec myth, these figures locate the city of Tenochtilán; they are Mexican emblems today. There are also the bird-serpent portents which appear to Agamemnon and Afrasiyab.

The hero himself may be associated with the bird, as Osiris with the hawk. Seth becomes the serpent. In still other myths there is a composite feathered serpent. Because of its widespread distribution this is a fascinating epic symbol—the Piasa Monster, Quetzalcoatl, Chinese funerary figures, and Inca textiles.

In most cases the bird-serpent symbol signifies a resolution of two powers as the Yin-Yang. Flamel's *Figures peintes d'Abraham le Juif,* an alchemic treatise, illustrates the combat between the fixed wingless symbols and the volatile winged symbols. There is a precarious balance of power, which may be displaced in either direction. Above, the Divine Breath fecundates the mysterious Philosophic Tree.[66]

Of course, the bird or serpent may be associated with another powerful animal such as the solar bull, Marduk, or the winged lion, Nergal, the Garudas and Kinnaras, the griffin and the chimera, the bird-man figure of the Etowah repoussé plate.[67] Now, if the process of mythopoeism remains constant, the only difference will be in the multivalent symbolic elements selected.

There appear to be several variant processes of symbolization in the bird-serpent complex. First, there is the *Gestalt example* of a picture which can be interpreted either as two kissing faces or as a chalice. Myth fuses the two into the idea of a talismanic loving-cup. When the two elements fused are opposites, the result is an Orwellian idiom of love-hate—or the embodiment of love-death or weakest-strongest which are frequent mythic paradoxes.[68]

Other possibilities are the process of transformation and mutation and the symbolization of the most powerful. Finally, there is syncretism and the opposition of cults.

In the transformation process the myth-maker wishes to create a hybrid with the bird's liberating aspects and the serpent's demoniac qualities. Iconographically, the artist expresses the idea by trapping the animal as half-and-half. Centaurs, swan-maidens, and werewolves fall into this category. (The centaur's ability to change is lost.)

If the objective is to portray the idea of the most powerful, the myth-making process combines power symbols. The Horus hawk and the asp serve as the familiars, or protective spirits, of the pharoahs. The condensation of symbols can conceivably represent the actual fusion of two different cults as in Egypt. This is religious syncretism.

Combination with the serpent symbol results in frightening

Medusa-like thaumaturgic figures. There is the Iroquois Atatarho and the Jainist Parshvanatha. The legendary imperial rulers of China, Fu-hsi and Nuwa, emerge from entwined serpents. The same caduceus-like motif occurs among the Mayas and on an early sacrificial goblet of King Gudea of Lagash.[69]

In the opposition of cults, the symbols are not fused. This theory provides a rational explanation for Apollo's victory over Python.[70] In the French narrative of St. Martha and the dragon, St. Martha expels a horrid monster. Archaeological evidence confirms the monster's existence—in statuary form. St. Martha therefore qualifies as a genuine dragon-slayer.[71]

Such theories appear to explain the feathered serpent symbol. Plutarch has a more generalized theory of the Egyptian gods:

> For that the Gods, being afraid of Typhon, changed themselves into these animals . . . is a foolery . . . And among those who would assign some political reason for these things, there are some that affirm that Osiris in his great army, dividing his forces into many parts . . . at the same time gave every one of them certain ensigns . . . with the shapes of several animals upon them, which in the process of time came to be looked upon as sacred. . . . Others say again, that the kings of after times did, for the greater terror of their enemies, wear about them in their battles the golden and silver heads. . . . of fierce animals. But there are others that relate (that princes observed the mercurial nature of the Egyptians and) . . . therefore taught them a perpetual kind of superstition, to be the ground of endless quarrels and disputes among them. For the various animals which he commanded different cities to observe and reverence, being at enmity and war with one another . . . (they were) drawn into the quarrels of their beasts.[72]

The Egyptians were ingenious at creating sphinx-like forms; their versatility occasioned Juvenal's remark that even their kitchen gardens yielded gods (XV:10). Almost every member of the great Ennead had an animal form. Buto was a serpent, and Sebek, a crocodile. In Tibetan mythology, Dong sum mila had eighteen animal-headed sons.

The tested hero frequently encounters such demonic figures. Krishna attacks Kaliya, the thousand-headed serpent demon of the River Jumna. He fights Bachhasura, who is in the form of a crane; Kesin, a wild horse; Byomasur, a wolf; Arishta, a bull; the demons, Dhenuka and Pralamba and his witch-nurse, Putana. A picture shows the hero bitten in the heel by a serpent and triumphantly bruising the serpent's head.[73]

As a child, Krishna plays with the herdsman's children, his foster brothers. They enter what they suppose to be a cave. It is really the jaws of the serpent-king Aghasura. Krishna expands to burst through the monster and release the children. The National Geographic expedition has discovered a similar deity's statue—in Central America.[74]

Descent to the Underworld

The Aino have a parallel myth, "The Hunter in Hades." The story distinctly introduces the next phase of tested heroism, the descent to the Underworld, the swallowing by the Whale, or the "harrowing of Hell." The Danish hero, Ereik, is one of the few who uses the dragon's jaws as a pathway to Paradise. Hsüan Chung and his horse Pai Ma are devoured by a dragon, which transports them to the Western Paradise to procure the sacred books of Buddhism. The Aino myth incorporates the encounter with the Bear Goddess, the world-tree, the forbidden fruit, the fall, and the heroic descent:

> (The hero follows a bear into a dark cave and finds himself in another world.) There were trees, houses, villages, human be-

ings. With these, however, the young hunter had no concern. What he wanted was his bear, which had totally disappeared. The best plan seemed to be to seek it in the remoter mountain district of this new underground. So he followed up a valley, and, being tired and hungry, picked the grapes and mulberries that were hanging on the trees, and ate them as he trudged along.

Happening suddenly, for some reason or other, to look down upon his own body, what was not his horror to find himself transformed into a serpent. . . . (The pine-tree goddess appears to him in a dream and tells him that the only way he can recover his human shape is to climb a pine tree and jump.). . . . Crash he went. On coming to his senses, he found himself standing at the foot of the tree, and close by was the body of an immense serpent, ripped open as to allow of his having crawled out of it.

On reaching his home, he went to bed, and dreamt. . . . It was the same goddess of the pine-tree, that appeared before him and said: "I have come to tell you that you cannot stay long in the world of men after eating the grapes and mulberries of Hades. There is a goddess in Hades who wishes to marry you. She it was who, assuming the form of a bear, lured you into the cavern, and thence to the underworld. You must make up your mind to come away."[75]

Parts of the primitive myth might be accompanied by Mozart's *Die Zauberflöte.* The heroic descent is a conventionalized episode. Often the myth localizes around dark and forboding caverns, St. Patrick's Purgatory, Souli, or Lake Avernus.

The descent often develops into an initiation rite. The neophyte enters the sanctuary's holy portals, which are guarded by terrifying statues of Gog and Magog. A psychopompus or Charonic figure conducts him into the mysteries. After he passes the threshold, the priests catechize and initiate him. He views the holy of holies. After the lustrations in Lethe and perhaps an oath of silence, the hero emerges triumphant. This interpretation applies to the Eleusinian rites according to the Rev. William

Warburton in *The Divine Legation of Moses Demonstrated* (1738–41). Edward Gibbon was unimpressed.[76]

Of course, *facilis descensus,* the trip down is easy, but why do the gods permit the hero to return? The answer covers almost every facet of the monomyth. It combines man's faith in immortality with man's fear of becoming a "sinner in the hands of an angry God."

In the apocryphal *Gospel of Nicodemus,* Christ descends to liberate the prophets. In a Winnebago myth, heroic altruism merits release. After a series of ordeals, the "two friends who became reincarnated" reach Earthmaker's lodge:

> in order to pass the test of the Old Woman who rids the soul of all the recollections belonging to the earthly life, each soul must be solicitous not of its own welfare but of the welfare of the community.[77]

In stark contrast to the love of humanity of this myth is the "harrowing of hell" by the Chinook Blue-Jay:

> The ghosts buy Ioi, Blue Jay's sister for a wife, and Blue Jay goes in search of her. Arriving in the country of the ghosts he finds his sister surrounded by heaps of bones, to which she alludes as her relations by marriage. The ghosts take human shape occasionally, but on being spoken to by Blue Jay become mere heaps of bones again. He takes a mischievous delight in reducing them to this condition.[78]

There are many artistic examples of the harrowing in the Western tradition, Fra Angelico's picture in the Florentine Regia Gallery; Tintoretto's in the church of San Cassiano in Venice, and the windows in King's College Chapel.[79]

"Visits to the Region of the Souls" are frequent among the American Indians. The Ojibwa eponymic hero descends and returns. Tylor comments on the Algonquin beliefs:

> Their experiences have been in great measure what they were taught in early childhood to expect, the journey along the path of the dead, the monstrous strawberry at which . . . the ghosts refresh themselves, but which turns to red rock at the touch of their spoons, the bark offered them for dried meat and great puffballs for squashes, the river of the dead with its snake bridge, or swinging log, the great dog standing on the other side, the villages of the dead beyond.[80]

Similar tests occur in the *Popol Vuh,* where the brothers descend to play ball; they encounter the house of leopards and the house of fire, recalling Daniel and Shadrach. The classical parallels are numerous and better known. Pausanias tells of Theseus and Pirithous (X:28:1). Lucan mentions Eukrates' looking into a chasm of Hades. There are also Antyclos, Nikander, and Kleodemos.[81]

In general the descent myth has one of several objectives: securing a magic talisman, power symbol, or ritual; illustrating the consequences of a broken taboo or injustice, a repetition of the "first disobedience"; consulting with ancestors or seers; searching for eternal life or a rescue from death; or seasonal etiology.

As Owen Glendower says to Hotspur: "I can call spirits from the vasty deep." Hotspur replies: "Why so can I, or so can any man,/ But will they come when you do call for them?" Obtaining power over the spirit-world is the most important motif of the descent stories. A familiar example is Aladdin. The hero receives a ring as a talisman and armed with this, he descends. He passes the jewel-trees, follows the instructions of the African magician, and secures the lamp. The ring and the lamp command the genii and exemplify power over the spirit world.

Another example of this myth form occurs in the Navaho *Nightway.* The wind gods abduct the hero. They force him to undergo several tests: sweat-houses which cause blindness, distaffs which distort the body, and people who chop up their victims. The wind gods then enchant him and transport him underground. He loses his reason, but Talking God rescues him. Before he can return home, he must learn a ritual. Also he must accept food only from the inexhaustible bowl of his divine protector.[82] The purpose of this descent myth is to explain the origin of a ritual-controlling power. The cliff-dweller's descent through the *sipapu* into the kiva reenacts the myth.

Power, Myth, and Ritual

By descending, the shaman obtains his claims to power. In a Kwakiutl text the shaman boasts: "I was carried to the lower world because I am a real shaman."[83] In the Milne Bay Prophet Movement, Tokeriu claims a visit to the other world, where he learned of a tidal wave which would destroy all unbelievers.[84] In the tale of the Sons of Aymon, the magician Malagigi descends to retrieve his horse Bayard.[85]

Campbell discusses the relationship of shamanism to the heroic descent:

> On his laborious journey . . . the shaman has to encounter and master a number of differing obstacles. . . . The most difficult stages of the adventure now begin, when the depths of the underworld with their remarkable manifestations open before him. . . . After he has appeased the watches of the kingdom of the dead and made his way past the numerous perils, he comes at last to the Lord of the Underworld, Erlik himself. And the latter rushes against him, horribly bellowing, but if the shaman is sufficiently skillful he can soothe the monster back again with promises of luxurious offerings. The moment of the dialogue with Erlik is the crisis of the ceremonial.[86]

After such an experience the shaman returns to become a venerated and feared figure in the community. As a spokesman for the spirit powers, he can direct the political powers and influence the decision-making authority.

The quest for power symbols or talismans occurs in the Enkidu-Gilgamesh cycle. *Pukku* and *mikku*, presumably ceremonial objects, fall into the Underworld. Enkidu is sent to retrieve them. Gilgamesh cautions him against a number of tabooed acts; Enkidu disobeys and is unable to reascend. Gilgamesh goes first before Enlil and then before Enki, the god of wisdom. The latter orders the sun-god Utu to pierce a hole in the darkness and allow Enkidu to return.[87]

The heroes of the *Kalevala* go to Poholya to take the magic Sampo. Cuchulainn descends to Dun Scaith. He passes the tests of the serpent pit, the house of toads, and the sharp-beaked monsters. He carries off cows and a cauldron.

Broken taboos are present in many descent myths. The most common form is the Orpheus-Eurydice story. The Japanese Shintoist parallel tells of Izanagi who goes to the Land of the Yellow Stream to recover his sister-spouse. The Zuñi story tells of the flute-god and the disappearance of the corn maidens. The myth of Persephone and Demeter includes the tabooed pomegranate. In this case the eating of the fruit explains seasonal change.[88]

The broken taboo is somewhat different when the crime is committed on earth. Then the theme is retributive justice as in the punishments of the damned. It occurs in Oriental tales, imitated by Beckford's *Vathek*. An illustrated leaf from the Jaipur Manuscript of the *Razamnamah* vividly depicts the "Tortures of Hell." Bramanicides are punished more severely than insecticides—but both are punished, as are heretics and kings who oppress their subjects.[89]

The Quest for Immortality

The search for everlasting life inverts the theme of eternal punishment. The quest for immortality occurs in the descent of Maui into Hine-nui-te-po. Maui, like Gilgamesh, fails only by accident. The Norse gods unsuccessfully attempt to rescue Balder; Innana descends to visit Tammuz. Hell is literally harrowed in the search for the body members of Osiris. When the rescue is successful, the return marks the conquest over death. When Miao Shan descends, the condemned are released to hear her pray. Buddha gives her the peach of immortality. Another example is the Indian story of Savitri, which parallels Hercules' rescue of Alcestis.

When Savitri becomes nubile, her father, King Aswapati, sends her to the many kingdoms of India to choose a husband. At last she selects Satyavan, the son of the blind, exiled, hermit, King Dyumatsena. A court sage divines Satyavan's predestined death a year from their wedding day. Savitri serves her husband with unexampled constancy and devotion for the year. She conceals her anxiety.

Finally, the fateful day arrives; Satyavan goes into the forest to chop wood. Savitri begs to accompany him, and he reluctantly grants her wish. While cutting down a tree, Satyavan suddenly faints, and a grisly figure, dressed in blood-red, appears. He has coppery eyes and bears a noose in his hand. The story continues:

> Savitri stood up, and with joined hands asked him respectfully who he was. "I am Yama god of death," he said. And without another word he tore the soul out of Satyavan's body. . . . Savitri followed the god of death. After going some distance Yama looked back and saw Savitri. "Woman why do you follow me?" "God of justice," said Savitri, "your worship knows the sacred laws better than I. It is written in the scriptures that a husband

and wife are one, and even death has no power to part them. I will follow my lord wherever he goes."

"Thy words," said Yama, "pleaseth me. And thy devotion to thy husband is praiseworthy. Ask thou, therefore, any favor of me except the life of thy husband."

Savitri asked for the restoration of the eye-sight of her father-in-law. . . . (The sequence recurs; the next favor is the restoration of Dyumatsena's kingdom. Then comes the third favor.)

Savitri asked for a hundred sons for herself and Yama granted her the boon. "But, my lord," said Savitri, "how can I have sons without my husband? It now becomes incumbent on you to grant the life of my husband."[90]

In the African Akikuyu parallel, Wan-ji-ru, the maiden rain-sacrifice, is rescued by her lover.[91]

Swallowed by the Whale

In a common variant of the descent myth, the Leviathan swallows the hero. Iconographically, this theme is the Matsya avatar of Vishnu, the Assyrian figure with a piscine vestment, the Khorsabad figure.[92] It occurs on a vase in the Vatican Etruscan collection, "The Return of Jason," and possibly in Glaucus, Neptune, and the mermen.[93] The holy man Markandeya wanders as a pilgrim through Vishnu's body.[94] The best-known version is the story of Jonah and the Whale. Mishe-Nama, "King of Fishes" swallows Hiawatha; Holy Boy in the Navaho *Male Shooting Way* undergoes a similar experience.

According to Frobenius, the Eskimo of the Bering Straits relate the trickster Raven's descent into the Whale. Raven darts into the open jaws of a whale-cow; he takes his fire sticks. There he encounters a beautiful girl. He is well-fed, but given one injunction. There is a tube running through the ceiling from which sweet oil drips. He is not to touch the tube; however, in order to get at the oil he breaks it. The tube is one of the heart arteries of the whale. The whale dies. The girl never returns. The whale finally washes ashore, and Raven escapes. He tells the people that finding fire-sticks in a whale is an evil omen. They leave the feast to him.[95]

Wipunen swallows Wainamoinen, who searches for the magic ship-building formula. Once inside, he forces Wipunen to divulge the information. The same search for knowledge occurs in Odysseus' consultation with Teiresias; Aeneas' visit to Anchises, and Saul's meeting with the Witch of Endor. A gourd-shaped container consumes Monkey; he tricks the demons into giving him the gourd and captures them in the imp or genii-in-the-bottle style.[96]

Commonly associated with the descent is the escape-transformation-pursuit in which the hero evades the Death God and returns to the upper world. The *Dance of Death,* as illustrated by Holbein, and Gottfried August Bürger's *Lenore* have a different end result. Eliade describes the pursuit motif:

> (T)he fundamental point of the story is the escape of a young hero from the kingdom of death, pursued by a terrifying figure who personifies Death itself . . . we should find in it all the elements of anxiety, of the supreme effort to escape from an imminent danger, to free oneself from a dreaded presence.[97]

The pursuit and transformation may take the form of an obstacle course. A Kwakiutl hero receives these instructions:

> In case you should be pursued by Cannibal-at-the-North-End-of-the-World, when he comes near you, throw this stone behind you and it will at once grow and become a mountain and as soon as he comes near you again, throw behind you this comb, it will become a thicket . . .[98]

Hair oil becomes a pond, and cedar wood, cedar trees. The closest parallels are in Russian fairy tales. It is not entirely impossible that Russian influence in this area is responsible for the similarity. The Tibetan hero, King Kesar of Ling, owes much of his success to his metamorphoses. He becomes at various times, a boy, a goddess, a cairn, a giant, and a bee with iron wings. In the last form he enters an enemy and kills him. The magical escape from the death figure is the final triumph of tested heroism.[99]

Magnanimity and Epic Heroism

The product of tested heroism is the combination of power with honor. The actions of the epic hero serve as models for emulation, The epics thereby establish cultural mission and values. Moral purpose and magnanimity temper the will to power and the quest for power. This fusion of ethics and politics makes the epic co-organic.

In the Job-like Hindu story of Harischandra, power is subordinated to moral purpose:

> Once a discussion arose in the court of Indra as to who, in the three worlds, was the most truthful and righteous person. The sage Vasishta maintained that none could excel Harischandra, the then Emperor of Aryavartha. . . . (Vasishta was not prepared to withdraw his remarks when challenged, and a violent argument broke out with the sage Viswamitra.) . . . At last Viswamitra said: "Harischandra is king and can well afford to practice the various virtues. . . . Give me leave to test him under adversity, and I will very soon show what sort of a man he is!" . . . (The gods consent and Viswamitra appears before the king as a poor Brahmin; he complains that he is starving and begs a favor.) The wily Brahmin . . . asked for the kingdom of Harischandra. The king,

> without showing hesitation or displeasure, immediately abdicated. . . . Now, no gift to a Brahmin could be properly ratified without a minor gift. . . . Viswamitra, on receiving the kingdom, promptly demanded Harischandra's weight in gold.[100]

Since Harischandra has given away his treasury, he and his family are sold into slavery. Their oppressive taskmaster is the keeper of a cremation ground. A large number of tests vindicate the King. In the myth, power yields to virtue. *Per contra,* the story of Duryodhan exemplifies the insatiable lust for power and its reprehensible outcome. The conflict of power and virtue is a common mythic theme.

In the tales of epic heroism the "point of honor" is a fulcrum on which the action turns. Heroes are expected to be as sedulous as parliamentarians and as sensitive as prima donnas when their honor is at stake. The best-known example is the contention over Briseis by Achilles and Agamemnon. There is also the critical argument between Roland and Oliver on the blowing of the horn to summon aid at Roncevalles. Some African myths pose the unresolved point as a moral dilemma to the audience. This requires the audience to decide between two conflicting claims. Conflicts of loyalty are common. Such myths highlight areas of social tension and allow participation in the myth. The story sometimes ends: "If this thing would come to you, which would you choose?"[101]

The carnage of hand-to-hand combat, vivid as an animated anatomy text, fills the epic. Such personal duels magnify the sense of honor. Peteguelen fights Tucapel in the *Araucana.* The sage Colocolo addresses the combatants:

> Why do we in anger struggle . . .
> And indulge in civil squabbles . . .
> Why do we, inflamed with fury,
> Break our adamantine union,

While we, trampling cherished privilege
Justify the worst injustice?[102]

The answer is that injured honor must be restored. After the hero has proved his point, he can and must be magnanimous. Achilles can afford to be gracious and condescending to Agamemnon; he can afford to return Hector's body to Priam.

Ruskin calls such magnanimity, "the great measuring virtue, which weighs in heavenly balances all that may be given, and all that may be gained, and sees how to do noblest things in noblest ways."[103] The nature of honorable action and magnanimity is not constant from culture to culture. McNamee makes an interesting study of the transitions in these concepts:

> Every society no matter how primitive has its heroes whom it admires and honors but what men find admirable and honorable in their heroes is, from society to society and from age to age, forever subtly changing. Since the epic is structured precisely to elicit our admiration for the hero, the great man of the society out of which it comes, it should be an excellent place in which to discover correctly what a nation's or a culture's concept of human greatness actually was.[104]

The blood-and-thunder of Achilles dictates a code of personal morality and valor, a primitive code of rugged individualism, courage, and military greatness. Achilles' notion of honor is different from Aeneas' *pietas,* the mandate to a Ciceronian civic duty. Indeed as McNamee indicates, Achilles and Turnus have the same heroic choice. For Homer, Achilles' desire to distinguish himself in a meteoric career is right, even laudable; for Vergil, Turnus is wrong, tragically wrong.

With the advent of Pauline Christianity with its message of service, duty, and "love thy neighbor," the epic hero becomes a Christian man. Barely emerging from paganism, there is Beowulf, demonstrating both pagan and Christian concepts of honor. The Thomistic ideal of honor appears in Tasso. Tancred is the virtuous courtier of Castiglione. Spenser describes the ideal of the public servant in "Mother Hubbard's Tale":

And in his Prince's service spends his dayes,
Not so much for to gaine, or for to raise
Himselfe to high degree as for his grace,
And in his liking to winne worthie place;
Through due deserts and comely carriage.
In what so please employ his personage,
That may be matter meete to gaine him praise;
For he is fit to use in all assayes . . .
. . . for wise and civill governaunce
For he is practiz'd well in policie . . .[105]

Spenser writes to Sir Walter Raleigh of another hero: "in the person of Prince Arthure I sette forth magnificence in particular which, vertue for that (according to Aristotle and the rest) it is the perfection of all the rest, and conteineth in it them all."[106] The *Flos Regum Arthurus* establishes the ideal of the chivalrous hero, especially beloved by the British. In the Arthurian legend the theme of tested heroism validates the king's legitimacy and power. One of the best-known of heroic feats is the provenance of Arthur's sword. The first, drawn from the rock in the churchyard, establishes Arthur's right to the kingship. The Lady of the Lake presents the second, Excalibur, as a power symbol.

Sometimes the hero is literally annealed in power. In the Ossete poem, Batrazd goes to Kuldalagon, the heavenly smith, and asks to be put into the furnace:

At last you have tempered me! How uselessly you continue!
Take me quickly, cast me into the sea.
And the heavenly smith takes his pincers,
With the pincers he takes the Nart by the knees,

Cast him at once into the blue sea,
The sea foamed and hissed and bubbled,
And the sea became dry that very day.
So the body of Batrazd was tempered,
His body turned to blue steel.
Only his liver remained untempered;
No water touched it, all vanished in steam,
When steel Batrazd came out of the sea.[107]

The excess of power, the magical heat, is a characteristic of the epic hero. Cuchulainn is an example. In the *Rig-Veda,* the cosmic Prajapati must become heated through extreme asceticism in order to create the world. In the jataka tales, the person's merit causes Sakka's throne to heat up. There is a parallel in the story of St. Martin of Tours, related by Sulpicius Severus (*Dialogues* II, 5). St. Martin visits the Emperor Valentinian, who refuses to receive him. St. Martin warms the Emperor's throne.

In Tasso's epic the heat is also that of Christian inspiration. Godfredo desires peace in the crusader's camp:

He ceased and felt a strange unwonted heat
  Course thro' his veins, by Heaven itself infused
Whence, with firm hope and strength sublime replete.
  That made him bolder and his brow suffused.[108]

Milton's "sacred ecstasy" of the "Fifth Elegy" is similar. The mystic fire is sometimes an aureole or oriflamme, sometimes an "inner light."

Many heroes possess magic talismans or power attributes. Siegfried and Perseus share the helmet of invisibility; Alberich has the magic ring; Gustavus Adolphus and the Freischütz, the silver bullet—with due apologies to Fran Striker. A magic mist conceals Indrajit; this enables him to defeat both Rama and Lakshman.

The eponymous hero transfers the power symbol to the culture-at-large. It becomes part of a standard, an imperial eagle or star and crescent. Such symbols generate a psychological attachment which effects patriotism.

Anti-Heroic Functions

Besides outright villainy which simply inverts the heroic order, there are many anti-heroic functions in the myths. "Thersitical," for example, is synonymous with scurrilous attacks on power. Thersites denounces Achilles and Odysseus in the Achaean council. By goading the latter into action he disperses the tense atmosphere. The anti-hero is not necessarily black-mustached and mortgage-foreclosing. He is often a trickster, a transformer, an unpromising hero, a clever hero, or a punished wanderer.

Social leveling is the function of the anti-hero as trickster. By constantly breaking social taboos, he liberates the community from conventional morality. This theme is the basis for an entire genre of picaresque literature. In Aristophanes' *Frogs,* the hero becomes the enemy of social boundaries. He chooses the costume of Hercules for his descent into the Underworld; he flees in terror before Empusa and hides among his own priests. Hercules himself *may* play such a comic role in Euripides' *Alcestis.*

The African trickster, Edshu, in a bicolored hat, appears to two tribe members on different sides of the road. They fall into arguing over the color of the hat and involve the entire social system in their quarrel.[109] In a Balochi tale, a tiger is eating up all the foxes. One clever fox tells the tiger that there is another tiger in competition. He takes him to a well where the tiger sees his own reflection and jumps in; end of tiger.[110] Such is the Machiavellian politics of foxes. Coyote is a popular trickster among the Indians; in the fire-theft myth he sneaks in among the fire people. He steals the fire in his cedar-bark headdress.[111]

The trickster is the despair of the nobility, the Emperor's tailor in Andersen's tale.

The trickster readily fits into the cathartic and social protest functions of the political myth. Radin concludes that the trickster serves as a *speculum mentis* "wherein is depicted man's struggle with himself and with a world into which he had been thrust without his volition."[112] The trickster also serves as an object for social satire. Discussing a Winnebago myth, Radin comments:

> We have here, in short, an outlet for voicing a protest against the many, often onerous, obligations connected with the Winnebago social order and their religion and ritual . . . the chief of the tribe . . . is here and in other parts of the cycle so repeatedly criticized . . . he was the symbol of order, and the proponent of peace, one whose function it was to interfere in all kinds of situations. Moreover he, in a civilization where prestige was primarily associated with warfare, could not go on the warpath.[113]

Such is also the satire of Petronius and Rabelais; such, also the Roman pasquinades. The irreverent Beaumarchais brandishes Figaro's razor over the heads of the privileged classes.

The trickster carries with him the atmosphere of Carnival; he is a mud-faced "delight-maker."[114] He inverts the cultural order; he recreates the Roman Saturnalia or the Babylonian Sacaea. The Tarahumara have a dust festival; the Thai, a water festival. By creating mock kingdoms, the trickster purges tendencies toward revolution. By institutionalizing heresy through Abbots of Unreason, he staves off challenges of religious authority. The leveling function appears in the Asiatic mysteries.

> In the circles of the mystics, Asiatics mingled with Romans and slaves with high functionaries. The adoption of the same faith made the poor freedman the equal and sometimes the superior

> of the decurion and the *clarissimus.* All submitted to the same rules and participated in the same festivities, in which the distinctions of an aristocratic society and the differences of blood and country were obliterated.[115]

During the Middle Ages the devil was a favored victim of the trick. The devil is unbelievably stupid, and some of this tradition rubs off in *Paradise Lost.* One man, disguised as a sack of flour, eludes the Callicantzaros. In the story of the Freischütz, the hunter outwits the devil who cannot identify a strange creature. It is the hunter's wife adorned in feathers and molasses. Gambrinus, a jilted lover, makes a pact with Beelzebub, good for thirty years. He invents lager beer, and the Holy Roman Emperor creates him Duke of Brabant and Count of Flanders. At the end of the prescribed time, Beelzebub sends Jocko to claim Gambrinus' soul. Jocko gets drunk and lacks the nerve to return to his master in that condition.[116] In a later story of "Jack O' My Lantern," the devil finds himself treed in a cross-marked apple tree. When the carver dies, the devil refuses him admission to Hell. The devil says: "Shet de do' an' don' let dat man come in hyah, he done treat me scanlous."[117]

In an amusing Russian story, St. Nicholas plays the trickster. He outwits St. Elias in a land transaction. A peasant who is a devotee of St. Nicholas but not of St. Elias is punished by the latter with a crop failure. However, in the nick of time St. Nicholas arranges for the sale of the land to a priest of St. Elias.[118] Another series of trickster stories is stuck to the little monster, the tar-baby.

As in so many cases when one person does something, it is tricky or deceptive; when others do it, it is witty or clever. Frequently, the genuine hero resorts to tricks or transformations to obtain his purposes; the trickster himself may be a benefactor.

Hun Apu and Xbalanque trick the earth giant with an artificial crab; they also disguise themselves as doctors, as well qualified as Molière's *médecin.*[119] Kesar of Ling also resorts to the doctor trick. The hero may feign madness, acting as a jester or simpleton to protect himself. The ability to transform is a mark of shamanism. Marina, the daughter of King Sigismund of Poland: "Changed herself into a magpie,/And away she flew out of the palace."[120]

A Chinese tale illustrates the honorable trick of the clever hero in its best form:

> One of the greatest legendary Chinese generals, Chuko Liang, having a reputation somewhat like that of Ulysses among the Greeks, is famous as a strategist who, even with a small number of soldiers, is never outwitted, defeats all by baffling ruses, and avoids the sacrifice of men in battle. His most famous trick is the stratagem of the "Empty City." Having only twenty soldiers to defend Hsi Cheng, he throws open the gates to the attacking army and appears in a watchtower playing a guitar. The enemy listens to the music, debates, and then withdraws without entering the city, fearing a trap from the craftiest of all generals.[121]

Another aspect of anti-heroism is the unpromising hero. This may be the "little man lost in the crowd." Bowra mentions the heroes of Greek nationalism:

> When a country is under foreign domination, there is a tendency for every man to become a hero who resists or fights the conquerors. . . . Many Greek poems of the last two centuries tell of otherwise obscure persons who have struck a blow for their people. . . . There is a captain, Malamos, who refuses at the last minute to make submission to the Turks. . . . There is Xepateras, who fights alone and is threatened by a whole army. . . . There is Master John of Crete, who raises a rebellion. . . . There is the mother of the sons of Lazos who denounces her sons for leaving their stronghold in Olympus and says she will curse them if they

> join the Turks. There is the patriarch Gregory who is hanged by the janissaries in front of his church.[122]

A related myth of unpromising heroism is the well-known Cinderella tale. In myths of this type the heroine appears as a foundling or social outcast, persecuted by the unjust authority of a wicked stepmother.[123] Kesar of Ling is called "The Street Boy of Bad Descent." Suddenly he rises to undreamed-of heights of power and status. Sometimes the hero is unleavened, but the feeling of popular identification is so strong that he nearly rises. In this class is Millet's *Man with the Hoe* and Van Gogh's *Potato Eaters.*

Such degraded humanity may live in the Dostoyevskian underground, the house of the dead. He may be the proletarian figure of Gorki, bitterly and desperately searching for a new life. These shrouded *penitentes* go persecuted through the world, institutionalized criticisms of all authority, portraits of misery and dejection—"pale, ire, envy, and despair." Hopelessly branded, insane, they are nihilists who cannot stand to be "I" but demand to be "we": revolutionary attackers of myths, destroyers of the social order. They are the possessed and the dispossessed, attackers for the sake of attacking, destroyers for the sake of destroying, Marxists; they are vitriolic, restless dead souls, mingling *horreur* and *terreur,* misery and hatred.

The hero himself is sometimes reduced to this pathetic state; the wandering hero becomes conscious of his heroism. The wandering stranger is a common mythic type; there is the pathos of the Anglo-Saxon "Wanderer" and the revolution of Euripides' *Bacchae.* Lear and Oedipus undergo transformations in their wanderings; they elicit our sympathies. The character of the anti-hero regresses, rather than progresses, under such conditions. He is transformed as Satan in Monk Lewis' novel. He becomes the punished wanderer, the wild huntsman with his pack of hounds, Vishnu, Dietrich von Bern.

The figure which most appeals to the romantic temperament is the "Wandering Jew." Sue develops this myth in a social novel. In the anti-heroic agony, the fiery eyes transfix the viewer of the Jew in the Gothic etching by Doré. The eyes are those of Ethan Brand, of the one who ripped the veil off the image at Saïs. The stark nakedness of the human soul is bared to the elements. The Wanderer is unbounded by the limitations of society; indeed he is punished by not being permitted to remain in society. The text on which the legend of the Jew is based is his rebuke to Christ on the *Via Dolorosa:*

> Vade Jesu, vade, quid moraris?
> Ego vado, et tu expectabis, me donec redeam.

Shelley uses the legend in *Queen Mab* as a destructive, iconoclastic myth:

> There is no God!
> Nature confirms the faith his own death groan sealed . . .

The Jew, Ahasuerus, however, is summoned to testify:

> Is there a God! Aye, an almighty God,
> And vengeful as Almighty . . .
> Tyrannous omnipotence . . .
> Planted a tree of evil . . .
> I cried,
> "Go! Go!" in mockery
> A smile of god-like malice reillumed
> His fading lineaments, "I go,"
> He cried,
> "But thou shalt wander o'er the unquiet earth,
> Eternally . . ."[124]

Finally, Ahasuerus compares himself to:

. . . a giant oak
Which Heaven's fierce flame
Had scathed in the wilderness to stand
A monument of fadeless ruin there,
Struggling with the whirlwinds of agony . . .

There is also Byron's Manfred. The Jew appears in "Hellas," "Thalaba," the "Curse of Kehama," the demons of the Lake Poets. But above all, Melville chooses "Queen Mab" as the title for a chapter in *Moby Dick* and transfers Ahasuerus to Ahab. In this novel, the cosmic struggle between good and evil convincingly repeats the holocaust and the theme of the wanderer. The struggle between the hero and the dragon recurs; the dragon emerges, destroying himself in destroying the hero. But the heroic, epic cycle is renewed with a "They call me Ishmael."[125] The wanderer participates in the antipolitics of withdrawal. In this variant the statesman nauseated with responsibility retires from society. Sometimes it is an enforced exile. Cowper's "Retirement" (1782) and Po Chü-i's poem fall into this category:

So always, the Counsellors of Kings;
Favor and ruin changed between dawn and dusk . . .
And amid the grass, a road that leads to the hills . . .
At last he has made a "coup" that cannot fail![126]

Notes to Chapter III

1. R. W. Emerson, *Essays,* Lovell edition, n. d., p. 220.

2. W. Y. Elliott in *Fugitives' Reunion Conversations at Vanderbilt,* May 3–5, 1956, Rob Roy Purdy, ed. (Nashville, Tenn.: Vanderbilt University Press, 1959), pp. 34–35.

3. W. Y. Elliott, "The Constitution as the American Social Myth," in Conyers Read, ed., *The Constitution Reconsidered* (New York: Columbia University Press, 1938), pp. 209–24. Other "condensation symbols," or epic symbols, are the "swastika, cross, caste marks, the horns of Satan, the three-forked crossroads of Hecate, the falcon of Osiris."

4. Neumann, op. cit., pp. 32–33.

5. C. M. Bowra, *From Vergil to Milton* (London: Macmillan & Co.; New York: St. Martin's Press, 1945), p. 213; *Paradise Lost,* V:571–76; cf. Jitendra N. Banerjea, *The Development of Hindu Iconography* (University of Calcutta, 1956).

6. C. M. Bowra, *Heroic Poetry* (London: Macmillan & Co., 1961), p. 410; cites T. E. Lawrence, *Revolt in the Desert* (London: Jonathan Cape, 1927), p. 94.

7. Maurice B. McNamee, *Honor and the Epic Hero,* "A Study of the Shifting Concept of Magnanimity in Philosophy and Epic Poetry" (New York: Holt, Rinehart, and Winston, 1960).

8. J. Walter Fewkes, "Ancestor Worship of the Hopi Indians" *Annual Report of the Smithsonian Institute,* Government Printing Office (Washington, D.C., 1921), pp. 485–506.

9. Hans Kohn, *Nationalism* (New York: D. Van Nostrand, Anvil Books, 1955), p. 183; cites Jawaharlal Nehru, *Toward Freedom* (New York, John Day, 1941), pp. 269–75.

10. W. J. Cash, *The Mind of the South* (New York: Vintage Books, Random House, 1960), pp. 66–68, 127–28, 241.

11. Sidney Hook, *The Hero in History* (Boston: Beacon Press, 1955).

12. James Joyce, *Finnegan's Wake* (New York: Viking Press, 1934), p. 581.

13. Cited in Chase, op. cit., p. 10; Cox's *Manual* was published in 1867.

14. Schneider, *The History of World Civilization,* Vol. I, p. 24; Vol. II, p. 439.

15. Lord Raglan, op. cit., p. 179ff.; also Lord Raglan, "The Hero of Tradition," *Folklore* (1934), Vol. 45, pp. 212–31; Watu Gunung is Javanese; cf. Sir Stamford Raffles, *History of Java,* Vol. I, pp. 421–24; Nikawng is Sudanese; cf. D. S. Oyler, "Nikawng and the Shilluk Migration," and "Nikawng's Place in the Shilluk Religion," *Sudan Notes and Records* (1918), Vol. I, pp. 107ff. 283ff.

Cf. Charles Baudouin, *Le Triomphe du Héros* (Paris: Plon, 1952)—psychoanalytic treatment of the epic heroes.

16. Cp. Mildred O. Waugh, "Legends of the Child," *The American Scholar* (1948), Vol. 18 No. 1, pp. 19–30.

17. Propp, op. cit., p. 20.

18. Ibid.

19. Cf. Clyde Kluckhohn, "Recurrent Themes in Myth and Mythology," *Daedalus,* p. 269; Spencer, op. cit., pp. 31–37.

20. W. Y. Elliott, "The Constitution as the American Social Myth," p. 209.

21. Joseph Campbell, *The Hero with a Thousand Faces* Bollingen Series XVII (New York: Pantheon Books, 1949), pp. 32–33 also in Bollingen Series XVII (copyright 1949 by Bollingen Foundation), reprinted by permission of Princeton University Press.

22. Rank, *The Birth of the Hero,* p. 65.

23. Thomas Bulfinch, *Legends of Charlemagne* (New York: Mentor Books, New American Library, 1962), p. 390.

24. Von Schiefner, op. cit., p. 273.

25. Rank, op. cit., p. 15

26. Ibid., p. 74 n. 2; cf. A. H. Krappe, "La Naissance de Moïse," *Revue de l'Histoire des Religions* (1933), Vol. 107, pp. 126–33. Pausanias, III:24.

27. Ibid., p. 63.

28. *Kalevala,* pp. 499–500.

29. Graves, op. cit., p. 130.

30. Rank, op. cit., p. 18; Campbell, op. cit., pp. 321, 346; Elsie Clews Parsons, *Tewa Tales,* p. 194; *Memoirs of the American Folklore Society,* XIX (1962).

31. J. N. B. Hewitt, "A Constitutional League of Peace in the Stone Age of America," *Smithsonian Institute Annual Report* (Washington, D.C., 1918), p. 536.

32. Sir George Grey, *Polynesian Mythology,* "And Ancient Traditional History of the New Zealand Race" (London: John Murray, 1855), p. 18.

33. Cf. D. L. R. Lorimer, "An Oral Version of the Kesar Saga from Hunza," *Folklore* (1932), Vol. 42, pp. 105–41. M. W. Stirling, "Concept of the Sun Among American Indians," *Annual Report of the Smithsonian Institute, 1945* (Washington, D.C., 1946), p. 394.

34. W. Crooke, "The Legends of Krishna," *Folklore* (1900), Vol. XI, pp. 7–10.

35. Bowra, *Heroic Poetry*, p. 95.

36. Guerber, op. cit., p. 273.

37. Cf. Piazzetta's *Elijah Taken up in a Chariot of Fire*, National Gallery of Art. There is also a picture of the Ascension in the Heliosform preserved at the Monastery of St. Apollonaris in Egypt, Herbert J. Spinden, "Sun Worship," Pl #4, *Annual Report of the Smithsonian Institute* (Washington, D.C., 1933). The solar boat of the Pharoahs is a similar case.

38. Matthew Arnold's "Balder Dead," cf. A. H. Krappe, "The Myth of Balder," *Folklore* (1923), Vol. 34, pp. 184–216.

39. Gaster, *Thespis*, p. 295f.

40. Cited by W. Y. Elliott, *Western Political Heritage*, prefatory quotations.

41. R. Piddington, *Essays in Polynesian Mythology* (New York: Cambridge University Press, 1959), pp. 113–53.

42. Rev. D. Emslie, "Folklore Tales of Central Africa," *Folklore* (1892), Vol. III No. 1, pp. 99–100.

43. Ibid., p. 34. There is an interesting reversal of the myth which tells of an unsuccessful rebellion in which the ousted chief attempts to gain power. A chief is driven away by a successful revolt and wanders in the mountains scheming how he is to regain his former position . . . on the eve of success he goes out, "when the moon is bright," to "confer with the spirits of his fathers." He sees a "hili" or an "incanti," and the next morning his companions find his body lying on the bare earth, face downwards, and "quite shrivelled up." They disperse in terror and never revisit that spot again. As for the chief, his spirit wanders forever, "calling his people." Ibid., p. 341.

44. Rhys, op. cit., p. 184 et seq.

45. R. B. Tate, "Mythology in the Spanish Historiography of the Renaissance," *Hispanic Review* (1954), Vol. 221, pp. 1–18.

46. Squire, op. cit., pp. 90–92. Cf. Robert H. Lowie, "The Test Theme in North American Mythology," *JAF* (1908), Vol. XXI, pp. 97–148.

47. Lang, op. cit., p. 95.

48. William Jones, "The Culture-Hero Myth of the Sauks and Foxes" *JAF* (1901), Vol. XIV No. 55, p. 234.

49. Jung, op. cit., p. 124 et seq.

50. Grey, op. cit., pp. 66, 73.

51. Jung, loc. cit., at note 49.

52. Werner, op. cit., p. 386.

53. Michel Bréal, *Hercule et Cacus,* "Étude de Mythologie Comparée" (Paris: Chez A. Durand, 1863), p. 177.

54. Feldmann, op. cit., pp. 97–99.

55. *Gesta Stephani,* s. 33 (London: Thomas Nelson and Sons, Ltd., 1955).

56. Gaster, op. cit., p. 148.

57. Thurman Arnold, *The Folklore of Capitalism* (New Haven: Yale University Press, 1937), pp. 36–37.

58. Plutarch, op. cit., p. 110.

59. Cited by Charles Long, *Alpha: The Myths of the Creation* (New York: George Braziller, 1963), pp. 135–36. From Germaine Dieterlen, *Africa: Journal of the International African Institute* (London: Oxford University Press, 1957), Vol. XXVII, pp. 126–35.

60. Jung, op. cit., p. 119.

61. Howey, op. cit., p. 372.

62. Walter J. Fewkes, "Sun Worship," *Annual Report of the Smithsonian Institute* (Washington, D.C., 1918), p. 507.

63. Statius, cited in Howey, op. cit., pp. 150–51.

64. Cp. Erich Neumann, *The Great Mother,* Bollingen Series #47 (New York: Pantheon Books, 1955).

65. Joseph Campbell, ed., *The Arabian Nights* (New York: Viking Press, 1952), pp. 767–77.

66. M. Caron and S. Hutin, *The Alchemists* Evergreen Profile Book #27 (New York: Grove Press, 1961), p. 134.

67. *The Missouri Archaeologist,* Vol. 18 #3, October 1956, p. 39.

68. Long, op. cit., p. 18.

69. Zimmer, op. cit., Fig. 8; p. 71 (on the use of *vahana* or vehicles in Hindu iconography); *nagakals,* twined-serpent motif; p. 72ff. s. 3, "The Serpent and Bird." Spinden, op. cit., Pl#4.

70. Joseph Fontenrose, *Python* (Berkeley: University of California Press, 1959).

71. Mrs. Gutch, "St. Martha and the Dragon," *Folklore* (1952), Vol. 44, pp. 193–204.

72. Plutarch, op. cit., pp. 129–30.

73. Crooke, op. cit., esp. p. 12; Howey, op. cit., p. 41.

74. Matthew W. Stirling, "Expedition Unearths Masterpieces of Carved Jade"

("Deity in Serpent's Jaws"), *The National Geographic Magazine,* September 1941, Vol. 80 #3, p. 309.

75. B. H. Chamberlain, *Aino Folk-Tales,* (London: privately printed for the Folk-lore Society 1888), pp. 40; also p. 42, "An Inquisitive Man's Experience in Hades." (The hero tests the underworld's reality.) Attis is closely connected with the pine. There is some affinity to the *Gilgamesh* myth in which the hero slays the dragon at the base of the world-tree. At the top is the Zu bird and in the branches the house of Lilith, the Maid of Desolation, Kramer, op. cit., p. 33; another variant converts the prince into a monster. Cf. G. L. Kittredge, *A Study of Gawain and the Green Knight* (Cambridge: Harvard University Press, 1916).

76. Kuhn, op. cit., pp. 1108–10.

77. Cf. Tylor, op. cit., II, p. 54.
Claude Lévi-Strauss, "Four Winnebago Myths: A Structural Sketch" Diamond, ed., op. cit., p. 353.

78. Miss S. R. Burstein, "The Harrowing of Hell," *Folklore* (1928), Vol. 39, p. 128.

79. Tillyard, op. cit., p. 30.

80. Tylor, op. cit., Vol. II, pp. 44–50.

81. Ibid., pp. 53–54.

82. Spencer, op. cit., pp. 158–59.

83. Boas, op. cit., II, p. 101.

84. Worsley, op. cit., pp. 51, 101.

85. Guerber, *Myths and Legends of the Middle Ages,* p. 199.

86. Campbell, op. cit., p. 100.

87. Kramer, op. cit., p. 33.

88. Some of these myths are collected in Padraic Colum's *Orpheus Legends of the World* (New York: Macmillan Co., 1930).

89. N. W. Thomas, *Epics, Myths, and Legends of India,* 4th ed. (Bombay: D. B. Taraporevala Sons and Co., 1949), p. 60, pl. XXXIX.

90. Ibid., pp. 63–65.

91. Feldmann, op. cit., p. 271.

92. William Simpson, *The Jonah Legend* (London: Grant Richards, 1890), frontispiece and title page.

93. Campbell, op. cit., p. 247, Fig. 12.

94. Zimmer, op. cit., p. 38.

95. Leo Frobenius, *Das Zeitalter des Sonnengottes* (Berlin, 1909), pp. 85–87; cited by Campbell, op. cit., pp. 90, 207–9.

96. Margaret Mead and Martha Wolfenstein, *Childhood in Contemporary Cultures* (Chicago: University of Chicago Press, 1955), p. 246ff.

97. Eliade, op. cit., p. 103.

98. Boas, op. cit., Vol. II, p. 387.

99. "The Epic of King Kesar of Ling," *Journal of the Royal Society of Bengal*, viii, 1942. A. David-Neel, *The Superhuman Life of Gesar of Ling* (London, 1932). Although the identification Caesar-Kaiser-Kesar is considered tenuous, Spenser speaks of "kesars and kings . . ." several times. Cp. metamorphoses of Dionysus Zagreus and George B. Grinnell, "A Cheyenne Obstacle Myth," *JAF*, (1903), Vol. 16, pp. 108–116.

100. Thomas, op. cit., pp. 105–7.

101. Feldmann, op. cit., p. 202.

102. *Araucana*, p. 165.

103. John Ruskin, *Works*, "A Joy For Ever" (London: G. Allen, London, 1905), Vol. XVI, p. 56.

104. McNamee, op. cit., p. x.

105. Cited by McNamee, p. 139; "Mother Hubbard's Tale," II:773–793.

106. Ibid., p. 145.

107. Bowra, *Heroic Poetry*, p. 139.

108. Tasso, op. cit., p. 197.

109. Leo Frobenius, *Und Afrika Sprach* (Berlin: Vita Deutsches Verlagshaus, 1912), pp. 243–45; Campbell, op. cit., p. 45.

110. M. Longsworth Danes, "Balochi Tales," *Folklore* (1892), Vol. III No. 3, p. 51ff.

111. James A. Teit, "Thompson Tales," in *Folktales of Salishan and Sahaptin Tribes*, Fraz Boas, ed., p. 2, *Memoirs of the American Folklore Society*, Vol. XI (1917); cf. Frazer, *Myths of the Origin of Fire* (London: Macmillan & Co., 1930), pp. 173–74, 182–83.

112. Radin, *The Trickster*, p. x.

113. Ibid., p. 152, 153.

114. Adolf Bandelier, *The Delight-Makers* (New York: Dodd-Mead, 1890). Cf. Jung, *On the Psychology of the Trickster Figure*, Radin, ed. (New York: Philosophical Library, 1950).

115. Cumont, op. cit., p. 28.

116. Fiske, op. cit., pp. 125–29.

117. W. W. Newell, "The Ignis Fatuus, Its Character and Legendary Origin," *JAF* (1904), Vol. XVII, pp. 36–60.

118. Magnus, op. cit., p. 216.

119. *Popol Vuh,* p. 213.

120. Bowra, *Heroic Poetry,* p. 505.

121. Orrin Klapp, "The Clever Hero," *JAF* (1954), Vol. 67, pp. 21–34.

122. Bowra, *Heroic Poetry,* p. 113.

123. Marian Roalfe Cox, *Cinderella,* Folklore Society (London: David Nutt, 1893).

124. P. B. Shelley, *Poetical Works,* W. M. Rossetti, ed. (New York: John W. Lovell, 1860), p. 50.

125. John Livingston Lowes, *The Road to Xanadu* (Boston: Houghton Mifflin, 1927); I personally feel that Coleridge's "Ancient Mariner" belongs in this group. Werner Zirus, *Der ewige Jude in der Dichtung, Palaestra,* #162 (Leipzig: Mayer und Mueller, 1928).

126. Po Chü-i in Arthur Waley, trans., *Translations from the Chinese* (New York: Alfred A. Knopf, 1941), p. 188.

IV. THEORY OF POLITICAL MYTH

• • •

Like a living portrait by El Greco, Dostoyevsky's Grand Inquisitor speaks for tormented humanity:

> There are three powers, three powers alone, able to conquer and to hold captive forever the conscience of these impotent rebels for their happiness—those forces are miracle, mystery, and authority.[1]

Myth is the bond between "miracle, mystery, and authority." Political myth is the mechanism of charisma, linking the hero to the community. Myth is a primary source for legitimizing and maintaining political power. The deprivation of myth is the beginning of power politics. Myth-custodians are power-holders. Myth establishes moral consensus in the community and is accompanied by social sanctions. Myth stabilizes the relationship of the individual to politics by restricting the purely organic state with the element of moral purposiveness. Myth as political is co-organic.

Myths and Politics

Myths contain the stereotypes which condition political behavior. They limit meaningful alternatives for social action. Myths may stratify society into castes and determine leadership. They may create political factions, struggling over allegorical or literal meanings. Myths dictate social norms and accepted values. Because of their relative immunity to factual attack, myths effectively preserve customs, rituals, and ceremonies.

The *rites de passage* instruct the youth of the community in mythology. This is the initiation of citizenship. Secret societies often have the dual function of education in myths and the maintenance of discipline. Other myths catalyze loyalty and insure continuity in the transfer of power. Myths may also serve as social cathartics, diverting political discontent. As social satire they serve as a safety valve, releasing accumulated frustration. Myths are the vehicles for propaganda and iconoclastic attacks.

Myths, which frequently manipulate fear and superstition, may also assure invulnerable security—even give dangerous illusions of false security. Myths evoke the shared emotions of nationalism. Myths create social cohesion and stimulate the social consciousness of group politics. Myths are among the imponderables which send the calculations of social science awry.

Notorious for their ethnocentricity, myths frequently provide cultural defense mechanisms. They provide a psychological insulation which enforces cultural solidarity. Some peoples maintain myths pertinaciously even in the face of external attack. As systems of belief, myths tend to be extremely antipragmatic. Myth systems in conflict are punctuated by fanaticism and violence.

The widespread popularization of certain myth themes provides a basis for international understanding. Comprehension of myths is vital to cultural dynamics. The failure to appreciate native myths is a characteristic failure of imperialism—it leads to war and revolution. With such thoughts in mind Sir George Grey approaches the myths of the Maori:

> I soon perceived that I could neither successfully govern, nor hope to conciliate a numerous and turbulent people with whose language, manners . . . and modes of thought I was quite unacquainted . . . it was necessary that I should be able thoroughly to understand their complaints. . . . Only one thing could, under such circumstances, be done and that was to acquaint myself with the ancient . . . traditional poems and legends to induce their priests to impart to me their mythology.[2]

Such perception greatly improves colonial administration. Although traditional myths may be temporarily overturned by conquest or revolutionary conditions, political dynamics demands at least an attempt to return to traditional forms.

Myths are associated with the human predicament and the existential problems which impinge upon politics. Myths exist because of social tensions. Myths function to bridge the tensions between man and God; man and nature; man and society; man and himself. Myths recount man-searching for power, knowledge, security, or eternal life. The most noticeable element of myth is humanity. Man's aspirations and sufferings are basic to political myth. Sumner points to the "invincible tendency of the human masses to mythologize."[3] This tendency is part of man's constant search for adequate myth-forms for self-expression.

Myths attempt to structure society in such a manner as to avoid mass loneliness and alienation. They structure society in anticipation of the formal devices of constitutionalism. Myths serve as the archetypes of legality and persist as custom in the face of statutory law.

Myths in their political capacity are related to myths in their aesthetic capacity. They are situated at a point where politics meets literature and art. The epics and epic heroes perform definite political functions, which introduce myth as a construct in political theory.

Political myths can best be studied by the polarizing process of placing the epic myths in their anthropological context. This chapter will also discuss historical consciousness and progress in the idea of freedom. There are two objectives: a unified theory of POLITICAL MYTH and a systematic analysis of the correlations between myth and social conditions and the dynamic cultural transitions associated with changing political mythology. The following table outlines the theory of politics and mythology.

THEORY OF POLITICAL MYTH

State of Society	*Type or Function of Myth*
Formative	Civilizing; Demoniac-Rational; Culture-Heroes
Revolutionary	Iconoclastic; Utopian; Cultural Catastrophism; Messianism
Response	Appeal to Traditional Myths; or None; Myth Vacuum
Stabilizing	Legitimizing Government; Social Establishment
Stable	Legality; Traditional Patterns Heroic Virtue; Paideia, Citizen's Education; Moral Purpose; Power Myths; Pure Entertainment
Growth Process	Historical Myths
Internal Power Challenge	Social Satire or Criticism
Response	Cathartic; Social Cohesion; Witch-hunting; Scapegoats

External Power Challenge	Cultural Defense Mechanism; Extreme Bi-polarity; Children of Light and Children of Darkness; Propaganda; Racial and Ethnic Myths
Oppression	Myths of Freedom; Escape into Myth World; Messianism.

Political Conditions for Myth-Formation

Myths systematically respond to the "cry of the times." Cultural change results as one myth-group challenges another. The prevalent type of political myth is inherently a function of the social milieu.

Common causes of myths are pathological, such as social dislocation, collective insecurity, economic disorganization, or psychological depression. Other myths have an antibiotic effect which attempts to stabilize society. The Hobbesian "war of all against all" is an ideal vivarium for myth. The Leviathan itself appears under such conditions. Often myth is an attempt to adjust to the unusual social tensions and pressures of a "time of troubles." Myth is the antidote for a disturbed status quo. The customary ingredients of the myth-formula are rationalization, escapism, and legitimation.

For example, myths of a promised land mitigate the hardships of migration. Conquest produces myths of ethnic superiority and invulnerability. Cultural degeneration may cause myths of a lost golden age. The gap between unequal civilizations or social strata results in a messianic myth. Insecurity in power requires a legitimacy myth; collective insecurity requires a scapegoat or cathartic myth. Epic myths effect spiritual regeneration after a crushing defeat.

Myths are the product of cultural crises; they are a response to the challenges of politics. During the formative phases of social development, Nature limits decision-making. Natural catastrophes cause myths of "divine" wrath and appeasement. The people "were like so many beasts, without religion or government."[4] In the Kesar of Ling saga, the government of earth is chaotic, and the King of Heaven is induced to send his son to set things aright.

Many myths contain remnants of the struggle between barbarism and civilization. Such is the subjection of the Titans. The irrational, demonic, or deformed yields to the civilizing.

Another series of myths recounts the Neolithic "agrarian revolution" and the domestication of maize. Perhaps the best-known variant is the tale of Mon-daw-min, collected by Schoolcraft:

> "It is my friend!" shouted the lad. "It is the friend of all mankind! It is Mondawmin! We need no longer rely on hunting alone; for as long as this gift is cherished and taken care of, the ground will give us a living . . . . The Great Spirit has listened to my voice, and sent us something new, and henceforth our people will not alone depend on the chase or on the waters."[5]

Quiche and Cakchiquel myths from Meso-America manifest interesting similarities. There is a parallel in the Middle Celebes:

> The self-sacrifice of a man is the motif in a myth that calls to mind the Kaingang story about the self-sacrificing chief. A nobleman in the provine of Besoa . . . was much concerned about his serfs who had nothing to eat but roots . . . the nobleman . . . dressed in brilliant clothes . . . ran from right to left in circles, each time nearer to the edge of the field. The longer he ran, the more his body disappeared . . . and at last only his head was visible above the ground. But before his head disappeared, it spoke, "For the

future, you shall eat me who am your fellow man, for everything that is good to plant shall come out of me . . ."[6]

Myths also relate the grant of as much land as the hero can encircle with a cow's hide and the opportunistic hero who slices the hide into small strands to rope off the fields. Another civilizing myth is the Ugaritic text describing Baal's building activities, which may reflect the socio-economic crisis caused by the emergence of metallurgy.[7] Fire-theft myths from Maui to Prometheus commemorate a still earlier crisis.

The Sumerian "Creation of the Pickax, Cattle, and Grain" is another agrarian myth. The most comprehensive civilizing myth is the Sumerian "Transfer of the Arts of Civilization from Eridu to Erech." Inanna, the tutelary heroine-goddess, goes to Enki, who dwells in the watery abyss, the Abzu, to secure the civilizing powers. The intoxicated Enki loads them into the solar boat:

O name of my power, O name of my power,
To the pure Inanna, my daughter, I shall present
The exalted scepter staffs, the exalted shrine,
shepherdship, kingship . . .[8]

This ritual formula conveys some one hundred divine decrees, encompassing the totality of Sumerian institutions and culture: priestly offices, eldership, heroship, goodness and justice, the crafts, the shout of victory, judgment and decision.

The integration of nature and society creates a number of myths which develop according to the reasoning *post hoc ergo propter hoc.* Primitive magicians give meteorological explanations in this manner. At this point, scientific and religious myth are undifferentiated from the political form. Control, or supposed control, over the food supply, over animal reproduction, or rain is a decisive factor in the myth and in political power.

The politician appears as the Sorcerer of Trois Frères—a shaman.

Although his seriousness is open to question, Pepys makes this entry in his *Diary:*

> In the afternoon I went upon the river; it was raining hard upon the water. I put ashore and sheltered myself while the king came by in his barge. . . . But methought it lessened my esteem of a king that he should not be able to command the rain.[9]

Such a conflict of natural and social powers is a source for political theory. Moses, Joseph, and Elijah have even been accredited as rainmakers. This office is still of great importance among the Zulus and other African tribes as well as certain smaller towns of the American Middle West. Roosevelt receives credit for ending the drought—which was the fault of Cleveland.

The politician as magician is of utmost significance to understanding the relations between myth and primitive society. Lang writes:

> Even among those democratic paupers, the Fuegians, "the doctor-wizard of each party has much influence over his companions." Among those other democrats, the Eskimo, a class of wizards, called Agakuts, become a kind of civil magistrate because they can cause fine weather, and can magically detect people who commit offences. Thus the germs of rank, in these cases, are sown by the magic which is fetichism in action.[10]

The selection of a new king in Sofala, where the king's soul reputedly enters into a sorcerer, exemplifies the extent of shamanistic power. The magician then advises the government.[11] Chadwick discusses the observations of Livingstone and Shooter:

> The utterances of the seer Tlapone, from the Makololo on the Zambesi, give evidence of great political sagacity, though ut-

> tered in a fit of deliberately induced frenzy. The observations of the prophets of the Zulu and neighboring tribes recorded by early Europeans . . . bear witness to great political insight.[12]

Frequently the shaman's power in the community derives from the acquisition of mana, wakanda, or orenda, a mysterious power. The Great Plains tribes encourage individualism in obtaining power by the spirit dream. However, among the Jicarilla Apache, a myth tells how the shaman alone can be successful. "The episode . . . represents the victory of a socially anointed priesthood over the highly dangerous and unpredictable forces of individual endowment."[13] Such a myth marks the subordination of the individual to the shaman's power.

Mythopoeism

The Salem Witch Trials, a cathartic myth, and the Sioux Ghost Dance, a messianic myth, serve as the briefest sort of case examples. In the Salem Trials a series of characters from the *Malleus Maleficarum* parade in a macabre fantasy before a Puritan court. The social symptoms are insecurity, limited opportunity for expression, and a relatively stringent moral code. An unsettled social situation, nurtured in the hothouse of small-town Puritanism, becomes ample cause for accusations of witchcraft.[14]

Initially the hysteria directs itself against social outcasts. The result of the trials is a thorough catharsis and escapism. The myth provides a prophylaxis against attacks on established society. It also produces a canon to measure loyalty to social norms. A side effect of the myth, including the condemnation of Goody Good, was the continued need for exorcists—or at least experienced theologians capable of dealing with the dan-gers of the "invisible world." Witches create business for witch doctors, who traffic in social potions and political panaceas.[15]

Just as the Salem trials exemplify the formation of the social cathartic myth, the Sioux Ghost Dance typifies the formation of a messianic myth. Mooney describes the Sioux beliefs:

> The great underlying principle of the Ghost Dance doctrine is that the time will come when the whole Indian race, living and dead, will be reunited in a regenerated earth, to live a life of aboriginal happiness, forever free from death, disease, and misery . . .[16]

The Indian's utter despair fabricated a mythology; it was the promise of a millennial reinstatement in power. The causes were a complete dislocation of the tribes, defeat, starvation, and suffering. The condition which created the Ghost Dance was the converse of Frederick Jackson Turner's "safety-valve of the frontier." On the Indian's side the frontier was constricting; rebellion was quashed; channels for political expression were closed; opportunities for free action were restricted. There was a basic human need for a myth. The internalization and sublimation of the shock of contact with the whites produced a messianic myth. The myths attempted to reintegrate society and return to the old customs.

Traders, captives, official tribal representatives, and possibly Mormon missionaries circulated Ghost Dance myths. These were typical groups which caused the wide diffusion of myths.

These brief case studies have introduced the principles that unsettled political conditions engender political myths, and that the myth-type produced is correlative to the social need. The major Chinese myth-making periods, the overthrow of the Yin Dynasty and the anarchic Wars of the Three States, provide confirmation. Let us consider the variant forms of political myth as well as the associated social conditions.

Political Messianic Myth

Political messianism is a great historical apposition. The messiah complex fuses religious sociology with politics. Max Weber has described the charismatic messiah. Eric Voegelin examines the phenomenon in terms of kerygma, gnosis, and mythos. Voegelin's interesting analysis relates the gnostic movement of Joachim of Flora to the myths of modern totalitarianism.[17]

The "dying god," sometimes associated with ritual regicide and a vegetation cult, is the messianic prototype. Osiris and Tammuz belong to this category. Classical messianism is widespread. Pausanias reports that a serpent-child fought on the side of the Eleans against the Arcadians; he is named Sosipolis, "savior of the state."[18] In 307 B.C., when Demetrius restores the Athenian democracy, the people accord him the title *Soter.*[19] Of course, the Judaic expectations of a political messiah provide a familiar case. This tradition extends through the Essenes, Bar Kochbas, Serene of Syria, and Obayah Abu. The downtrodden condition of these people is ample cause for anticipating the appearance of the Isaianic messiah.[20]

The medieval epic stresses the political myth of the returning king. There is Aine's son:

> who was received into the fairy world after his death, and now lives under the surface of Lough Gur, in County Limerick, waiting like the British Arthur, for the hour to strike in which he shall lead forth his warriors to drive the foreigners from Ireland.[21]

France venerates Joan of Arc as her savior, and the cries of "Dieu et St. Denis" merge with those of "Dieu et Ste. Jeanne." In Spain there is the Cid and St. James of Compostella; among the Bhuddists, Milo, or Maitreya. There is the Shi'a belief in the second coming of the Imam, Mahdism; Alice, the latest African prophet; the Vailala Madness of New Guinea.[22] Such diversified messianic movements are uniformly associated with popular discontent. For instance, the Taiping Rebellion comes under the influence of Hung Siu-ch'üan:

> Some . . . had been favored with visions, others had become exhorters, denouncing those who behaved contrary to the doctrines; others essayed to cure diseases. . . . He became more and more possessed with the idea . . . that he had been commissioned to be Emperor of China; and one day his father found a slip on which was written "The Heavenly King of Great Reason, the Sovereign King Tsuen."[23]

Another messianic outbreak repeats the characteristic syndrome:

> In 1857, after a period of guerrilla warfare with the English in South Africa, resulting in the confiscation of the natives' territory, one of these tribes hastily embraced a messianic religion which promised salvation from these ills. An impostor . . . predicted that if the confederate tribes slaughtered all their cattle, destroyed every peck of corn, and left the ground untilled in the spring, that at a certain time their ancestors would rise and drive the English into the sea.[24]

Curiously, parallel messianism periodically disturbed the American Indians. The earliest occurrence, other than Quetzalcoatl, is in the Pueblo Revolt of 1680 in which Popé:

> a medicine man of the Tewa, had come back from a pilgrimage to the far north, where he claimed to have visited the magic lagoon of Shipapu, whence his people traced their origin and to which the souls of their dead returned after leaving this life. By these ancestral spirits he had been endowed with occult powers

> and commanded to go back and rouse the Pueblos to concerted effort for deliverance from the foreign yoke.[25]

There was a continuous series of such outbreaks: Condorcanqui's Revolt, the Delaware Prophet, Kennekuk, Pathĕskĕ, Tävibo, the Smohalla Religion. Tävibo preached that the houses and goods of the whites would be swallowed by a great earthquake. However, the eminently practical Indians were uncertain that they, too, would not fall in. Tävibo, like Mohammed before him, received a new revelation, which explained that indeed the Indians would be buried, but only to be resurrected. The culmination of the Indian messianism was Wovoka and the Sioux Ghost Dance.

Seemingly somewhat removed from the mystic cults of the Paiute Prophet is Blake's "Jerusalem." Yet this poem, as Klopstock's "The Messiah," marks the incursion of the messianic myth into industrial society. The building of the new Jerusalem, the chariot of fire, and relentless militancy are common elements of the myth. The dark Satanic mills have produced the messianic components of modern nationalism and Marxism. Aggravated by an extreme inferiority complex and a sensitivity to historic deficiencies—and the reminders of them, messianism provides the mumbo jumbo which makes the native not "want to leave the Congo."[26]

Consider the role of Jomo Kenyatta as messiah. Sir Arden Clarke, the British governor, is cast as Pontius Pilate, and the Kikuyus are the "chosen people"—invulnerable to European bullets and the recipients of a mandate to expel the imperialists. The mystique and ritualism appeals to the savage mind:

> The book of the Kikuyu is Holy, it helps me to be good, It is my guiding principle when I go to join the Kikuyu. The Book is Kenyatta, it is he who leads me, It is he who saved me by his blood. . . . Kenyatta will come with a sword for the harvest, and

> with a seat for our people when we receive self-government ... God told Kenyatta in a vision "You shall multiply as the stars of heaven, nations will be blessed because of you."[27]

Speculations on the origin of such movements among the Mau Mau customarily begin with Garveyism and the Watchtower Movement. More distantly related is the Charleston slave revolt of Gullah Jack of the sacred crab claws.

The general causes of messianism interest Norman Cohn in *The Pursuit of the Millennium.* Prophecies are rampant during periods of rapid social change among people living on the margin of society. Insecurity is virtually an institution among the uprooted and disoriented.[28] Messianism, arising under such conditions, varies but slightly from its counterpart in Marxist mythology. Indeed Marxism capitalizes on such pseudo-theology and incorporates it into a political myth. Modern totalitarianism harnesses the millennial forces.

Russia has always been plagued by false Dmitris; the Communists are the latest such power claimants. It is true that the icons of St. Vladimir and Our Lady of Kazan have been replaced by photographs of the Kazan University Student, Vladimir Ilytch. Marxism has realized the visions of Filofei of a "Third Rome" and the *ex oriente lux* of Danilevsky's pan-Slavism. The charisma of its semimythic heroes and martyrs sustains Soviet power. Power is inherent in the right to reinterpret the myth. The disciples of Marx adhere to the frail promise of future world conquest and domination.

To some degree these Soviet myths have displaced the epic myths in Russia; but there is a great deal of continuity between the martial spirit of the *byliny* and the *Lay of Igor* and Soviet militarism; a great deal of continuity between the power quest of Afanasayev's folk tales and the Soviet power lust; a great deal of continuity between the "underground man" and Oblomov, who cannot find his place in society, and the Soviets. There is also a continuity between tsarist hero worship and the Stalinist "cult of the individual." It is not surprising that Soviet poets have expressed themselves in traditional heroic forms when writing of Lenin and Stalin. Marfa Kryukova tells in her versified "Life of Lenin" of an attack by a "fierce snake"—the assassination attempt. Another poet writes: "Then rose on his mettlesome legs/ The strong powerful young man,/ The warrior Josef Vissarionvich . . ."[29] In one form this is Masaryk's Caesaropapism—in another, the political messianic myth. And in a curious way, Marx resembles the "red slayer" of Emerson's "Brahma."

Millennial Myths and Cultural Catastrophism

Related to Marxist messianism is the prophecy of the impending destruction of capitalistic society. The millenarian-proletarian enthusiasm of Marx combines Pieter Brueghel with Hieronymus Bosch. The root of the myth is in Thomas Müntzer, the *Bauernkrieg,* and even before in the declarations of Tanchelm and Eudes de l'Etoile—that each was the son of God.[30] Enfantin, the Saint Simonist, followed them in a similar manifesto, but terminated his career as a successful railway director.

Worsley discusses the chiliastic myth. It is

> (a)mong people who feel themselves to be oppressed and who are longing for deliverance that they (millenarians) have been particularly welcomed especially by the populations of colonial countries, by discontented peasants and by the jetsam of the towns and cities of feudal civilization.[31]

The Ragnarok of the *Eddas* is the best expression of the myth of cultural catastrophism:

East of Midgard in the Ironwood
The old hag sat,
Fenrer's terrible race she fostered.
One of them
Shall at last in the guise of a troll
Devour the moon.

The hag's watcher,
The glad Edger,
Sat on the hill-top
And played his harp . . .

Beneath the earth
Crows another,
The root-red cock
In the halls of Hel . . .

Vala knows the future
More does she see of the
Victorious gods' terrible fall . . .

Mimer's sons play;
To battle the ancient gods are called
By the ancient Gjallar-horn . . .

Quivers then Yggdrasil
The strong-rooted ash,
Rustles the old tree
When the giant gives way . . .

The sun darkens;
The earth sinks into the ocean;
The lucid stars
From heaven vanish.[32]

Dasent notices that such pessimism greatly facilitated the Christianizing of Iceland. A race which expects its gods to be destroyed in a final holocaust can hardly be disturbed when the ancient prophecies begin to come true.[33]

A prototype of the epic millenarian myth is Plutarch's description of Sulla's activities during 87 B.C.:

> One day when the sky was serene and clear, there was heard in it the sound of a trumpet, so shrill and mournful that it frightened and astonished the whole city. The Tuscan sages said that it portended a new race of men, and a renovation of the world, for they observed that there were eight several kinds of men, all differing in life and manners; that heaven had allotted to each its time, which was limited by the circuit of the Great Year; and that when one race came (to the end of its time) . . . it was announced by some wonderful sign from either earth or heaven. . . . Such was the mythology of the most learned and respectable of the Tuscan soothsayers.[34]

Plato's narrative in the *Statesman* parallels this myth. Its successors are Hegel's *Spiritus Mundi* and Spengler's pessimism. The cyclic catastrophism in history permeates Aztec and Hindu thought.

The murder of the Emperor Constans in 350 gave rise to the prophecies of the Triburtine Sibyl, predicting a "time of sorrows" followed by a golden age. The *Triburtina* introduces the "Emperor of the Last Days," who also appears in the prophecy of Pseudo-Methodius, an effort to console Syrian Christians in their uncomfortable role as a minority. The prophecies themselves were far more durable than the causative political events.[35]

The ranks of the prophets of doom are numberless. In 1524,

> Europe was awaiting in an agony of prayerful terror a second deluge. . . . As the fatal month drew nigh, dwellers by the waterside moved in crowds to the hills, and the President Aurial, at Toulouse, built himself a Noah's Ark.[36]

Fired with a zeal to save humanity, the prophets are more often than not rejected by a humanity that does not want to be saved—thus Cassandra, thus Laocoön. The modern texts of catastrophism are from *Jeremiah* and *Revelation*. The refrain is from Thomas of Caelano's hymn, *Dies irae*.

On one side then is the advocate of fire contending with the glacial theorist. On the other, incidentally, are the opponents of catastrophism, the rosy glaziers of illimitable human progress, such as Condorcet.

Worsley summarizes the millenarianism of the cargo cults:

> In these movements, a prophet announces the imminence of the end of the world in a cataclysm which will destroy everything. Then the ancestors will return or God, or some other liberating power, will appear, bringing all the goods the people desire. . . . The people therefore prepare themselves for the Day by setting up cult organizations . . .[37]

Chiliasm, catastrophism, and vaticinations of doom generate a social hysteria. Rational politics is also set aside in the Berserker rage or the peyote cult—rationality is not a requisite of myth. The politics of despair may even mythologize suicidal tendencies in the form of the Mayan Ixtab, the Greek "hanged Artemis," or the Hindu Kali.

> Some fever of the blood and brain,
> Some self-exalting spell,
> The scourger's keen delight of pain,
> The Dervish dance, the Orphic strain,
> The wild-haired Bacchant's yell.[38]

Myths of Legitimacy and Social Establishment

As a social process, messianism is marked diminuendo. The high emotional pitch of the movement is difficult to sustain.

Society must "routinize the charisma" in order to conserve its power. Myths of legitimacy and social establishment perform this function by stabilizing and institutionalizing the community.

Rousseau ponders over the problem of legitimacy: "Man is born free, but everywhere he is in chains. What can make it legitimate?" Rousseau's answer is the rather nebulous "general will." The political myths relieve the uncertainties and insecurities of power-holding. Myths erase the bar sinister from the usurper's armorial bearings. They pardon the crimes behind the crowns. Myths minimize the amount of "naked power" required to retain control of government. They ordain, validate, and substantiate the "powers that be." In the epics the theme of tested heroism indicates the legitimate authority claimed by the hero. Myths justify loyalty to the heroic credo.

Legitimizing myths are of two types: those which legitimize governments, usually by investing the hero with a divine right, and those which establish a caste system or an elite.

The desire to be more-than-equal is rooted in human nature; this possessive, status-seeking tendency requires a mythology to defend its position. In this manner a myth legitimizes caste or class. Each class must manufacture its own pseudo-celestial arcana as a means of self-preservation. Frequently the establishing myth catalogues the enormity of the debt which society owes to the caste's heroic founder. Myths may also maintain the *need* for a certain group. Thus, a military elite encircles the country with assorted ferocious dragons. Williams reports the following syllogism:

> The whole universe is subject to the gods; the gods are subject to the spells . . . the spells to the Brahmans; therefore the Brahmans are our gods.[39]

Establishment myths are intensely conservative; they portray challenges to the social structure as futile, illegal, moreover sinful. In one of the most meaningful social passages in *The Faerie Queene* is Artegall's meeting with the egalitarian Giant:

There they beheld a mighty Giant stand
Upon a rocke, and holding on hie
An huge great paire of ballance in his hand,
With which he boasted . . .
That all the world he would weigh equallie,
If ought he had the same to counterpoys . . .

For-why, he sayd, they are all unequall . . .
And had encroached upon others share . . .
And so were realmes and nations run awry.
All which he undertooke for to repaire . . .
And all things would reduce unto equality.

Therefore the vulgar did about him flocke,
And cluster thicke . . .
Like foolish flies about an honey-crocke,
In hope by him great benefite to gaine.
And uncontrolled freedome to obtaine.

Therefore I will throw downe these mountains hie,
And make them levell with the lowly plaine;
These towring rocks, which reach unto the skie,
I will thrust downe into the deepest maine . . .[40]

The myths which Spenser satirizes are an attack on the myth of establishment. James Blish comments on similar myths:

from the point of view of the rational humanitarian *most* myths are offensive because they impede the spread of social justice . . . myths which actually retard social justice seem particularly loathsome . . . if they seem to command . . . belief.[41]

Class myths severely restrict social privileges. Among many peoples even survival after death is a mythic prerogative of the nobility. The mass burials, excavated by Sir Leonard Wooley at

Ur, as well as the Pharaonic *ka* of Egypt are part of this belief. Weber notes that in India transmigration is an adjunct of caste. The usual post-mortem continuity of class imposes an entailed inheritance of ancestor worship. Myths in which social status ceases after death have a pronouncedly democratic flavor which appeals to the nonestablished classes.[42]

Such an anticipated reversal, raising mudsills and the proverbial "bottom-rail," appears in a post-bellum Negro song:

> We's nearer to de Lord
>   Dan de white folks and dey knows it;
> See de glory gate unbarred;
>   Walk up, darkeys, past de guard;
> Bet a dollar he don't close it . . .
>
> Hallelujah! t'anks an' praise:
>   Long enuff we've borne our crosses;
> Now we's de sooperior race;
>   We's gwine to hebben afore de bosses.[43]

A common form of the caste-establishing myth is the Platonic myth of the metals. In the Incan parallel, the Sun, acting as demiurge, founds the city of Cuzco. There are three eggs, one gold, one silver, another copper; from these emerge kings, priests, and slaves. In the Tibetan *Kah-gyur* is a tale regarding the marital restrictions of the city of Vaisali with towers of gold, silver, and copper, marking the three classes.[44]

In an interesting American myth, the citizens of Xibalba are sentenced to become "hewers of wood and drawers of water":

> Since neither your great power nor your race any longer exist, and since neither do you desire mercy, your rank shall be lowered. Not for you shall be the ball game. You shall spend your time making earthen pots and tubs and stones to grind corn.[45]

These myths which legitimize caste are closely allied to those which establish government by a ruling class. With an unusual attention to the Aristotelean rationale, this type of myth states that some are born to rule; others, to obey. The myth defines the qualifications for leadership, which are virtues of the epic hero. The hero himself founds the dynasty.

The formula is that of the *Lusiads.* Lusus, a companion of Bacchus, fathers the line which rules Lusitania; ergo, the Portuguese kings possess divine protection and descent; and if Lusus is wanting, St. James will serve. The *Popol Vuh* terminates in the finding of a legitimate symbol of power: "This is a remembrance which I leave for you. This shall be your power . . ."[46] The *credenda* and *miranda* of legitimate power, the loyalty-evoking symbols, originate in the political myth. The legacy of such coronation rituals is security.

The myth often contains divine right, or the mandate of heaven. Shamanism is often the source of royal powers of magic healing. The frontispiece of the *Eikon Basilike* shows the divine emanations about the monarch. If this light is eclipsed, a shadow falls on the ruler's legitimacy. This myth inconveniences the Emperor Ming Ti:

> We have heard that if a sovereign is remiss in government, God terrifies him by calamities and portents. These are divine reprimands sent to recall him to a sense of duty. Thus eclipses of the sun and moon are manifest warnings that the rod of empire is not wielded aright.[47]

On the other hand, a similar belief ends a revolt against Tiberius.[48] Such a rudimentary notion of "natural law" is readily manipulated in the service of legitimacy.

In spite of the relative absence of divine right theory during the Middle Ages, the *benedicite* of a legitimizing myth is of the utmost importance. The papal power of "binding and loosing" drives Henry to Canossa. The myth also unites tradition, ritual, taboo, and custom against political schismatics and reformers. The legitimizing myth routinizes the messianic myth and stabilizes society.

Myths of Legality and Community

As society stabilizes, legal order and institutions are defined. The idea of "natural law" clarifies from the original legitimacy myth. Before the codification of the law, myths control the community. In fact, by creating a *consensus iuris*, myths structure the ethical framework of the community and thereby establish the community itself. Durkheim advances the idea that the objects of totemic worship in the elementary forms of religious life are actually symbolic social groups.[49] Temporary order may be achieved by force, but permanent order requires a myth, embodying social prohibitions and sanctions. In *God Without Thunder*, John Crowe Ransom pictures the mythmaker as legislator.[50]

"Primitive" society has a highly developed sense of lawfulness and community. As one Indian chief says:

> The Indians on the prairie before there was the white man to put him in the guardhouse had to have something to keep him from doing wrong.[51]

The Nahua of Mexico are "those who live by rule," distinguishing themselves from the lawless barbarians. The demonic spirit of nihilism opposes such an ethical community. Nihilism attacks the "Dragon Thou Shalt" and the moral mythology.

Codified law becomes depoeticized but retains its mythic basis. It becomes ritual. Usually a divine-origin myth substantiates the legal code. A Babylonian stele depicts Shamash granting the tablets of law. Such figures as Pachacutic and Manu fuse legislator, culture-hero and myth-maker.

There are several characteristics of these early legal myths: the divine origin of the law, the immanence of justice and retribution, the homeopathy of the law with frequent blood feud and blood revenge, the role of the priesthood in ascertaining guilt, the maintenance of conformity through the fear of a secret society. Myths frequently idealize a prelapsarian condition of peace and justice.

The foundations of primitive justice are lost in a mythic world of superstitions:

> To test the guilt or innocence of an accused person, put a rooster under a pot and let all suspects touch the pot. When the thief touches it, the rooster will crow . . . To test the guilt or innocence of an accused person, place two chairs back to back and rest a sifter between them lightly. Then say:
>
> "By Saint Peter, by Saint Paul,
> By the Lord who made us all,
> If (supply name) did this,
> Turn sifter, turn and fall."[52]

A Chinese belief, based on sounder physiological evidence, was that a guilty person cannot chew dry rice.

Although it is difficult to speculate on the origins of these legal myths, an anecdote told by W. E. Gladstone from Rousseau's *Confessions* seems apropos:

> Equally primitive and childlike was Rousseau's train of thought on the memorable day at Les Charmettes, when distressed with doubts as to the safety of his soul, he sought to determine the point by throwing a stone at a tree, "Hit, sign of salvation; miss, sign of damnation!" The tree being a large one and very near at hand . . .[53]

Such logic is certainly adaptable to the legal requirements of "noble savagery." Rousseau's treatment of myth and civil religion is naturally "romantic," but it not only anticipates the freedom-themes of the later romantic, but also the totalitarian "cult of the state." A similar thought process fabricates sophisticated "legal fictions." These are conveniences capable of converting a maxim of Roman water law into a requirement for parliamentary representation.

Since the legal myths provide a mechanistic formula for justice, it is only reasonable to appeal to the divine, legitimizing myth in determining the rightness of a cause. The powers of animism and animatism testify. In 1642 Jacques Aymar discovers the Lyons' murderers with a divining rod. Chauvin hypothesizes that the murderer's body exudes a detectable substance.[54] In a jataka tale, a goblin gives the hero a similar crime-detecting power. Many myths relate that certain objects, owned by the victim of a violent death, will bleed. This is contagious magic.

Now, if myths can detect criminality through magic, it is only reasonable to entrust the legal process to a well-qualified witch doctor, skilled in the cabala:

> Quakery, the Ju-Ju king of New Calabar . . . told de Cardi that, if the king tries to detect robbers it would have little effect, because the king was a man like themselves from whom they would steal if they got the chance. "But if I sent round a notice that if the thieves did not immediately bring me the stolen articles, my Ju-Ju would cause them (the thieves) to swell up and burst, you would see how quickly they would come to me and deliver up the stolen goods."[55]

The Apache medicine man has as one of his principal functions the scaring up of thieves.[56] Fear of the law becomes fear of gods—*Primos in orbe deos fecit timor.* "Temples of justice" house the courts, where the law is "enshrined," where the high priests wear archaic black robes. The manipulation of myth, fear, and law becomes a function of the secret society.[57] Indeed the myths of infallible justice may become so potent that the innocent believes he is guilty as accused.

Gradually legal experts extract the forms and processes of the law from legal myths. The myth atrophies, and the law emerges. A homeopathy of law develops in which "like punishes like." Formulas of blood feud and blood revenge, the vendetta, the *wergeld*, and trial by ordeal, occur. Lawson compares legal customs in Antiphon's ancient Maina and in the same modern area:

> In Maina it is held that, if the next of kin fail to avenge the dead man, no matter to what cause the failure be due he falls prey to the dead man's wrath. Antiphon on the contrary asserts that, if the next of kin have honestly done his best to bring the murderer to justice, he will not be punished for failure therein; and yet he does not represent the dead man as inactive in such a case, but dares to threaten the jury that the murdered man's anger will now descend . . . upon the jury . . . In modern Maina the kinsman who should have recourse to law . . . would be accounted a recreant.[58]

Many situations require expiation of a criminal act.

The myth of the broken taboo and its punishment is a common legal myth. The Kaonde hummingbird brings down the wrath of the god Leza for opening the forbidden calabash before delivering it to the first man and woman.[59] The broken taboo theme is typified in a Clackamas myth, "Fire and His Son's Son":

> Such disobedience or nullifying of parental admonition is a frequent motif in Northwest states' literatures, and invariably the culture's conscience intervenes to punish the youth who has shown disrespect towards a parental trustee of standards.[60]

Parsons considers a number of myths of this type:

> In New Guinea, Kiwai Island initiates fear being seized by incurable disease. Among the Elema as other tribes to reveal that the bull-roarer is man-made will result in the curse of Tiparu, the equivalent of death. A Koita child who stayed in the bush at night would encounter a *vadavada,* a man, who travels by night and who brings sickness and death to those he meets . . . The Euahlayi tribe of New South Wales have a bogey called Gineet Gineet . . . He goes about with a net across his shoulders into which he pops any children he can see . . . 'N*e*naunir of the Masai is a kindred monster; he is an invulnerable stony-bodied creature with the head of a beast of prey . . .[61]

The human tendency to disobey sometimes is cast in terms of a myth of archaic rebellion against authority. The gods transform the rebels into beasts or inanimate objects. They may exile or expel the wrongdoer into the lawless world. Both the Egyptians and Manichaeans believed in penal transmigration. In the Canaanite Aqhat myth, the goddess Anat punishes the hero when he fails to yield to her the silver bow—possibly a lunar power symbol. Plagues follow crimes against the people; this is Oedipus' first punishment. Similarly there is God's judgment against Bishop Hatto of Fulda—the Mausthurm.

God decrees taxation in a Shilluk myth:

> One day Dok was out hunting and he came to a great tree . . . A voice called to Dok to bring his father. When Nikawng was brought, God announced the penalty to be inflicted on them for fighting the sun. He said that their people would be compelled to pay tribute, and that is the reason that the Shilluks are required to pay taxes to the government.[62]

Myths provide severe punishments for abuse of power. Mythic judgments are inexorable, whether they be by the relentless Erinyes or in the afterlife of a Platonic Hades, populated by the convicts of Minos, Aecus, and Rhadamanthus. *Dike* follows *hybris*, as Tantalus and Sisyphus testify. The myth details the agony of retribution. The Guinea natives tell of a great priest before whom they must appear after death. The priest will send the good to a happy place but will kill the wicked a second time. The fear of revenants is also a check on crime.

Man's interest in legal formulas often involves an abstract myth of justice. The mythological figure, whose attributes are blindfold and scales, personifies this concept. The Egyptians mythologize *Maat*, or right order. The handless judges' statues of ancient Thebes symbolize incorruptible honesty. Antigone immortalizes the "spirit of the laws."

The Oresteian trilogy relates the quest for justice. The antique notion of the *lex talionis* and the pre-Olympian religion comes into conflict with the Delphic code. Apollo enjoins Orestes to kill Clytemnestra—the next of kin must revenge the murdered man and then be ritually cleansed. Neither system of justice is adequate. A new retributive agency is furnished by Athena's institution, the Areopagus:

> Guard well and reverence that form of government
> Which will eschew alike licence and slavery;
> And from your polity do not wholly banish fear.
> For what man living freed, from fear, will still be just.
> Hold fast such upright fear of the law's sanctity,
> And you will have a bulwark of your city's strength.[63]

In Tasso's epic, Godfrey articulates the ideal of impartial justice. He replies to Tancred, who opens the dialogue:

> . . . It is not wise
> To the same level punishment to adjust;
> In different ranks the same crime different is:
> "Twixt peers alone equality is just."

"The lowliest should," the pious chief replies,
"Obedience learn from those of high estate . . .
What were my power if I but swayed the base,
And o'er the mob alone dominion bore? . . .
And now preserving strict equality,
No difference make 'twixt vassals and their lords."[64]

The ultimate ideal of social justice, tempered by mercy and humanity, occurs in the Chinese myth of Kwan Yin, who intercedes for the accused:

My wish is . . . to heal humanity of all its ills . . .
I wish to equalize all classes.[65]

Power Myths

"Mythology is a shrewd device of the legislator to keep the people in subjection," claimed Critias in an Athenian debate. Myths *are* the medium which transmits political power. Van der Leeuw defines myth as "the reiterated presentation of some event replete with power."[66] Fontenelle writes that "all the gods which the pagans have imagined, have been dominated by the idea of power."[67] This idea is inherent in Jupiter and possibly in Minerva.

In an African fable, tortoise claims equality in power with elephant and hippopotamus, even deigning to address each as "friend." He challenges them individually to a tug of war; attaches them to opposite ends of a long rope and thereby validates his power claims.[68] The Russian fairy tales betray an almost pathological obsession with power. The power quest, the power test, and the superhuman power of the hero are all part of the epic, political myth.

Societies in which animatism prevails draw power myths from many sources. Eliade comments on Ablott's *The Keys of Power,* which analyzes ritual and belief in Indian society:

> Indeed, if one perseveres to the end of the book, one is unable to say what in the eyes of an Indian, is *not* capable of having power.[69]

Jambuka, the wise bird of the jataka tales, philosophizes on the role of power in India:

> Amidst the great ones of the earth a five fold power we see,
> Of these the power of limbs is, sure, the last in its degree.
> And power of wealth, O mighty lord, the next is said to be,
> The power of caste without a doubt is reckoned fourth in fame
> And all of these a man that's wise most certainly will claim.[70]

A Jicarilla storyteller is almost gnostic:

> The plants, rocks, fire, water, all are alive. They watch us and see our needs. They see when we have nothing to protect us, and it is then that they reveal themselves and speak to us.[71]

A multiplicity of power sources derive from analogy to nature. *Mana* in power myths can be extremely vague. In fact, among the Fiji "a thing has *mana* when it works, it has no *mana* when it doesn't work."[72] Van der Leeuw states:

> To the primitive mind . . . the thing is the bearer of a power . . . During an important expedition, for example, an African negro steps on a stone and cries out: "Ha! are you there?" . . . Again: an Ewe tribesman in West Africa enters the bush and finds a lump of iron there; returning home, he falls ill, and the priests explain that a *tro* (a divine being) is manifesting its potency in the iron, which in the future should be worshipped.[73]

The custodians of this power are often magicians. The Melanesian chief's power lies in his ability to communicate with the ghosts. Even Dr. Dee and Cagliostro have exerted some political influence. The possession of regalia and magic talismans insures power; by corollary, their loss spells disaster. For example, there are the palladium and xoanon, power objects of ancient Troy, and the sacred medicine bundles of the American Indians. The latter are often a childlike omnium-gatherum.

Secret societies may also be the trustees of myths. As Webster informs us:

> In communities where the political powers of the chiefs are as yet in a formative stage, the secret societies provide effective social restraints and supplement the governmental activities of the earliest rulers.[74]

Power myths adapt to the needs of primitive society, agrarian, hunting, or military.

Agrarian power myths are of utmost value in a society dependent on irrigation or rainfall. The "Young Corn God" in Harvard's Peabody Museum is a sublime expression of Mayan agrarian civilization. The king may hold power as a tenant farmer, responsible for droughts and famines, capable of ordering Nature at will. An interesting case is the punishment of the Italian saints who fail to provide rain.[75]

Such are the powerful spirits who rule "the corn and the wild." Their cults have comprised powerful political organizations. The most important offshoots are the ritual regicides in Frazer's pattern. Ritual regicide discourages actual regicide—at the same time it reminds the king that he is expendable. Such practices also supply scapegoats to alleviate the sufferings caused by crop failure.[76]

Nomadic peoples invoke hunting gods to maintain power. Examples are Nimrod, the hunter hero, and Nerrivik, the old Eskimo "woman of the sea." Such mythic figures are often dreadful and malignant. Hunting societies accumulate political power. Hunting myths occur among the Navaho:

> Hunting is practiced as a valued means of subsistence. In addition certain rules of conduct for hunting are indicated. Ritual transgression and excess in taking game are pictured as punishable offenses subject to supernatural sanctions.[77]

Military power myths are extremely common. Among the Winnebago, the head of a war party must possess a supernatural warrant. In other words, the warrior must be ingenious enough, philosophical enough, to create a myth before leading an army. Terrifying war gods contribute to successful martial power.

There are usually extensive protective taboos on the body of the leader or king. The friseur is as important as M. Beaucaire. Great danger attends the haircut; so the king simply evades it; and so do the English scholars and the beatniks. The chiefs of the Sandwich Islands were accompanied by portable spittoons.

Power myths in general serve as a centripetal force to maintain cohesion, conformity, and orthodoxy. Such myths minimize individual self-assertion and place an emphasis on absolute obedience to the power holders. Malinowski writes:

> Let us realize that in primitive conditions, tradition is of supreme value for the community and nothing matters as much as the conformity and conservatism of its members. Order and civilization can be maintained only by strict adhesion to the lore and knowledge received from previous generations. Any laxity in this weakens the cohesion of the group and imperils its cultural outfit to the point of threatening its very existence.[78]

A rather uncommon variant stresses the *abnegation of power*. The Tibetan "Dumb Cripple" pretends to be handicapped to avoid being invested with kingship. After reigning sixty years in a previous existence, his reincarnation was in hell.[79]

Iconoclastic Myths

Opposed to the myths of social establishment, legitimacy, and power are the popular iconoclastic myths. These usually challenge the social system from within; often they are myths of social criticism. To offset these myths, society must produce a cathartic myth. Sometimes this myth takes the form of a scapegoat or permissible *social* satire—a retreat into the world of Yahoo and Brobdingnag. When the challenge to society is external, a mythic cultural defense is needed. Frequently this myth assumes the apocryphal form of "children of light and children of darkness."

Social satire is apparent in Aristophanes' comedies. *The Knights* attacks Cleon; *The Clouds* assails Socrates and the new tendencies in philosophy and rhetoric. *The Wasps* exposes the absurdities of the Athenian jury contest. *Lysistrata, Thesmophoriazusae,* and *Ecclesiazusae* satirize varying aspects of Athens and especially women in politics. Pope's *Dunciad* similarly reveals social idiosyncrasies.

Such social satire is also evident in the myths of the trickster. Klapp describes a hectic episode in the life of Till Eulenspiegel:

> Eulenspiegel is commissioned to paint a picture for some noblemen. He spends his time eating and drinking and delays his patrons with excuses. Finally, when ready, he shows them a picture of nothing but a blank canvas in a frame, telling them

> that those who are low born will see nothing in it. Each pretends that he sees the picture.[80]

Expressed as an etching and as a direct social criticism, we discover a Goya, a Daumier, or a Nast.

Another myth of social criticism is the story of Shemyak the Russian judge. A lawsuit occurs between a rich peasant and a poor peasant. The poor man stands behind the judge with a cloth-wrapped rock. Shemyak, thinking that he is being offered a bribe, greedily decides the case in favor of the poor peasant.[81]

Such myths may be classified as iconoclastic or cathartic, depending on the extent to which the regime sanctions them. The ruler may institutionalize catharsis in the form of a scapegoat. The Peruvian Aymara expelled the plague with a black lama. Frazer comments:

> In Tibet the ceremony of the scapegoat presents some remarkable features. The Tibetan new year begins . . . the government of Lhasa . . . is taken out of the hands of the ordinary rulers and entrusted to the monk of the Debang monastery who offers to pay the highest for the privilege. The successful bidder is called the Jalno . . . The Jalno exercises his authority in the most arbitrary manner for his own benefit. (The Jalno, representing the Grand Lama, plays at dice with the "King of the Years.") If the King of the Years wins, much evil is prognosticated. . . . Fortune, however, always favors the Jalno, who throws sixes with unvarying success, while his opponent turns up only ones. Nor is this so extraordinary as at first sight it might appear, for the Jalno's dice are marked with nothing but sixes. . . . When he sees the finger of Providence thus plainly pointed against him, the King of the Years is terrified and flees away. . . . His face is still painted half white and half black. . . . Thus driven out of the city, he is detained in the great chamber of horrors at the Samyas monastery, surrounded by monstrous . . . devils . . . thence he goes away to the mountains of Chetang, where he has to remain an outcast.

If he dies before the time is out, the people say it is an auspicious omen. . . . In the Jalno we may without undue straining discern a successor of those temporary kings, those mortal gods, who purchase a short lease of power and glory at the price of their lives . . .[82]

The "King of the Years" is a substitute's substitute.

The *enemy of the people*, be it Chénier or Dr. Stockmann, releases accumulated social tensions and political pressures into myth-created channels. Prophylactic rites occur in Babylonian society, with a specific rite for every evil. By keeping the intellectual classes occupied in squabbling over the meaning of myths and the lower classes awed and entertained, both by the myths and by the squabbling, the government diverts the revolutionary tendencies in these groups.

Iconoclastic myths on the other hand are the propaganda of social or religious reform. Many Utopian myths portray society as-it-is-not-but-might-be. The Leninist tendency is to couch such myths in an Aesopian language in the interest of avoiding censorship. Nineteenth century political novels conceal a great corpus of these myths. Dickens and Zola head the conscious literary onslaught against industrial society. At the same time capitalism nurtures the orphaned newsboy-bootblack of Horatio Alger as a cultural defense myth. Unfortunately, Andersens' little match girl has not been blessed by having read Herbert Spencer.

The Faerie Queene contains several propaganda myths. The most important political creation is the portrait of the "false Duessa," Mary Queen of Scots. Elizabeth's vanity more than tinges the portrayal. Diplomatic history records James VI's official complaint to the English ambassador.[83]

Most iconoclastic myths mask a marked anxiety over social status, bringing the social-inversion myth to the fore again. The poverty-stricken hero becomes the ideal of the Russian tale of

Danilo the Unfortunate.[84] In this story Prince Vladimir ends up covered with mud. The myth of defensive response shows the poor as utterly incapable of governing. Sancho Panza's kingdom approximates this type.

An attack on the established mythology may result in skepticism, pessimism, materialism, or general disillusionment. A paralyzed society may make no response. Heresy, however, is usually risky and rarely of any rewarding nature, except for some personal satisfaction. In the 1700s the Canton of Uri sentenced one Freudenberger for publishing the opinion that the Tell myth had a Danish origin.[85]

One myth system, confronted by a rival, may absorb the opposing doctrines. Typical situations are the absorption of Greek and Irish myths by Christianity and the relation of Roman paganism to the Oriental cults.

Examination of the stories of SS. Dionysus and Demetra illustrate the effect of co-existence, attack, absorption, and response. St. Dionysus was on the way to Naxos; he placed the first grapevine, as it grew larger, in the leg bone of a bird, a lion, and an ass:

> And so he came to Naxos. And when he came to plant . . . he could not sever the bones. . . . Then the vine grew and bore grapes and men made wine and drank thereof. And first when they drank they sang like birds, and when they drank more they grew strong as lions, and afterwards foolish as asses.[86]

It does not require a great deal of imagination to see Bacchus leering behind the facade.

> St. Demetra was an old woman. . . . She had a daughter who was very beautiful past all imagining. . . . A Turkish lord of the neighborhood of Souli who was a wicked man and versed in magic saw her one day . . .[87]

Myths may even more openly commemorate cultural symbiosis; such is the marriage of Krt in the Ras-Shamra texts. This myth quite plausibly associates the Semitic and Hurrian peoples in northern Syria.[88]

Bowra discusses several examples of myths yielding to political and religious expediency. Among the Uzbeks the bey's distaste for democratic heroes caused the suppression of this poetry; the Revolution revived the proletarian pieces. Another group converted Rustum into a god-fearing Mohammedan.[89]

There is a dialectical intellectual process by which the myths of variant cultures confront each other. The same process operates between heresy and orthodoxy in the mythology of a single culture. Close agreement of the versions *can* facilitate intercultural understanding. Just as frequently minor doctrinal variations cause bitter contention and bloodshed. This is especially the case where the interpretation of myth has political overtones as in the Arian heresy. The achievement of consensus on variant forms of myth by peaceful means is an ideal of international relations.

Myths and Values

Three tendencies occur in value-creating myths: an extreme tendency toward autochthony, toward stereotyping other peoples, and toward bipolarity, or ethical dualism.

Autochthony is the mythological association with parts of the known and familiar landscape. By a process of mythic transmutation this becomes a powerful fantastic landscape by association with violence and legend, or by imagination. These myths are fondly tendered by the local antiquarians. It is little wonder that Homer's birthplace is authentically located in over half of Grecian territory in Asia Minor. A local mythology of haunted forests and places, *Kinderbrünen, Loesskindern,* is a unique inheritance which separates one group of people from their neighbors. These traditions unify the larger community, or nation. St. Patrick performs such a role for the Irish. Antaeus-like, the people draw strength from such myths. Eliade writes:

> The rite of depositing them (children) on the soil implies the idea that there is a substantial identity between the Race and the Soil. This idea is expressed, indeed, in the sentiment of autochthony which is the most vivid of all those that we discern in the beginnings of Chinese history: the close alliance between a country and its inhabitants is so profoundly believed in, that it has remained at the heart of the religious institutions and of public rights.[90]

Among the Karadjeri, two brothers are born from the earth in the form of dingoes. They become culture heroes and introduce the sacred mysteries to the tribe.

Not only is there a tendency in political mythology to idealize the indigenous, but there is a corresponding stereotyping of cultural enemies. The latent belief is that all Hyperboreans are cannibals. Myths segregate the children of light and the children of darkness; thereby they create a bipolar ethics. "Iphigenia in Aulis" expresses the dichotomy between Greek and barbarian.

War myths of two California tribes, Yuki and Nomalaki, illustrate the same point. Nomalaki, "Indian Bear," slays Yuki and blood payment is demanded and refused. In the Nomalaki version:

> Many Yuki were killed. . . . Yuki at that time were a most war-like and vicious people—caught poaching contrary to inter-tribal law . . . they often robbed and made raids . . . and were dissatisfied with their territory. . . . The Yuki heard the roar of guns and saw their men being mowed down. They became very frightened

and fled. . . . They thought that the United States Army was after them.[91]

It seems but a short transition to the myths associated with the slogans *"Mehr Raum"* and *"Drang nach Osten."* In the Yuki version of the conflict, needless to say, there is only one Yuki casualty while the tribe slays a thousand war-mongering Nomalakis.

The "mythology of dark and fair," which has interesting psychological implications, arises frequently in situations of intercultural tension.[92]

Sebba cites this interesting Southern "Why Story":

> An old lady in the deep South, plantation-born and plantation-raised, explained why Negroes have pale lips. . . . God originally created all men black. But the better ones wanted to be pure and white like God; and God in his mercy created a pond in which anyone could dip and come out pure and white. And so all the young, strong, intelligent, God-loving people rushed to the pond and emerged white. The stupid, lazy, slow ones dawdled on the way; when they got to the pool, there was no water left . . .[93]

The enemy inverts the values established by the national mythology. In Greek folklore, he is insolent, violent, lawless, and impious. Tylor stresses this point:

> In any country an isolated or outlying race, the lingering survivor of an older nationality, is liable to the reputation of sorcery. It is thus with the Lavas of Burma, supposed to be the broken-down remains of an ancient cultured race and dreaded as man-tigers, and with the Budas of Abyssinia, who are at once the smiths and potters, sorcerers and werewolves, of their district.[94]

In a similar fashion Procopius describes the Kingdom of Arawn:

> . . . to the effect that no man could live there for half an hour on account of the unwholesomeness of the air, and that it was infested with vipers and all kinds of noxious beasts.[95]

Myths may preserve the remnants of an intellectually superior, but conquered people or the memory of genuinely barbaric enemies. Several queer peoples appear in Herodotus such as those south of the Sahara with eyes in their breasts.

The racial myths and myths of national character create such stereotypes. Political theory is burdened by such myths from classical times through the writings of John Barclay to modern racism.[96] These myths lead to all sorts of fantastic illusions of superiority. Woltmann claims Giotto, Alighieri, Bruno, Ghiberti, Vinci, Arouet, and Tasso as being of good German stock—Jothe, Aigler, Braun, Wilbert, Wincke, Arwid, and Dasse. The humor of this mythic outburst is nullified by the bloodshed which defended it.[97]

Myths are notoriously ethnocentric. The tale is told of the African village in which the commonly held view of the world is that the village stands in the center of a disc-shaped world. On the periphery are the United States and Belgium—also Portugal, as there was a Portuguese trader in the next village. Of course, not all the natives are so naive; at least one has a more sophisticated view, possibly the result of a zealous trinitarian education. His cosmology describes the world as triangular; the village was still at the center.

The conquered is often expected to assimilate the myths of the conquerors. The stock image, evoked by Dr. Emerson, is one of the dusky children of French Africa, reciting "Our ancestors the Gauls . . ."[98] Nation after nation has proclaimed itself alone capable of salvaging humanity, of a *mission civilatrice*, of shouldering the "white man's burden." The least harmful versions are the grandiose visions of Mrs. Jellyby in *Bleak House* for the colonization of Borrioboola Gha. Race after race has mythologized its neighbors into "half devil and half child."

Such myths recount how one people is chosen to lead the crusade or establish the human race—how Delhi or Delphi is the navel of the world—*Te Pito Te Henua*. Sumner reports that the Caribs claim to be the only people; so do the Yaghan of Tierra del Fuego. He continues elsewhere:

> The most important fact is that ethnocentrism leads a people to exaggerate and intensify everything in their own folkways which is peculiar and which differentiates them from others. It therefore strengthens the folkways.[99]

A related element, which stimulates national feeling, is the collection of myths and folklore. Mythology functions to form a people in the same manner as language. Again there is a tendency to extract the shared cultural heritage. For example, the annexation of Finland by Russia in 1809, motivates Castren's collection of the *Kalevala*. The *Mabinogion* plays a similar role in the Celtic Renaissance. The unpromising Norwegian hero Askeladden reawakens national consciousness in the 1870s.[100]

Melville Herskovits summarizes this idea:

> The study of folklore has always been marked by a strongly nationalistic emphasis, and its investigation, often conducted under governmental subsidies, has been focused on local or regional areas within specific domains . . . folklorists have always been concerned more with studies of the folk literary forms . . . among their own people.[101]

Myths and Moral Purpose

One of the most important functions of the political myth is the ethical education of the citizen. The myth details his obligations and responsibilities in the community. Lord Russell recounts a story told of Confucius:

> In passing by the side of Mount Thai, Confucius came on a woman who was bitterly weeping by a grave. The Master pressed forward and drove quickly to her; then he sent Tze-lu to question her. "Your wailing," said he, "is that of one who has suffered sorrow on sorrow." She replied, "That is so. Once my husband's father was killed here by a tiger. My husband was also killed, and now my son has died in the same way." The Master said, "Why do you not leave the place?" The answer was, "There is no oppressive government here." The Master then said, "Remember this, my children, oppressive government is more terrible than tigers.[102]

Myths forcefully convey such moral precepts. Doubtlessly such passages give pause to the modern Chinese censor. Because of this morality of mythology, governments are frequently at pains to censor the circulating tales. The imperial government of Hunan Province felt that the "pathetic fallacy" in *Alice in Wonderland* might be subversive.[103] Tales which mix little white rabbits and little black rabbits are also "immoral" in some areas.

Myths create the types for cultural achievement and the acceptable moral values. These values are widely diversified. As Eliade points out: "Oriental cultures succeeded in conferring positive values on anxiety, death, self-abasement, and upon chaos."[104]

Radcliffe-Brown's work demonstrates that:

> The function of the myths and legends of the Andamanese is exactly parallel to that of the ritual and ceremonial, (they are) the means by which the individual is made to feel the moral force of the society acting upon him.[105]

Myths capsulize and make palatable the community's ethical system; *le conte moral* associates political prudence and proverbs. Many myths teach respect for authority, social norms, sacred tradition, loyalty, and friendship. Webster lists a few of the mythic virtues:

> Obedience to the elders . . . bravery in battle, liberality towards the community, independence of maternal control, steadfast attachment to the traditional customs and the established moral code.[106]

Didactic myths have always been valued as educational devices. Greek educators used the Homeric cycles extensively. In late Greece, Homeric study became an affectation. Dio Chrysostom reported a colony that read almost nothing else but the *Iliad.* It is little wonder that Plato, interested in myth as a device for moral civic education, took alarm at the Homeric myths and attacked them in the *Republic.*

The proposed Platonic recension of the Homeric epics illustrates the problems of the educational use of myths. Plato maintains: "All mythology and poetry is a narrative of events, either past, present, or to come."[107] To adapt a Platonic myth, mythology, properly used, guides us from the shadows of the Cave to a vision of philosophical truth. This vision can only be seen through myths. Plato's treatment of myths as political raises the great dilemma of mythology, toleration versus the "closed society."[108]

Plato's allegation against the Homeric myths is that they are untrue and therefore unsuited as educative devices. He pictures Homer as a sophist, unskilled in government. The particulars of the indictment are numerous. These are some of the objectionable propositions taught in Homeric myths: that Justice is a thief; that the gods are the authors of evil; that the gods are changeable, emotional, intemperate, senders of lying dreams, and susceptible to bribery; further, that famous heroes are passionate.[109]

Plato singles out several passages which he considers to be especially obnoxious:

> I would rather be a serf on the land of a poor portionless man . . . than rule over all the dead who have come to nought. . . . He feared lest the mansions grim and squalid which the gods abhor should be seen both of mortals and immortals.[110]

Such lines, he says, are not "for the ears of boys who are to be sons of freedom and are to fear slavery more than death."[111]

On the other hand, Plato frequently uses passages from Homer to illustrates his philosophic principles. He evinces a great love for Homer:

> Although I have always from my earliest youth had an awe and love of Homer, which even now makes the words falter on my lips . . . a man is not to be reverenced before the truth.[112]

The allowable use of poetry, lyric or epic, in the Platonic state includes hymns of praise to the gods or famous men. And after the purgation of Homer:

> Then in this, I said, Homer will be our teacher, and we too, at sacrifices and on like occasions will honor the brave with hymns.[113]

The student of myth becomes the good citizen and the myth-educator, the statesman. This is a theme from Jaeger's *Paideia:*

> The function of the myth within the dialogue is to sum up. . . . The essence of the Platonic myth lies in its cooperation with the logos. . . . Long after the reader has forgotten the tortuous complications of Plato's logical arguments, he can remember the picture given by the myth, which becomes a symbol of the philosophical meaning of the whole . . .[114]

The Neo-Platonist, Sallustius, felt somewhat differently on the use of Homeric myths in education:

> Now myths represent the Gods themselves and the goodness of the Gods—subject always to the distinction . . . (between) that which is clear and that which is hidden, since, just as the Gods have made the goods of sense common to all, but those of the intellect only to the wise, so the myths state the existence of Gods to all, but who and what they are only to those who can understand. . . . But why have they put in the myths stories of adultery, robbery, father-binding, and all other absurdity? Is not that perhaps a thing worthy of admiration, done so that by means of the visible absurdity the Soul may immediately feel that the words are veils and believe the truth to be a mystery?[115]

The ability to apperceive the meaning of the myths is part of the educational process.

Epic, Myth, and Historical Consciousness

The first chapter introduced a number of problems in regard to Euhemerism and the myth-history relationship. These aspects of myth as well as their projection as the idea of freedom are the final topics for discussion.

Several authors have intimated that an intensive interest in historic myths as well as historiography is symptomatic of cultural decadence. Of course, if we observe Miniver Cheevy's going around mourning "the ripe renown," we may expect the result to be a "bullet in the head." An interest in historical myths, however, can also be part of the growth process of a normal society. Indeed, the myth, as Eric Voegelin suggests, is a record of historiogenesis, a social claim of maturity.

Certain characteristics of the mythic treatment of history are especially prominent: the dissolution of the time barrier, the utopianism, the search for continuity, the tendencies toward concentration and patternism, myths as historical sources, and fatalism.

The temporal parallel of the "seven-league boots" which dissolve space is time dissolution in historicity. In this paradoxical concept, then is now. Man arrests or escapes from time. Sometimes there is a removal to a remote and indefinite period—"Once when the world was very young." In other myths there is an actual time lapse. Irving uses this theme several times, including *The Adelantado of the Seven Cities.* The hero, Don Fernando, departs on an exploring expedition. After spending a "short time" on a mysterious island, he returns to find that several generations have elapsed.[116] The awesome mythic concept of the dissolution of time into infinity occurs in the Hindu myth, "The Parade of the Ants."[117]

A second tendency of historical myths is "to look before and after," to orient the myth toward the beginnings or end of time. There is an acute sense of loss in looking backward, a sense of degeneration, a recollection of *temps perdu.* The Cargo Cult has prophesied the return of a "Golden Age." Mansren will plant a coconut palm which will arch over until it touches Miok Wundi—then "no more work, and no 'Company' (i.e., the Dutch), no forced labor and no taxation."[118] The vision of such times contrasts with the stark realities of politics. It memorializes the loss of freedom and appears in the form of a lost earthly paradise in almost all mythologies.

The utopian myth functions in a similar manner. Lord Acton has theorized that this type of myth is generated "whenever great intellectual cultivation has been combined with the suffering which is inseparable from extensive changes in the condition of the people."[119] Many *nowheres* provide an escape from politics—where the reformer can create his Icaria undisturbed.

Third, historical myths manifest a genealogizing tendency, a search for patterns. Most men are not as easily satisfied as the hero of Cooper's *Monikons,* who is able to trace his lineage back only a single generation. Manetho's king lists conveniently fill the lacunae in Egyptian history. The Holy Roman emperors attempt to connect their office with that of Romulus Augustulus in an unbroken succession, In Hebraic history, the patriarchs, the *toldoth,* preserve continuity with the original *berith* and the *toroth.* As Widengren tells us: ". . . genealogy renders immense service by linking up mythical and truly historical figures together in one single chain."[120]

Lord Raglan rails against this tendency:

> We thus see arrayed in defense of false genealogy the powerful forces of religion and patriotism; of custom and tradition; of family pride and individual vanity; and of Euhemerism and rationalization.[121]

Raglan succeeds in demonstrating that some local traditions are false; this leads to the *non sequitur* that all such myths are false. Even if they are false, the reasons behind the fabrications are significant.

The establishment of ancestral continuity is necessary in societies where ancestor worship is prevalent. Tylor writes:

> On the continent of Africa, manes-worship appears with extremest definiteness and strength. Thus Zulu warriors, aided by the "amatongo," the spirits of their ancestors, conquer in battle.[122]

This is essentially a power myth, frequently associated with legitimacy. For example, there is the legend of Prince Vladimir in which Augustus sends his brother, Prus, to organize the people on the Vistula.[123] Rurik is his descendant.

Examine the Greek genealogical tables which connect the dynasties of the ancient world with the gods. All the branches terminate in eponyms. Ion, for example, gives his name to the Ionians. Aegyptus and Nilus are the distant kin of Dorus, Aeolus, and Achaeus via the gods. The neat order of historical evolution is striking. This evolutionary tendency is a recurrent pattern in historical myths.

There is an almost proto-Comtian idea of historical stages in an Incan myth of the systems of worship. The four brothers and sisters in the myth of Pacari Tampu establish successively: *paccariscas,* or holy places, fetishes, Viracocha, and sun worship.[124] The four Aztec ages in the *Codex Vaticanus* are water, wind, fire, and famine. In Hindu mythology there are the four cyclic *Yugas,* ending in the cultural catastrophism of the Kali Yuga. The Chinese have a similar progression of epochs. The Navaho recognize four ages: beginnings, animal heroes, gods, and patriarchs. The Maori traditions tell of six aeons of darkness, followed by the growth of civilization or consciousness:

> From the conception, the increase,
> From the increase, the swelling,
> From the swelling, the thought,
> From the thought, the remembrance,
> From the remembrance, the desire.[125]

Frequently evolutionary myths betray a marked intuitive acquaintance with biogenesis. Regarding this point, Furneaux states:

> The idea of evolution by natural selection seems to be contained in the story of one Iroquois clan, who believed that their ancestor, the turtle, had been forced to take up his abode on dry land by the drying up of the pool in which he lived.[126]

Here is an awareness of the theory of "progress to prevent change" which states that in order to conserve the environment an organism must often adapt.

Myths themselves seem to undergo an organic evolution. Such a process, however, is difficult to substantiate even as a hypothetical structure. Frequent "jumps" are involved for any one culture. Most contemporary anthropologists are chary of such a scheme. Radin, in fact, holds:

> The cardinal error is and always has been the assumption that every element in culture must have had an evolution and one generally comparable to that which exists in the animal world.[127]

Mythology and the philosophy of history also share the biological tendency to analogize the decline of culture with the organic life cycle. A Creek ceremony marks decay and renewal by allowing the pardon of all crimes except murder. Similarly, there is the Babylonian belief in the "eternal return of things"; Nietzsche, who vaunts his discovery of this phenomenon, is somewhat preceded by Berosus. Frazer traces this belief in a "Great Year" to a very early social stage in which:

> . . . men, ignorant of the secret processes of Nature and of the narrow limits within which it is our power to control and direct them, have commonly arrogated to themselves functions which

> . . . we should deem superhuman . . . The illusion has been fostered and maintained by the same causes which begot it, namely, the marvelous order and uniformity . . . (of) Nature . . . He forsees them (cyclic occurrences) and forseeing them mistakes the desired recurrence for an effect of his own will.[128]

The tendency toward patternism stereotypes the myths and makes them of questionable value as sources of history. This, however, depends on what is meant by history. Lord Raglan, with several scholarly tricks up his sleeve, reduces it to factual chronology.

Raglan cites several ahistorical myths: the Trojan Wars, Herodotus' histories, and the details of the Serbian Battle of Kosovo. He also mentions Bédier's scholarly analysis of the ahistorical character of William of Orange, Girard de Rousillon, Ogier the Dane, and Raoul of Cambrai. The Russian *byliny* "are probably compiled by monks with the object of claiming for their monasteries the formal possession of religious preeminence and the widest territorial rights."[129]

One of Raglan's statements is especially revealing:

> Is there nothing in the stories of the Punic Wars which would afford material for the poets of epics and dramas? Of course there is plenty but it could not be used because the basis of epics and dramas was not historical.[130]

In the first place, Raglan has "forgotten" Naevius' poetry and the *Punica* of Silvus Italicus. In the second, the historicity of the *Pharsalia*, the *Araucana*, the *Lusiads*, and the *Henriade* is not open to question in general. The Serbian epic was incidentally a source used by vonRanke, whose penchant as a "realist" is unquestionable also.

Myth has a naughty and embarrassing propensity for proving its historical validity: consider Schliemann, Evans, the discovery of the Toltec city of Tula. The last events led to some uncomfortable remarks regarding the "vague science of anthropology and the exact art of myth."[131]

Malinowski's valued opinion subscribes to a different view of myth and history:

> (Myth) is the historical statement of one of the events which once and for all vouch for the truth of a certain form of magic. Sometimes it is the actual record of a magical revelation coming directly from the first man to whom magic was revealed in some dramatic occurrence. More often it bears on its surface that it is merely a statement of how magic came into the possession of a . . . community.[132]

Bowra's view must also be heard. In his *Heroic Poetry,* he separates shamanistic and heroic poetry. Bowra takes the position that the heroic poet rarely takes an interest in historical accuracy. The hearers of the poem accept the narration as fact. For example, the Athenians substantiated their claims to Salamis with Homeric passages. Some poems refer to an eponymic king; others, such as the "Death of the Emperor Constantine Drazagis," do give explicit dates—the fall of Constantinople was May 29, 1453—a Thursday![133]

One Kara-Kirghiz bard explains the poetic-historic dilemma:

> Everything in this tale you'll find,
> Entanglement of false and true,
> All happened very long ago,
> Eye-witnesses are hard to find.[134]

Bowra concludes his argument:

> Heroic poetry is a well of information on what people think and feel, and even when it reports history incorrectly, it is none the less informative because it shows how facts affected living men

> and women and made them find their own interpretations and form their own myths.[135]

The examination of the epic myths leads to Geyl's conclusion that myth and history are often inextricably fused.[136] Yet Tylor makes the critical ability to separate myth from history the test of the true historiographer. Such an *historiolysis* destroys much that is of value to intellectual history; the end products are a few geographical and migratory patterns. There are Kiche and African parallels to the diaspora after the Tower of Babel; the Leni-Lenape have a curious ice-migration myth.[137]

The problem of separating myth and history is not new. The classical problem was Stesichorus' claim that Helen spent the War in Egypt, not Troy. He did, however, write a palinode, cited by Plato in the *Phaedrus:*

> That was a lie of mine when I said that thou never embarkedst on the swift ships, or wentest to the walls of Troy.[138] [243]

Herodotus also reports Helen's presence in Egypt. Another example is the text dealing with Sennacherib's devastating victory over Hezekiah, who ends up like a caged bird. Either the old wolf had a tolerably good propagandist or the fold was destroyed. How different the version of II *Kings:* 18–19.

In this subsection on myth and history all but one of the aspects of historical myth has been discussed: dissolution of time, utopianism, patternism, continuity, and organic evolution. Fatalism introduces the complex problems of human responsibility and freedom.

Physical determinism sometimes influences the pervasive fatalism of the epic myths. Here is the tradition of Manilius: *Fata regunt orbem, stant omnia lege.*[139] As St. Augustine views the problem:

> What seems . . . particularly impious in the worship of heavenly bodies, as well as a danger to morals, is that such worship implies a denial of human liberty and can only end in a discouraging fatalism.[140]

Cumont comments on the spread of fatalism in the ancient world:

> Of course, the more the idea of fatalism imposed itself and spread, the more the weight of this hopeless theory oppressed the consciousness. Man felt himself dominated and crushed by blind forces that dragged him on irresistably as they kept the celestial spheres in motion. His soul tried to escape the oppression of this cosmic mechanism, and to leave the slavery of Ananke . . .[141]

Fatalism runs as a theme through the Teutonic and Anglo-Saxon myths with their sense of pessimism and omnipresent doom. In the stories of combat between friends or fathers and children there is Unamuno's *sentimiento trágico de la vida.* The great self-obliterating battle, willed by fate, is repeated between Tancred and Clorinda, Sohrab and Rustum, the d'Ailly's Hildebrand and Hadubrand, and in New Zealand, Kokako and Tama-inu-ko. In *Samson Agonistes,* Milton writes of the "inevitable cause/ At once both to destroy and be destroyed."

The fatalistic myth negates free action. It provides an escape for those oppressed by politics. There is a memorable passage in Tolstoy's *Diary:* "I . . . went to the peasants . . . they don't want their freedom." *"They don't want their freedom."*[142]

The Greek *Moira* has a more protective aspect. Fate is not a "blind Fury." In fact, fate may confront man with a choice as in the *Agamemnon:*

> So he put on,
> The harness of Necessity.[143]

Progress of the Idea of Freedom

If fatalistic myths abdicate responsibility, other myths search for freedom. That search may require endless wanderings looking for the "River of the Arrow" and freedom from "the wheel of things." It may be expressed as the sense of loss—of freedom, the Promethean agony, or it may retreat into an alchemic "as if." Modern scientific thinking tends to seek emancipation from myth; yet the persistent theme of history is emancipation only through myths. The presence-absence of epic may correlate with the degree of freedom.

There is an old Indian proverb to the effect that "Poetry is a flower that grows only in free soil." Man's search for freedom concludes the study of political myth because freedom is myth's highest objective. Political mythology progresses toward creative freedom. As Eliade writes:

> the desire for absolute freedom ranks among the essential longings of man, irrespective of the stage his culture has reached and of its forms of social organization.[144]

There are many expressions of the idea of freedom in epic and myth. The many variant interpretations of the Prometheus myth are representative. Most epics contain remnants of freedom from necessity. There are myths of the golden ages. There is also freedom from the demoniac and the fear of barbarism. Here the slaying of the dragon returns. In the immortality search, there is freedom from natural boundaries: time, space, and death. Spengler feels that the symbolization of space is basic to our culture. In the myths of escape and messianism, there is freedom from tyranny and civil disorder. Myths of man's first disobedience express the problem of free choice and moral responsibility. In the myths which illustrate moral duty, freedom is construed as perfect obedience. Freedom as toleration of diversity is the motivating principle of the *Henriade.* Free expression and other civil liberties are anticipated in this epic. There are the many forms of spiritual freedom. At the same time many epics contain the theme of fatalism as the escape from freedom.

Several of these concepts deserve further discussion. The myth as "free choice" occurs infrequently. There is, however, an interesting parallel to Plato's "Myth of Er" in a Batak story. These people believe that the *tondi* may exercise free will prior to its incarnation. It is responsible for an unwise choice. Sometimes the result is "half-man." If so, the god may say:

> well and good but do not complain again, I allow all people to choose the good, but if they refuse, then they must suffer the consequences.[145]

Myths attempt to reconcile freedom and necessity in many respects. Man tries to free himself from the oppressive sense of law and uniformity of nature, or from death. The most common forms of the myth are the ascensional complex, the search for immortality, and the death-game.

In a southwestern Indian story, Coyote decides that death is necessary to decrease the surplus population, then he changes his mind:

> Desperate he makes himself wings of sunflowers . . . and tries to fly upward, but the leaves wither, and he falls back to earth and is dashed to death.[146]

Remember Daedalus and Icarus! Many people venerate winged dieties for their ability to soar above earth-bound reality. There are Psyche and Cupid, the scarabaic wings of Egypt, the Etruscan "angels" at Orvieto, and the Mercuric petasus. Each symbolizes an escapist freedom.

The search for immortality is a common mythological theme. As has been seen, freedom from death is nearly achieved, but the hero meets an accident. A little bird's laughter causes Maui to be entombed in the jaws of death. The serpent steals Gilgamesh's immortality herb. Freedom from death may also be tied to a game as in the pyramid text which recounts the Pharoah's tests in the underworld. He recovers his freedom by winning the snake game. An American Indian myth tells how "He-Who-Wins-Men" enslaves humans by inducing them to stake their freedom in a game. This myth is reminiscent of Coleridge's lines: "The game is done, I've won, I've won."

Finally there are the myths which treat freedom as an escape from tyranny. Of this type is Lugh's speech to his men: "Fight bravely, that your servitude may last no longer, it is better to face death than to live in vassalage . . ."[147]

Progress in the idea of freedom is progress away from man's fears. Myths which idealize freedom are an awesome reflection of the human spirit. They are in the truest sense POLITICAL MYTHS. The ultimate goal of myth and epic is the rational liberty, idealized by Barlow in the preface to *The Columbiad:*

> The real object of the poem embraces a larger scope it is to inculcate the love of rational liberty, and to discountenance the deleterious passion for violence and war; to show that on the basis of the republican principle all good morals, as well as good government and hopes of permanent peace, must be founded; and to convince the student of political science that the theoretical question of the future advancement of human society, till states as well as individuals arrive at universal civilization, is held in dispute because we have had too little experience of organized liberty in the government of nations to have well considered its effects.[148]

Notes to Chapter IV

1. Fyodor Dostoyevsky, *The Brothers Karamazov*, trans. Constance Garnett (New York: The Modern Library, Random House, 1950), p. 303.

2. Grey, *Polynesian Mythology*, pp. iii-viii.

3. Sumner, *Folkways*, p. 160.

4. Garcilaso de la Vega cited in Adolf F. Bandelier, "Aboriginal Myths and Traditions Concerning the Island of Titicaca, Bolivia," *American Anthropologist*, Vol. VI No. 2, p. 212. Cp. Lucretius, *The Nature of the Universe* (Baltimore, Md.: Penguin Books, 1951), V:925-1010.

5. Longfellow used this myth in "The Song of Hiawatha," cf. N. H. Dole, ed. (New York: T. Y. Crowell, 1898), pp. 271–76 (notes on Schoolcraft as a source). Diamond, ed., op cit., p. 432; Suzanne W. Miles, "Mam Residence and the Maize Myth," cf. Maud Oakes, *The Two Crosses of Todos Santos*, Bollingen Series, Vol. 27 (1951). Paul Radin, *Sources and Authenticity of the Ancient Mexicans*, Vol. 17, "University of California Publications in American Archaeology and Theology" (1920).

6. Gudmund Hatt, "The Corn Mother in America and Indonesia," *Anthropos* (1951), Vol. XLVI, p. 887. Kruyt, *De West-Toradjas op Midder-Celebes* (Amsterdam, 1938).

7. Julian Obermann, *Ugaritic Mythology* (New Haven: Yale University Press, 1948), p. 84.

8. Kramer, *Sumerian Mythology*, pp. 43–66, esp. p. 66.

9. Frankfort cites Pepys, op. cit., p. 312.

10. Lang, op. cit., p. 237.

11. Tylor, *Primitive Culture*, Vol. II, p. 134.

12. N. Kershaw Chadwick, *Poetry and Prophecy* (Cambridge: University Press, 1942), p. 30. Shooter, *Kafirs of Natal and the Zulu Country* (1857), p. 167ff.; Livingstone, *Missionary Travels and Researches in South Africa* (London, 1857), p. 86f.

13. Campbell, *The Masks of God*, p. 238.

14. David Levin, ed., *What Happened in Salem?* (New York: Twayne Publishers, Inc., 1952), Preface, esp. pp. 11–12.

Witchcraft charges have always been convenient devices for the removal of political opponents. John XXII participated personally in the trial of Bishop Hugo of Cahors, accused of *envoûtement, anglicisé*, pin-sticking, against the Pope. Richard G. Solomon, "The Grape Trick," Diamond, ed., p. 532. Cf. C. Hentze, *Chinese Tomb Figures*, "A Study in the Beliefs and Folklore of Ancient China" (London: Edward Goldstein, 1928), pp. 15–16.

15. Cf. H.C. Lea, "The Endemoniadas of Queretaro," *JAF* (1890), Vol. III, pp. 33–39; cf. B.B. Whiting *Paiute Sorcery*, Viking Fund Publications in Anthropology #15 (1950), discussed by E. Adamson Hoebel, *The Law of Primitive Man*, "A Study in Comparative Legal Dynamics" (Cambridge: Harvard University Press, 1954). The Shawnee Prophet, Tenskwatawa, directed an antiwitch campaign against his political opponents.

16. Mooney, op. cit., p. 777.

17. Max Weber, *The Theory of Social and Economic Organization*, trans. A.M. Henderson and Talcott Parsons (Glencoe, Ill.: The Free Press, 1947), p. 64f. Eric Voegelin, *The New Science of Politics*, Charles R. Walgreen Foundation Lectures (Chicago: University of Chicago Press, 1950).

18. Lawson, op. cit., p. 273.

19. Frazer, *The Golden Bough*, p. 390.

20. W.D. Wallis, "Individual Initiative and Social Compulsion," *American Anthropologist* (1915), Vol. 17 No. 4, p. 657. T.H. Gaster, ed., *The Dead Sea Scriptures* (New York: Doubleday and Co., 1956), p. 58.

21. Squire, *Celtic Myth*, p. 246.

22. Katesa Schlosser, *Propheten in Afrika* (Brunswick: A. Lembach, 1949).

23. S. Wells Williams, *The Middle Kingdom* (New York: Charles Scribner's Sons, 1882), Vol. II, pp. 584, 589.

24. Wallis, op. cit., pp. 653–54; cites McDonald, *Journal of the Royal Anthropological Institute*, Vol. 19, p. 280. A. E. Jenks, *The Bontoc Igorot* (Manila, 1893), pp. 204–5.

25. Mooney, op. cit., p. 659; cf. C. W. Hackett, *Revolt of the Pueblo Indians of New Mexico and Otermin's Attempted Reconquest*, 1680–1682 (Albuquerque: University of New Mexico Press, 1942); Condorcanqui claimed to be the reincarnation of the Inca. Francis Parkman, *The Conspiracy of Pontiac*, 2 vols. (Boston 1886); Alice C. Fletcher, "The Indian Messiah," *JAF*, Vol. IV, pp. 57–70; G. B. Grinnell, "Account of the Northern Cheyenne Concerning the Messiah Superstition"; Edgard Blochet, *Le Messianisme dans l'heterodoxie musulmans* (Paris: J. Maisonneuve, 1903). Romano Guardini, *Der Heilbringer in Mythos, Offenbarung und Politik, eine theologischpolitische Besinnung* (Zurich: Thomas Verlag, 1946). W. D. Wallis, *Messiahs, Their Role in Civilization* (Washington, D. C.: American Council on Public Affairs, 1943). Jung even relates flying saucers to the messiah complex.

26. Dr. A. K. Coomaraswamy mentions the principle of *land-nama*, which in our culture calls for New Zions, Sharons, and Bethels. Campbell, *The Masks of God*, p. 199. Handel's *Messiah* and *Judas Maccabeus* are comparable compositions.

27. Thomas Hodgkin, *Nationalism in Colonial Africa* (New York: New York

University Press, 1956), p. 14. R. S. Thompson, "Kenyatta: A Messiah of African Politics," *Harvard Politics* (1961), Vol. I:1. Invulnerability is also a feature of the Shawnee Prophet's messianism.

28. Norman Cohn, *The Pursuit of the Millennium* (London: Secker and Warburg, 1957). Cf. A. H. Fauset, "Black Gods of the Metropolis," *Publications of the Philadelphia Anthropological Society*, Vol. III, 1944.

29. Bowra, *Heroic Poetry*, pp. 116–17, 471.

30. Cohn, op. cit., pp. 33–40.

31. Worsley, op. cit., p. 225.

32. Cf. "The Völuspá," H. A. Bellows, trans., *The Poetic Edda* (New York: American-Scandinavian Foundation, 1923), pp. 1-27; the cited lines are Morris' rendition. The underscored passages have an interesting literary parallel in Ibsen's *The Master Builder*. Ragnar is a character in the play.

33. G. W. Dasent, "The Norsemen in Iceland," *Oxford Essays* (1858), pp. 165–214.

34. Petrie cites Plutarch, op. cit., pp. 9, 118.

35. Cohn, op. cit., pp. 16–17.

36. Tylor, op. cit., Vol. II, p. 131.

37. Worsley, op. cit., p. 11.

38. J. G. Whittier, "The Brewing of Soma," *The Pennsylvania Pilgrim* (Boston, 1872).

Of course, Durkheim and LeBon feel that such outbursts give evidence of a "group mind." Such a postulation is valuable in explaining catastrophism and the apparent *thanatos*-drive. Men do react in a group context. For studying myth, however, it is unnecessary to reify the "group mind" beyond the status of a convenient device for explaining such reactions.

39. Monier Williams, *Religious Thought and Life in India* (London, 1883), Vol. I, p. 207f.; Frazer, op. cit., Vol. I, p. 226. J. Muir, *Original Sanscrit Texts on the Origin and Progress of the Religion and Institutions of India*, Part I, "The Mythical and Legendary Accounts of Caste" (London: Williams and Norgate 1858).

40. Spenser, op. cit., V:ii, pp. 30–41.

41. James Blish, "Rituals of Ezra Pound," *Sewanee Review* (1950), Vol. LVIII, p. 206; cited in C. A. Ward, "The Good Myth," *University of Kansas City Review* (1958), Vol. 24:4, pp. 272–76.

42. Ernst Topitsch, "World Interpretation and Self-Interpretation, Some Basic Patterns," *Daedalus*, pp. 318–20.

43. Cited in *Harper's New Monthly Magazine* (1869), Vol. 38, p. 862.

44. Spence, op. cit., p. 258; Plato, *Republic,* III:415; von Schiefner, op. cit., p. 77.

45. *Popol Vuh,* p. 161.

46. Ibid., p. 208.

47. Campbell, *The Masks of God,* p. 455.

48. Tylor, op. cit., Vol. I, p. 333.

49. Cf. Alan W. Watts, *The Two Hands of God: The Myths of Polarity* (New York: George Braziller, 1963), p. 14.

50. Cited by C. A. Ward, "Myths: Further Vanderbilt Agrarian Views," *University of Kansas City Review* (1958), Vol. 25:1, p. 54.

51. E. A. Hoebel, *The Law of Primitive Man,* "A Study in Comparative Legal Dynamics" (Cambridge: Harvard University Press, 1959).

52. White, ed., op. cit., pp. 490–91.

53. *Confessions* I:vi; W. E. Gladstone, *Juventutus Mundi,* "The Gods and Men of the Heroic Age" (Boston: Little, Brown and Co., 1869).

54. Lang, op. cit., pp. 191–93; Magnus, op. cit., p. 271; Müller, op. cit., p. 248.

55. Cited by Elsie Clews Parsons, "Links Between Morality and Religion in Early Culture," *American Anthropologist* (1915), Vol. 17, pp. 42, 53; C. N. de Cardi in *Journal of the Anthropological Institute* (1899), Vol. 29, pp. 51–52.

56. J. G. Bourke, "Medicine Men of the Apache," *Ninth Annual Report of the American Bureau of Ethnology,* 1887–88, p. 461.

57. Cf. Frazer, op. cit., Vol. I, pp. 52–77; Alldridge in "The Sherbro and Its Hinterland, *Journal of the Royal Anthropological Institute* (1899), Vol. 29, pp. 153–59. Maxim: Petronius Arb. Frag.; Statius, *Thebaid,* iii:661.

58. Lawson, op. cit., pp. 443–44.

59. Feldmann, op. cit., p. 116.

60. Jacobs, op. cit., p. 141.

61. Parsons, op. cit., p. 47. (Several important secondary sources are cited on the Papuans, Masai, and Euahlayi.)

62. D. S. Oyler, "Nikawng and the Shilluk Migration," p. 114.

63. "Eumenides," 696–701; Aeschylus, *The Oresteian Trilogy,* trans. Philip Vellacott, (Baltimore, Md.: Penguin Books, 1956).

64. Tasso, op. cit., Vol. I, p. 103.

65. Werner, op. cit., p. 221.

66. Van der Leeuw, op. cit., p. 413.

67. Fontenelle, op. cit., p. 18.

68. Feldmann, op. cit., p. 208.

69. Eliade, op. cit., p. 131.

70. H. T. Francis and E. J. Thomas, *Jataka Tales* (Cambridge: University Press, 1916), p. 415.

71. Morris Edward Opler, *Myths and Tales of the Jicarilla Apache, Memoirs of the American Folklore Society* (1938), Vol. XXXI, p. 110.

72. Radin, *Primitive Man as Philosopher*, p. 152; Rudolf Otto, *Das Heilige*, (Breslau, 1917). Words of the M'N root often associate epic heroism with divine power and law: Manu, Manitou, Manes, Mana, Mandarin, Manabozo, and Min.

73. Van der Leeuw, op. cit., p. 37.

74. Webster, op. cit., p. 75.

75. Frazer, op. cit., Vol. I, p. 300.

76. Sidney Smith, "The Practice of Kingship in Early Semitic Kingdoms," Hooke, op. cit., p. 27. P. A. Talbot, "A Priest King in Nigeria," *Folklore* (1915), Vol. 26, p. 79. N. W. Thomas, "The Scapegoat in European Folklore," *Folklore* (1906), Vol. 17, pp. 258–88; S. G. F. Brandon, "Divine Kings and Dying Gods."

77. Spencer, op. cit., pp. 34, 55: "power becomes possession of the proper ritual objects."

78. Malinowski, op. cit., p. 22. Cohesion may possibly be measured by the extent of myth-variation in a society. A society which is extremely tolerant in this respect is not especially stable, although it allows the greatest amount of creative individualism.

M. Fortes, "Ritual Festivals and Social Cohesion in the Hinterland of the Gold Coast," *American Anthropologist*, Vol. 38 No. 4, p. 509f.; Gladys A. Reichard, "Individualism and Mythological Style," *JAF*, (1944), Vol. 57, pp. 16–26.

79. Von Schiefner, op. cit., p. lvi and No. 14.

80. Orrin E. Klapp, "The Clever Hero," p. 25. It is important to recognize that myths may perform a pure entertainment function, an antipolitical role. Thus when the explorer Rasmussen asks the point of a certain Eskimo story, the response is:

"It is not always that we want a point in our stories, if only they are amusing. It is only the white men that want a reason . . ." Cited by Ivar Lissner, *Man, God, and Magic*, p. 189. Lucian's Philocles in "The Pathological Liar" excuses the poets who use myths because of their entertainment value.

81. Magnus, op. cit., p. 173.

82. Frazer, Gaster, ed., pp. 304-5.

83. Spenser, op. cit., II: vi: 3.

84. Magnus, op. cit., p. 22.

85. Fiske, op. cit., p. 3.

86. Lawson, op. cit., p. 43.

87. Ibid., p. 80.

88. J. Gray, "The Krt Text in the Literature of Ras Shamra, A Social Myth of Ancient Canaan" (Leyden, 1955).

89. Bowra, *Heroic Poetry,* pp. 425–26.

90. Eliade, op. cit., p. 167.

91. Goldschmidt, Foster, and Essene, "War Stories from Two Enemy Tribes, Yuki and Nomalaki of California," *JAF* (1939), Vol. 52 No. 204, pp. 141–54.

92. Eric Berne, "The Mythology of Dark and Fair: Psychiatric Use of Folklore," *JAF* (1959), Vol. 72, pp. 1–13; Kenneth Burke, "Myth, Poetry, and Philosophy," *JAF* (1960), Vol. 73, pp. 283–306.

93. Sebba, op. cit., p. 151.

94. Tylor, op. cit., Vol. I, p. 113.

95. Procopius, *De Bello Gothico,* ed. Dendorf (Bonn, 1833), Vol. 2, p. 566; Rhys, op. cit., p. 10.

96. G. L. Gomme, *Ethnology in Folklore* (New York: D. Appleton, 1892), esp. Chap. III, "The Mythic Influence of a Conquered Race."

97. Radin, *The Racial Myth,* p. 44. John Barclay, *The Mirror of Minds* (London, 1633).

98. Rupert Emerson, *From Empire to Nation* (Cambridge: Harvard University Press, 1960), p. 53.

99. Sumner, op. cit., p. 28.

100. Jan Brunwand, "Norway's Askeladden, The Unpromising Hero, and Junior Right," *JAF* (1959), Vol. 72 No. 283, pp. 13–23

101. M. J. Herskovits, "Folklore After a Hundred Years, A Problem in Redefinition," *JAF* (1946), Vol. 59, pp. 89–100; E. J. Lindgren, "The Collection and Analysis of Folklore," Ch. XIV in *The Study of Society,* Bartlett, Ginsburg, Lindgren et al., eds. (London, 1939).

102. Bertrand Russell, *Power,* "A New Social Analysis" (New York: W. W. Norton, 1938), p. 273.

103. University of Kansas, *Library Bulletin,* "Burned Books" (Lawrence, 1955), p. 27.

104. Eliade, op cit., p. 12.

105. A. R. Radcliffe-Brown, *The Andaman Islands,* 2nd printing (London: Cambridge University Press, 1933), p. 327; cited by Campbell, *The Masks of God,* p. 370.

106. Webster, op. cit., p. 49; cf. David McClellan, *The Achieving Society* (Princeton, N. J.: D. Van Nostrand, 1961); Mead and Wolfenstein, op. cit., p. 236, "Tootle, a Modern Cautionary Tale adapted from David Riesman's *The Lonely Crowd,*" cf. H. V. Canter, *Mythological Paradigm,* 1933.

107. *Republic,* 329B, Jowett, trans.

108. K. R. Popper, *The Open Society and Its Enemies,* Vol. I, "The Spell of Plato" (London: Routledge and Kegan Paul, 1949); *per contra,* R. B. Levinson, *In Defense of Plato* (Cambridge: Harvard University Press, 1953).

109. *Protagoras,* 316D; *Republic,* 324A, 363A, 364D, 377D, 378D, 383D, 383A, 387B; *Hippias Minor,* 363AB.

110. *Odyssey,* xi, 459; *Iliad,* xx, 64.

111. *Republic,* 387B.

112. *Laws,* 595B; *Meno* 100A; *Cratylus,* 391–93; *Charmides,* 161A; *Phaedo,* 94D–95A; *Alcibiades I,* 697C, 700D.

113. *Republic,* 468CD.

114. Werner Jaeger, *Paideia,* "The Ideals of Greek Culture" (New York: Oxford University Press, 1943), Vol. II, p. 151.

115. Sallustius, "On the Gods and the World," pp. 192–93, appendix to Gilbert Murray, op. cit.

116. Washington Irving, *Wolfert's Roost and Other Papers* (Philadelphia: J. B. Lippincott, 1870), pp. 387–411.

117. Zimmer, op. cit., pp. 3-11.

118. Worsley, op. cit., p. 130. Herman Bauman, *Schöpfung und Urzeit des Menschen im Mythos afrikanischer Völker* (Berlin, 1936).

119. Lord Acton, *Essays on Freedom and Power* (Boston: Beacon Press, 1948), p. 270.

120. George Widengren, "Myth and History in Israelite-Jewish Thought," Diamond, ed., p. 476; Ernst A. Phillipson, "Die Genealogie der Götter in Germanischer Religion, Mythologie, und Theologie," *Illinois Studies in Language and Literature* (Urbana: University of Illinois Press, 1958).

121. Raglan, op. cit., p. 30.

122. Tylor, op. cit., Vol. II, p. 155.

123. Robert Lee Wolff, "The Three Romes, The Migration of Ideology and the Making of an Autocrat," *Daedalus*, p. 293.

124. Spence, op. cit., p. 305.

125. Radin, *Primitive Man as Philosopher* (New York: D. Appleton and Company, 1927), p. 293.

126. Furneaux, op. cit., p. 19.

127. Radin, op. cit., pp. 368–69.

128. Frazer, op. cit., Vol. II, p. 376.

129. Raglan, op. cit., p. 164.

130. Ibid., loc. cit.

131. Victor W. von Hagen, *The Aztec: Man and Tribe* (New York: Mentor Books New American Library, 1958), p. 41.

132. Malinowski, op. cit., p. 64.

133. Bowra, *Heroic Poetry*, pp. 28, 508.

134. Ibid., p. 41.

135. Ibid., p. 536.

136. Widengren, op. cit., p. 467.

137. Spence, op. cit., p. 231; Alexander, op. cit., p. 234; J. Alden Mason, "The Papago Migration Legend," *JAF* (1921), Vol. 34, pp. 254–68.

138. McDermott and Caldwell, op. cit. pp. 53–54.

139. Cumont, op. cit., p. 175.

140. Seznec, op. cit., p. 43; *City of God*, V:1–7.

141. Cumont, op. cit., p. 181.

142. Maude Aylmer, *The Life of Tolstoy*, Tolstoy Society (London: Oxford University Press, 1929), p. 152.

143. *Agamemnon*, trans. Vellacott, p. 27.

144. Eliade, op. cit., p. 106.

145. J. Warneck, *Die Religion der Batak*, pp. 8–24, cited by Radin, *Primitive Man as Philosopher*, p. 269.

146. Alexander, op. cit., p. 235.

147. Squire, op. cit., p. 111.

148. Joel Barlow, *The Columbiad* (Paris: F. Schoell, 1813), p. xii; cf. Books VIII-X.

CONCLUSIONS

• • •

Political Myth and Epic has pursued the Faustian search for meaning, conjured up some of the more unusual creatures of *Walpurgisnacht,* and even visited with Helen of Troy herself. The primary concern is the balance between myth and power.

Myth has largely been ignored by the quantitative anxiety of "social scientists," by positivists, behaviorists, and materialists. Myths, however, determine behavior, economics, and social structure. To evaluate the role of myth in politics is my purpose. The political approach synthesizes materials from related disciplines.

The hypothesis formulated consists of three parts: Myths are co-organic, inherently political, and the mechanisms of cultural dynamics.

Myths serve a moral purpose in structuring the community. They create a moral consensus with social sanctions and taboos. Myths also act according to the traditional organic theory in such aspects as diffusion and variation. As a purposive moral organism, myth is defined as co-organic.

Myth is inherently political. Myth is the means by which the political shaman maintains power. The specific functions of myth in the community can be formally classified: civilizing and cultural, messianic, legitimation and social establishment, legality, pure entertainment, education of the citizen.

There are also negative functions which include: iconoclasm, social satire and criticism, catharsis, cultural defense, and cultural catastrophism.

A systematic theory of political myth describes the co-organic relationship between the prevailing social conditions and these myth forms. Myths are examined in terms of response-reaction to periods of social stress and stabilization. Certain forms correspond to the civilizing struggle between rational and demoniac. Other types mark the cohesion of society. After an external or internal challenge to society, myths attempt to readjust the disturbed balance. Conflicting myth systems, such as bipolar ethnic myths, attempt mutual destruction, replacement, or absorption.

The basis for the co-organic theory of political myth is the social function of epic literature. Epics are national systems of myths which create patterns of patriotic virtue and leadership. Stress is laid on the moving "first principles," the progress in the idea of freedom, and the changing concepts of magnanimity.

The study focuses on the monomyth of the epic hero in order to confirm the elements of political myth. The hero is a queer national synecdoche, representing the whole people. The universality of certain heroic themes raises questions regarding mythopoeism. Why are the forms of myth more limited and predictable than those of history when history is restricted by human experience, but myth by human imagination? The answer may lie in the limited number of political forms. Mythic forms limit alternatives for social action.

Society is the first condition of heroic being; the hero is the eponymous hero, the culture hero. In spite of his initial rejection by society, he later validates the ethical basis of the community. His antitype is the lawless Polyphemus. The hero's stereotyped birth often creates an elite. His fight with the dragon is the struggle for civilization's survival. Tested heroism creates models of virtue and power; the hero acts as law-giver and myth-preserver. His searches for legitimacy, security, knowledge, and power are the human searches. The death of the hero is a cultural catastrophe.

The monomyth also creates a bridge between humanity and divinity. The myth fuses the personification symbols, the hero as representative of the community, with the epic symbols, such as the triskelion. The result is a magnification of man's spirit. The moral lesson is *pathei mathos.* The heroic myth is an epiphany which connects religion with politics.

The antiheroic functions are iconoclastic, cathartic, and antilegal. In antiheroism, the punished wanderer represents the spirit of rebellion, the destruction of power. The trickster is an intermediate heroic figure who breaks social taboos and thereby provides relief from social tensions. The scapegoat provides a catharsis for social inhibition and frustration. The "young stranger" is a revolutionary.

Although the formal study of epic heroism ends with Voltaire's *Henriade,* the book is intended as a stimulus to further research. Among the directions open are the pseudoreligious Marxist mythology and the myths of modern nationalism.

This study of political myth has attempted to reconstruct the architectonic principles of politics. The methods of research have included context analysis, content analysis, the comparative method, and functionalism. The approach attempts to integrate poetics and politics, science and religion. Indeed the myth-maker appears as philosopher, psychologist, meteorologist, and litterateur.

Again I acknowledge my debt to the insights of Dr. W. Y. Elliott, who has reemphasized the contemporary significance of myth and epic in an article for *The Harvard Review:*

> (U)nless Western Civilization can distill into some form partaking of the epic its own beliefs and affirmations, we are fighting against phantoms . . . the real battle is . . . with a mythology by

which the totalitarian systems have already foreshadowed the nature, if not the evolutionary form of what they would give as a human future. Few can doubt that Communism has become a pseudo-religion. But who can doubt that its greatest weakness is its lack of sense of beauty or the lack, even more, of the heritage of that human nature of which the epics are the enduring testimonials.

This book attempts to contribute a basis for understanding the conflict between democratic and totalitarian mythologies through the study of POLITICAL MYTH AND EPIC.

INDEX

• • •